THE FORCES IN AMERICAN ECONOMIC GROWTH SERIES

Giant Enterprise

Giant Enterprise

FORD, GENERAL MOTORS, AND THE AUTOMOBILE INDUSTRY

Sources and Readings

COMPILED AND EDITED BY

Alfred D. Chandler, Jr.

THE JOHNS HOPKINS UNIVERSITY

Harcourt, Brace & World, Inc.

NEW YORK · BURLINGAME

To Dougie

Library of Congress Catalog Card Number: 64–12560

THE FORCES IN AMERICAN ECONOMIC GROWTH SERIES

THE *Forces in American Economic Growth* series provides a documentary record of the building of the American economy. Each book in the series concentrates on the economic force or forces that generated the most compelling pressure for change at key junctures in American history. In each volume the men responsible for change speak for themselves. By presenting such a record the editors hope to enhance the reader's sense of economic reality, his awareness of underlying historic currents, and his ability to investigate and interpret business and economic change and growth.

The series attempts to achieve this goal by providing illustration and by permitting analysis. The documents presented are intended to show how new patterns of economic action occurred and how American entrepreneurs, managers, engineers, financiers, business analysts, workers, and labor-union leaders carried on their various activities at different periods of history. The record provides more than mere illustration. The documents have been collected and presented in a way to encourage analysis and interpretation. They raise questions of why and what as well as how. Why did new ways come when they did and in the way they did? What stimulated and what hindered change? What was the role of personality in producing innovation and bringing economic growth?

The series, in short, supplies the record, the source materials, that a reader can use to form his own judgment about the nature of economic and historical change. It will allow him to be his own historian and his own interpreter of the changing American business and economic scene.

ALFRED D. CHANDLER, JR.

CONTENTS

The Crisis of 1920–21   71

PART II
The Strategy of Competition
The Coming of Modern Management and Marketing

Ford Sticks to Tested Strategies   97

General Motors' Innovations in Management   111

EPILOGUE
The Industry and the Economy

PREFACE

THE growth of the auto industry has been dynamic—even explosive. At the very outset a succession of brilliant strategy decisions by Henry Ford increased his share of the swiftly expanding market from 19.9 per cent in 1911 to 55.7 per cent in 1921. Thereafter, Ford's domination of the market was challenged by other pioneers, with different skills. Pierre du Pont and Alfred Sloan—effective, rational innovators in management and marketing—boosted General Motors' share of total sales from 12.7 per cent in 1921 to 43.9 per cent in 1931, and to 47.5 per cent in 1940.

The penalties for inflexibility and conservatism were as immense as the rewards for bold innovation. While General Motors, with its new methods of management and marketing, was forging ahead, Henry Ford stuck stubbornly to the policies that had given him his dramatic start. His share of the market plummeted from 55.7 per cent in 1921 to 24.9 per cent in 1931, and to 18.9 per cent in 1940.

During the 1930's both Ford and General Motors faced a new challenge from organized labor. As the economy began to recover from the shattering depression after 1929 and as the automobile market began to revive, John L. Lewis and his associates decided the time had come to transform the industrial union into a significant force in the automobile industry and, indeed, throughout American industry.

The materials brought together in this volume serve to document this remarkable chapter in American economic history. They detail the strategy of expansion through mass production that served Ford so well from 1908 to 1920. In doing so these documents record the coming of the moving assembly line, the multi-purpose precision machine tool, the branch assembly plant and other methods and machines of modern production. These readings are followed by the record of the counterstrategy of expansion through financial combination so ably pursued by Billy Durant, Ford's opposite number at General Motors. This second set of readings, in turn, illustrates many of the methods of modern industrial finance.

As that early period unfolded, the forces that provided much of the excitement and sense of urgency brought with them the crisis of 1920–21. A brief but acute business recession then made Durant's personal financial position untenable, while only timely financing from the Du Ponts and the Morgans permitted General Motors itself to survive the crisis. Ford, meanwhile, faced with similar pressures, fell back on his far stronger financial position and thus easily weathered the storm.

During the 1920's management and marketing replaced production and finance as the major challenges in the automobile industry. By the mid-1920's most Americans who could afford a car had bought one. The market for automobiles leveled off at somewhat under 4 million passenger cars a year. General Motors' striking success in the resulting fiercely competitive battles resulted from the close attention its executives gave to the problems of administration. They created a new decentralized form of management at the very time that Henry Ford was deriding systematic management and was drawing the control of his vast industrial empire into his own hands and those of one or two "crown princes." Long-range success also lay in General Motors' restless search for new ways to sell to the mass consumer market through the development of an extensive product line, the annual model, massive advertising, the "trade-in," consumer financing, and systematic market analysis at the time when Ford stoutly maintained that his utility car could practically sell itself.

Another theme central to an understanding of automobile industry is the changing fortunes of the hourly worker from the early days of the then radical Ford policies (five dollars a day in 1914 was far above average) to the formation of one of the most effective and most powerful of the new CIO's industrial unions in the late 1930's. The documents describe the coming of new wage and personnel policies in American industry. They record the bitter conflict within the ranks of organized labor over the use of the industrial union to organize the non-unionized industries. Further, they tell of the success of the UAW and the CIO over General Motors through the use of the sitdown strike and describe the final victory of the unions over Ford.

In following the story the reader should keep in mind that these innovations and changes were having a critical impact on the growth of the American economy as a whole. From 1908 on the automobile industry added impressively to the national income. By 1925 an industry that had barely existed in 1900 ranked first in the value of its product, the cost of its materials, the volume added to manufacture, and wages paid. Moreover it became overnight a major market for steel, rubber, plate glass, aluminum, nickel, tin, copper, felt, leather, paint, and other products. The new market in turn encouraged technological and distribution innovations in these industries. For example, the automobile's requirements for lighter metals led the steel industry to develop alloys. The call for higher-powered fuel encouraged the petroleum industry to perfect ethyl and high-octane gasoline and to bring forth new, more efficient refining processes. The automobile's demands for rubber led to the development of better wear-resisting materials, and its needs for a tough type of glass to the coming of shatter-proof glass. The swiftly growing automobile industry also set off a major boom in the construction industries. Highway construction expanded enormously. For example, the forty-eight states spent $75 million for highways in 1918; fifteen years later they were spending over $1 billion a year.

This increased investment, along with the new salaries, dividends, and wages called forth by the coming of the automobile industry were a major factor in the rapid rise of the national income in the second and third decades of the twentieth century. The impact of the industry on the economy provides a subject for the statistical introduction which follows directly, and the analytical conclusion with which this volume ends.

Giant Enterprise

INDUSTRY STATISTICS

The Dynamics of Auto Growth, 1900–1957

Early Rivalries Flared and Subsided . . .

TABLE 1. COMPARISON OF NUMBER AND PROPORTION OF PASSENGER MOTOR VEHICLES SOLD BY THE PRINCIPAL MANUFACTURERS DURING ALTERNATE YEARS FROM 1911 TO 1937

YEAR	TOTAL NUMBER PASSENGER MOTOR VEHICLES SOLD BY ALL MANUFACTURERS a	CHRYSLER CORPORATION SALES	FORD MOTOR CO. SALES	GENERAL MOTORS CORPORATION SALES	SUBTOTAL, CHRYSLER CORPORATION, FORD MOTOR CO., GENERAL MOTORS CORPORATION PASSENGER-CAR SALES	SUBTOTAL, HUDSON, NASH, PACKARD, STUDEBAKER PASSENGER-CAR SALES	TOTAL PASSENGER-CAR SALES, 7 COMPANIES COVERED IN COMMISSION'S INQUIRY	ALL OTHER MANUFACTURERS' PASSENGER-CAR SALES, EXCEPT 7 COVERED IN COMMISSION'S INQUIRY
	Units	*Units*	*Units*	*Units*	*Units*	*Units*	*Units*	*Units*
1911	199,000	–	39,640	35,459	75,099	30,524	105,623	93,377
1913	462,000	–	182,311	56,118	238,429	44,004	282,433	179,567
1915	896,000	–	342,115	97,937	440,052	57,998	498,050	397,950
1917	1,746,000	–	740,770	195,945	936,715	75,348	1,012,063	733,937
1919	1,658,000	–	664,482	344,334	1,008,816	107,187	1,116,003	541,997
1921	1,518,000	–	845,000	193,275	1,038,275	120,459	1,158,734	359,266
1923	3,624,717	–	1,660,298	732,984	2,402,282	308,491	2,710,773	913,944
1925	3,735,171	134,474	1,494,911	745,905	2,375,290	515,066	2,890,356	844,815
1927	2,936,533	182,627	273,741	1,277,198	1,733,566	551,945	2,285,511	651,022
1929	4,587,400	375,381	1,435,886	1,482,004	3,293,271	563,405	3,856,676	730,724
1931	1,973,090	245,005	490,546	865,724	1,601,275	160,877	1,762,152	210,938
1933	1,573,512	399,912	325,506	652,023	1,377,441	104,731	1,482,172	91,340
1935	3,252,244	739,371	911,837	1,276,117	2,927,325	238,406	3,165,731	86,513
1937	3,915,889	996,005	836,696	1,636,671	3,469,372	358,246	3,827,618	88,271
	Per cent	*Per cent*	*Per cent*	*Per cent*	*Per cent*	*Per cent*	*Per cent*	*Per cent*
1911	100.00	–	19.92	17.82	37.74	15.34	53.08	46.92
1913	100.00	–	39.46	12.15	51.61	9.52	61.13	38.87
1915	100.00	–	38.18	10.93	49.11	6.48	55.59	44.41
1917	100.00	–	42.43	11.22	53.65	4.32	57.97	42.03
1919	100.00	–	40.08	20.77	60.85	6.46	67.31	32.69
1921	100.00	–	55.67	12.73	68.40	7.93	76.33	23.67
1923	100.00	–	46.05	20.23	66.28	8.51	74.79	25.21
1925	100.00	3.60	40.02	19.97	63.59	13.79	77.38	22.62
1927	100.00	6.22	9.32	43.49	59.03	18.80	77.83	22.17
1929	100.00	8.18	31.30	32.31	71.79	12.28	84.07	15.93
1931	100.00	12.42	24.86	43.88	81.16	8.15	89.31	10.69
1933	100.00	25.41	20.69	41.44	87.54	6.66	94.20	5.80
1935	100.00	22.73	28.04	39.24	90.01	7.33	97.34	2.66
1937	100.00	25.44	21.37	41.79	88.60	9.15	97.75	2.25

a U.S. Department of Commerce, Bureau of the Census, Statistical Abstract of the United States 1936, p. 363, for years 1911–19, and Census of Manufactures 1921–37. Figures for 1911–21 represent production and 1923–37 represent sales.

While Aggregate Sales Continued to Mount . . .

TABLE 2. MOTOR-VEHICLE FACTORY SALES AND REGISTRATIONS, 1900 TO 1957
[Number sold includes sales of military vehicles. Value of sales does not include Federal excise taxes.]

YEAR	MOTOR-VEHICLE FACTORY SALES				MOTOR-VEHICLE REGISTRATIONS			
	PASSENGER CARS		MOTOR TRUCKS AND BUSES		TOTAL	AUTO-MOBILES	BUSES	TRUCKS
	NUMBER	WHOLESALE VALUE	NUMBER	WHOLESALE VALUE				
		$1,000		*$1,000*				
1957	6,113,344	11,198,379	1,107,176	2,082,723	67,131,071	55,906,195	264,062	10,960,814
1956	5,816,109	9,754,971	1,104,481	2,077,432	65,153,810	54,200,784	258,764	10,694,262
1955	7,920,186	12,452,871	1,249,090	2,020,973	62,693,819	52,135,583	255,249	10,302,987
1954	5,558,897	8,218,094	1,042,174	1,660,019	58,510,253	48,461,219	248,346	9,800,688
1953	6,116,948	9,002,580	1,206,266	2,080,060	56,221,089	46,422,443	244,251	9,554,395
1952	4,320,794	6,455,114	1,218,165	2,319,789	53,265,406	43,817,580	240,485	9,207,341
1951	5,338,435	7,241,275	1,426,828	2,323,859	51,913,965	42,682,591	230,461	9,000,913
1950	6,665,863	8,468,137	1,337,193	1,707,748	49,161,691	40,333,591	223,652	8,604,448
1949	5,119,466	6,650,857	1,134,185	1,394,035	44,690,296	36,453,351	208,929	8,028,016
1948	3,909,270	4,870,423	1,376,274	1,880,475	41,085,531	33,350,804	196,726	7,537,911
1947	3,558,178	3,936,017	1,239,443	1,731,713	37,841,498	30,845,350	187,457	6,808,691
1946	2,148,699	1,979,781	940,866	1,043,247	34,373,002	28,213,336	173,585	5,986,081
1945	69,532	57,255	655,683	1,181,956	31,035,420	25,793,493	162,125	5,079,802
1944	610	447	737,524	1,700,929	30,479,306	25,566,464	152,592	4,760,250
1943	139	102	699,689	1,451,794	30,888,134	26,009,073	152,324	4,726,737
1942	222,862	163,814	818,662	1,427,457	33,003,656	27,972,837	135,957	4,894,862
1941	3,779,682	2,567,206	1,060,820	1,069,800	34,894,134	29,624,269	119,753	5,150,112
1940	3,717,385	2,370,654	754,901	567,820	32,453,233	27,465,826	101,145	4,886,262
1939	2,888,512	1,770,232	700,377	489,787	31,009,927	26,226,371	92,285	4,691,271
1938	2,019,566	1,241,032	488,841	329,918	29,813,718	25,250,477	87,664	4,475,577
1937	3,929,203	2,240,913	891,016	537,315	30,058,892	25,467,229	83,130	4,508,533
1936	3,679,242	2,014,747	782,220	463,719	28,506,891	24,182,662	62,618	4,261,611
1935	3,273,874	1,707,836	697,367	380,997	26,546,126	22,567,827	58,994	3,919,305
1934	2,160,865	1,140,478	576,205	326,782	25,261,710	21,544,727	51,530	3,665,453
1933	1,560,599	773,425	329,218	175,381	24,159,203	20,657,257	44,918	3,457,028
1932	1,103,557	616,860	228,303	137,624	24,391,000	20,901,401	43,476	3,446,123
1931	1,948,164	1,108,247	432,262	265,445	26,093,968	22,396,253	41,880	3,655,835
1930	2,787,456	1,644,083	575,364	390,752	26,749,853	23,034,753	40,507	3,674,593
1929	4,455,178	2,790,614	881,909	622,534	26,704,825	23,120,897	33,999	3,549,929
1928	3,775,417	2,572,599	583,342	460,109	24,688,631	21,362,240	31,982	3,294,409
1927	2,936,533	2,164,671	464,793	420,131	23,303,470	20,193,333	27,659	3,082,478
1926	3,692,317	2,607,365	608,617	484,823	22,200,150	19,267,967	24,320	2,907,863
1925	3,735,171	2,458,370	530,659	458,400	20,068,543	17,481,001	17,808	2,569,734
1924	3,185,881	1,970,097	416,659	318,581	17,612,940	15,436,102	–	2,176,838
1923	3,624,717	2,196,272	409,295	308,538	15,102,105	13,253,019	–	1,849,086
1922	2,274,185	1,494,514	269,991	226,050	12,273,599	10,704,076	–	1,569,523
1921	1,468,067	1,038,191	148,052	166,071	10,493,666	9,212,158	–	1,281,508
1920	1,905,560	1,809,171	321,789	423,249	9,239,161	8,131,522	–	1,107,639
1919	1,651,625	1,365,395	224,731	371,423	7,576,888	6,679,133	–	897,755
1918	943,436	801,938	227,250	434,169	6,160,448	5,554,952	–	605,496
1917	1,745,792	1,053,506	128,157	220,983	5,118,525	4,727,468	–	391,057
1916	1,525,578	921,378	92,130	161,000	3,617,937	3,367,889	–	250,048
1915	895,930	575,978	74,000	125,800	2,490,932	2,332,426	–	158,506
1914	548,139	420,838	24,900	44,219	1,763,018	1,664,003	–	99,015
1913	461,500	399,902	23,500	44,000	1,258,060	1,190,393	–	67,667
1912	356,000	335,000	22,000	43,000	944,000	901,596	–	42,404
1911	199,319	225,000	10,681	21,000	639,500	618,727	–	20,773
1910	181,000	215,340	6,000	9,660	468,500	458,377	–	10,123
1909	123,990	159,766	3,297	5,334	312,000	305,950	–	6,050
1908	63,500	135,250	1,500	2,550	198,400	194,400	–	4,000
1907	43,000	91,620	1,000	1,780	143,200	140,300	–	2,900
1906	33,200	61,460	800	1,440	108,100	105,900	–	2,200
1905	24,250	38,670	750	1,330	78,800	77,400	–	1,400
1904	22,130	23,358	700	1,273	55,290	54,590	–	700
1903	11,235	13,000	–	–	32,920	32,920	–	–
1902	9,000	10,395	–	–	23,000	23,000	–	–
1901	7,000	8,183	–	–	14,800	14,800	–	–
1900	4,192	4,899	–	–	8,000	8,000	–	–

And the Industry Became the Nation's Largest.

TABLE 3. RELATIVE IMPORTANCE OF THE MOTOR VEHICLE AND MOTOR-VEHICLE BODIES AND PARTS INDUSTRIES . . . 1899–1937

INDUSTRY AND YEAR	WAGE EARNERS (AVERAGE FOR THE YEAR)	WAGES	VALUE ADDED BY MANU-FACTURE	COST OF MATE-RIALS	VALUE OF PRODUCTS
Motor vehicles and motor-vehicle bodies and parts:	Rank	Rank	Rank	Rank	Rank
1899 [a]	–	–	–	–	150
1904 [a]	–	–	–	–	77
1909 [a]	20	–	17	–	21
1914 [b]	15	7	6	7	7
1919 [c]	7	5	3	2	2
1925 [d]	3	1	1	1	1
1931 [e]	2	2	2	2	4
1935 [f]	1	1	1	1	1
1937 [g]	2	2	1	1	1
Motor vehicles:					
1914 [b]	22	16	12	9	8
1919 [c]	9	7	6	4	3
1925 [d]	10	8	4	2	1
1931 [e]	12	12	8	3	2
1935 [f]	8	6	4	2	1
1937 [g]	8	4	5	1	2
Motor-vehicle bodies and parts:					
1914 [b]	34	25	38	49	47
1919 [c]	18	13	20	29	25
1925 [d]	8	6	8	8	9
1931 [e]	11	9	9	7	11
1935 [f]	4	2	6	5	5
1937 [g]	4	2	4	5	5

[a] U.S. Department of Commerce, Bureau of the Census, Thirteenth Census of the United States, 1910, vol. VIII, p. 45.
[b] U.S. Department of Commerce, Bureau of the Census, Abstract of the Census of Manufactures, 1914, p. 516.
[c] U.S Department of Commerce, Bureau of the Census, Fourteenth Census of the United States, 1920, vol. VIII, p. 16.
[d] U.S. Department of Commerce, Bureau of the Census, Biennial Census of Manufactures, 1925, p. 24.
[e] U.S. Department of Commerce, Bureau of the Census, Biennial Census of Manufactures, 1931, p. 30.
[f] U.S. Department of Commerce, Bureau of the Census, Biennial Census of Manufactures, 1935, p. 34.
[g] U.S. Department of Commerce, Bureau of the Census, Supplementary Report, Dec. 2, 1938, p. 2.

Ford's Long-Hidden Losses Were Coming to Light . . .

TABLE 4. FORD MOTOR CO. AND LINCOLN MOTOR CO. . . . SUMMARY OF SALES, PROFITS, DIVIDENDS, EARNINGS REINVESTED, AND SURPLUS BALANCE, . . . 1927 TO 1937 . . .

YEAR ENDED DEC. 31—	NET SALES	NET PROFIT AFTER TAXES	CASH DIVIDENDS, COMMON STOCK	SURPLUS ADJUSTMENTS ADDITIONS (NET)	SURPLUS ADJUSTMENTS DEDUC-TIONS (NET)	EARNINGS REINVESTED IN THE BUSINESS	SURPLUS BALANCE
1926	–	–	–	–	–	–	$698,987,075
1927	$ 355,975,669	$30,447,190 [a]	$10,358,700	$ 4,130,257	–	$36,675,633 [a]	662,311,442
1928	551,710,332	70,640,628 [a]	6,042,575	6,446,075	–	70,237,128 [a]	592,074,314
1929	1,144,688,097	91,531,572	6,042,575	4,791,056	–	90,280,053	682,354,367
1930	873,515,070	39,996,121	6,905,800	1,820,852	–	34,911,173	717,205,540
1931	460,069,223	37,181,192 [a]	8,632,250	–	$ 2,370,527	48,183,969 [a]	669,081,571
1932	254,680,008	70,851,153 [a]	–	473,037	–	70,378,116 [a]	598,703,455
1933	297,146,871	7,888,718 [a]	3,452,900	5,048,967	–	6,292,651 [a]	592,410,804
1934	531,926,851	21,362,118	7,769,025	–	10,316,080	3,277,013	595,687,817
1935	834,493,626	18,573,804	10,013,410	–	2,173,644	6,386,750	602,074,567
1936	760,487,306	21,463,529	11,221,925	–	13,243,390	3,001,786 [a]	599,072,781
1937	847,492,463	8,218,784	4,661,415	1,597,640	–	5,155,009	604,227,790
TOTAL	6,912,185,516	15,862,953 [a]	75,100,575	24,307,884	28,103,641	94,759,285 [a]	–

[a] Red figures.

While General Motors Was Earning Record Profits.

TABLE 5. GENERAL MOTORS CORPORATION AND CONSOLIDATED SUBSIDIARIE

	1927	1928	1929	1930
Net sales	$1,289,231,917	$1,481,745,323	$1,532,213,745	$1,005,327,9‹
Less factory cost of goods sold	889,760,528	1,032,987,511	1,103,555,492	732,224,8‹
Gross profit on sales	399,471,389	448,757,812	428,658,253	273,103,0‹
Commercial expenses	114,794,584	135,409,499	154,260,920	124,671,5.
Provision for doubtful accounts	399,493	163,930	566,121	779,7‹
Total expenses and doubtful accounts	115,194,077	135,573,429	154,827,041	125,451,2‹
Net profit on sales	284,277,312	313,184,383	273,831,212	147,651,8‹
Other income (net)	5,807,044	5,653,621	8,282,307	7,122,2:
Net profit on manufacturing operations	290,084,356	318,838,004	282,113,519	154,774,0:
Add income from outside investments:				
Dividends received	5,980,144	7,082,708	10,564,814	18,016,2‹
Provision for foreign dividend taxes	–	–	190,000[a]	499,3‹
Interest on Government, marketable, and other investments	2,164,705	5,633,584	4,085,288	1,850,5‹
Interest on accounts with General Motors Management Corporation	–	91,693	24,617	2,375,0‹
Total income from outside investments	8,144,849	12,807,985	14,484,719	21,742,5‹
Net income on total operations	298,229,205	331,645,989	296,598,238	176,516,5‹
Interest expense	887,346	1,429,822	2,018,131	2,335,4‹
Net profit after interest and before income taxes	297,341,859	330,216,167	294,580,107	174,181,0‹
Provision for State, Federal, and foreign income taxes	35,073,019	33,959,964	28,755,196	16,585,2‹
Net profit after income taxes [b]	262,268,840	296,256,203	265,824,911	157,595,8‹

ATEMENT OF INCOME AND EXPENSES, 1927 TO 1937

1931	1932	1933	1934	1935	1936	1937	Total, 1927–37
28,207,978	$440,899,312	$583,746,596	$862,672,670	$1,155,641,511	$1,439,289,940	$1,606,789,841	$12,225,766,736
96,671,671	358,461,453	428,024,934	685,840,349	900,096,946	1,094,059,974	1,286,004,580	9,107,688,243
31,536,307	82,437,859	155,721,662	176,832,321	255,544,565	345,229,966	320,785,261	3,118,078,492
10,331,532	84,199,336	72,578,858	76,877,898	81,513,876	91,214,218	97,484,428	1,143,336,684
1,131,787	1,426,097	1,077,063	211,816	125,372	380,787	67,673	6,329,900
11,463,319	85,625,433	73,655,921	77,089,714	81,639,248	91,595,005	97,552,101	1,149,666,584
20,072,988	3,187,574[a]	82,065,741	99,742,607	173,905,317	253,634,961	223,233,160	1,968,411,909
1,629,213[a]	1,847,144	2,017,053	3,402,836	3,337,887	1,849,839	3,321,186	41,011,935
18,443,775	1,340,430[a]	84,082,794	103,145,443	177,243,204	255,484,800	226,554,346	2,009,423,844
11,314,378	8,867,515	8,385,028	11,920,038	28,999,024	27,698,261	27,316,688	166,144,894
204,879[a]	488,114[a]	873,004[a]	1,191,455[a]	982,695[a]	1,335,516[a]	1,656,576[a]	7,421,585[a]
1,770,953	1,951,213	719,369	407,169	222,717	158,882	238,806	19,203,284
2,667,500	1,610,000	1,714,245	1,544,999	2,098,616	2,409,129	291,270	14,827,069
15,547,952	11,940,614	9,945,638	12,680,751	30,337,662	28,930,756	26,190,188	192,753,662
33,991,727	10,600,184	94,028,432	115,826,194	207,580,866	284,415,556	252,744,534	2,202,177,506
2,463,610	1,775,972	1,148,045	972,871	926,920	719,412	541,988	15,219,614
31,528,117	8,824,212	92,880,387	114,853,323	206,653,946	283,961,144	252,202,546	2,186,957,892
14,788,161	464,282	12,370,991	15,728,828	29,957,263	44,146,069	49,530,084	281,359,115
16,739,956	8,359,930	80,509,396	99,124,495	176,696,683	239,550,075	202,672,462	1,905,598,777

Deduction.
Net profit after income taxes is equivalent to "Net profit to stockholders' investment."

SOURCES

TABLE 1. Federal Trade Commission, *Report on the Motor Vehicle Industry* (Washington, D.C., U.S. Government Printing Office, 1939), p. 29.

TABLE 2. U.S. Bureau of the Census, *Historical Statistics of the United States, Colonial Times to 1957* (Washington, D.C., U.S. Government Printing Office, 1960), p. 462.

TABLE 3. Federal Trade Commission, *Report on the Motor Vehicle Industry* (Washington, D.C., U.S. Government Printing Office, 1939), p. 9.

TABLE 4. Federal Trade Commission, *Report on the Motor Vehicle Industry* (Washington, D.C., U.S. Government Printing Office, 1939), p. 649.

TABLE 5. Federal Trade Commission, *Report on the Motor Vehicle Industry* (Washington, D.C., U.S. Government Printing Office, 1939), pp. 525–26.

A GENERAL INTRODUCTION TO THE READINGS

As THE Preface and the tables have shown, few inventions have had a more profound impact on the American economy than the automobile. Nevertheless, the revolutionary changes created by the automobile and its production occurred in a larger historical context. The ways in which the industry grew and the ways in which the the automobile affected the United States were in good part determined by the nature of American business and industry in 1900.

The American Business Economy in 1900

In the first years of the new century, when the automobile was beginning to be produced commercially, the United States was climaxing its initial drive toward industrialization and urbanization. In 1850 the country had been a land of farmers and merchants. Its economic energies were concentrated on the growing and moving of cotton and foodstuffs for the more urban and industrial countries of Europe. The swift construction of railroads during the decade of the 1850's helped to launch the nation on its rise as an industrial power. The railroads themselves became a major market for iron and then steel, for coal, lubricants, copper, wood, felt, rubber, and other products. More important, improved transportation permitted the planters and farmers to reach European markets more quickly and cheaply. The increasing volume of trade not only encouraged a swift expansion of agriculture but enlarged the business of the merchants who serviced the farmers and increased the size and number of the cities in which they lived.

The coming of the railroads had another significant consequence for the future. Because individual railroad companies were so much larger than any other contemporary enterprise, they required brand-new techniques of financing and administration. The acquisition of the huge sums needed to build the roads led to the centralizing and institutionalizing of the American investment market in Wall Street. The administration of the great new private enterprises brought the earliest professional executives to American business. For the first time there was enough work within a single enterprise to require executives whose task was to coordinate, appraise, and plan the work of other men and even other managers. As early as 1860 the larger roads had administrators in charge of specialized functional departments handling motive power, maintenance of way, transportation, traffic, accounting, and legal affairs. They also had officers, such as general superintendents and general managers, who administered the work of the more specialized executives.

After 1880 American industry and American cities increasingly replaced Europe as a market for the nation's consumer products and replaced the railroads as users of the nation's producer goods. During the last two decades of the century the proportion of total output of wheat, meat, and refined petroleum shipped abroad dropped off quickly, as American cities and industries were tied together by the new railroad network into a truly national market. In addition, the city became the leading buyer of iron and steel beams, pipes, wire, and other metal shapes and products, as well as lumber, coal, paint, and many other items. Significantly, the most important new industry to be developed in the two decades before 1900, the electrical industry, grew by meeting the needs for urban lighting and transportation.

The swift growth of the urban and industrial market drove the American economy forward so that by 1910 the United States had the largest industrial output and one of the largest urban populations of any nation in the world. The high volume of business activity thus generated brought to American industry the great business enterprises that the railroads had initially developed. These huge business corporations grew as much through the addition of marketing and purchasing facilities as by expanding production. In the 1870's a manufacturing firm did only manufacturing. By 1900 many of the nation's most important industries were dominated by a few large enterprises that did their own purchasing, often controlled their own raw materials, and carried on their own wholesaling (and, in some cases, even their own retailing) activities. The creation of a distribution and sales network with its branch plants, warehouses, offices, railroad cars, delivery wagons, and so on usually proved expensive in terms of men, money, and materials as well as in entrepreneurial time and talents. Once a few firms within an industry had created their national distribution networks and had expanded production to meet the enlarged demand, the cost of entering the business on a national scale became almost prohibitive.

The Coming of the Automobile Industry

This, then, was the basic economic and business situation when Ransom E. Olds demonstrated the commercial feasibility of the automobile by selling more than 500 cars in 1900. As in the case of most new industries, the earliest years of the automobile industry were ones of technological innovations, improvements, and uncertainties. At first there was even a question as to how the new horseless carriage should be powered. Both new generators of power, the electric motor and the internal-combustion engine, as well as the older steam engine, were tested. By 1905 the gasoline engine had proven more flexible and easier to operate.

Then the more far-sighted entrepreneurs began to appreciate the sales potential of the automobile in the new national market. Among the first to see the possibilities were bicycle builders such as Albert A. Pope, Alexander Winton, and George N. Pierce and carriage makers such as the Studebaker

brothers and William C. Durant. These men had already built organizations
for large-scale selling. Engineers and mechanics, including Wilfred H. Leland,
the founder of Cadillac, and Henry Ford, also saw the potentialities. They
understood even more clearly than the bicycle and carriage makers the importance of developing a carefully designed, dependable product if the automobile was to be sold in any volume. And Henry Ford, more than Leland
or any other manufacturer, appreciated the huge demand awaiting a car priced
at under $1,000.

As the automobile makers began to move toward manufacturing for the
national market, they usually followed one or two standard strategies of expansion. The largest number, including Ford and Leland, built up their
distribution network of branch offices and concentrated on improving their
product and their production methods. Improved manufacturing methods
were to be particularly important, for speedier production increased output
and so lowered unit costs, thus permitting further cuts in price, which in
turn increased demand and further stimulated production. For such a strategy
the skills of the mechanic, the machinist, and the production engineer were
especially relevant.

The other road to expansion was through combination. The mass market
was to be met by accumulating existing assembling and marketing facilities,
as well as by obtaining control of producers of parts and accessories. Such a
strategy demanded expert financial and legal skills. After 1908 a number of
combinations appeared. They included the United States Motor Company
and the Everitt-Metzger-Flanders Company. Of the major combinations the
General Motors Corporation was the largest and most successful.

The first real growth of the industry, and with it the rise of the great national corporations, came immediately after the short business recession of
1907. In 1908, the year in which Ford first produced the Model T and
Durant formed General Motors, the industry produced 65,000 cars. In the
next year output doubled, reaching 130,986 vehicles. By 1915 production had
jumped enormously, running close to 1 million vehicles a year—nearly all
passenger cars. Within two years this output almost doubled, reaching 1.9
million. The entry of the country into World War I slowed down expansion, but in 1920 over 2.2 million cars were manufactured.

The Rise of Ford and General Motors

In this period of swift growth Henry Ford immediately took the lead.
His basic strategy was first to develop a product suitable for the mass market
and then to build a distribution network to sell it. In 1908 he put the dependable, light, sturdy, and inexpensive Model T on the market. As he improved his car, he and his able partner, James Couzens, completed their
national, indeed international, distribution network of dealers and regional
sales offices. By March 1913 the Ford Motor Company had branch houses
in thirty-one American cities and fourteen foreign ones. Its outstanding

product, marketed through such a comprehensive sales organization, brought a torrent of orders.

Supply simply could not keep up with demand. Ford and his associates began their ceaseless search for new ways to speed up the manufacturing and assembly processes. From these efforts came many elements of modern mass production, culminating in the innovation of the moving assembly line. By 1914 Ford's central Highland Park plant was turning out over 1,200 cars a day. Ford's production for the following year totaled 342,115 passenger vehicles, or just over 38 per cent of all automobiles sold by American manufacturers.

William Crapo Durant, the president of the Buick Motor Company, followed the other road to expansion. In 1908, a year in which 63,500 passenger cars were produced, Durant had began to prophesy an annual sale by the industry of 500,000 vehicles. To meet this potential he moved to combine a sizable share of the existing assembly and distribution facilities. He also appreciated the need to obtain control of companies making parts and accessories so as to assure his expanding assembly plants a steady flow of supplies. In organizing and financing his combination, the General Motors Company, Durant used little cash. Instead he paid for the securities of the companies he obtained by exchanging General Motors stock for theirs. Like most automobile manufacturers, Durant was able to raise funds for his initial capital investment, even for his exceedingly ambitious venture, without relying on Wall Street.

Nevertheless, an unexpected need for operating funds did bring the bankers to General Motors. Following the custom of the new industry, Durant counted on returns from the sale of his cars to pay his suppliers and labor force. In 1910, just as General Motors moved into increased production, a brief but unforeseen decline in demand suddenly caught Durant without money to meet his operating costs. In return for a loan of $15 million, a syndicate of New York and Boston bankers took control of the company. Durant then began to seek support outside the financial community and found it among the members of a wealthy industrial family, the Du Ponts of Delaware.

With Du Pont backing, Durant returned to General Motors in 1915, ousted the bankers, and embarked again on his policy of expansion through combination. The coming of World War I temporarily delayed his plans. But after the armistice he poured millions of dollars (raised from the Du Ponts and from the sale of securities directly to the public) into a massive expansion program. It involved building new plants and facilities as well as buying existing ones. Durant worked on such a vast scale that early in 1920 he needed still more financing. He had to call again on the Du Ponts, and then on their British associates, the Nobels, and finally on the illustrious banking house of J. P. Morgan and Company before the necessary funds were raised.

Then came the sharp and severe postwar recession. The war-engendered business boom petered out in the spring and summer of 1920. As it melted away, the demand for automobiles plummeted. Ford responded by slashing prices, demanding vigorous economies within his enterprise, and forcing his suppliers and dealers to carry him through the crisis. He accomplished the latter by abruptly canceling orders or making the suppliers sell at greatly reduced prices and by insisting that his dealers take and pay for cars that they could not sell at that moment.

General Motors fared far worse than Ford. Before demand returned again, General Motors was forced to write off a huge sum as dead loss. Only the success of the Du Ponts, the Nobels, and Morgan in raising funds earlier in the year saved the corporation from bankruptcy. Durant himself was less fortunate. His own financial difficulties resulting from the depression and his attempts to maintain the price of General Motors' stock brought about his final departure from General Motors. Pierre du Pont, who replaced him as president, began at once to reorganize the corporation's finances and administration as well as to reshape its production and marketing policies.

The Changing Market of the 1920's

For all his energy and activity Durant had succeeded only once, in 1919, in obtaining as much as 20 per cent of the market. Ford had close to 50 per cent. Since the rebuilding of General Motors under Pierre du Pont was to take time, Ford continued to reign supreme in the prosperous years immediately following the postwar recession. Those years saw the final burst of demand for automobiles. The industry's output rose from 1.5 million cars in 1921 to 2.5 million in 1922 and 4.3 million in 1923. But from 1923 until 1929 the market leveled off, taking an average of a little under 4 million cars a year. As had happened or would happen in so many American industries, the initial demand for the new product had reached the level permitted by the existing national income. Moreover, as has also usually been the case, production potential exceeded demand. By the mid-1920's the country's automobile plants had a productive capacity of over 6 million vehicles.

The automobile industry had therefore entered into the second stage of its history—that of competition rather than growth. Marketing now became a greater challenge than production. The underlying marketing problem was no longer to sell an individual his first car but to get the man who already owned one to buy a new car. And management became a greater challenge than finance. Effective coordination, appraisal, and planning were essential if costs were to be kept down and the market was not to be oversold.

Ford Sticks to Tested Policies

Henry Ford refused to take seriously these fundamental changes in the market. Having survived the crisis of 1920–21 by relying on his suppliers and dealers, he moved into the new period with full confidence in his old strategy. He continued to concentrate on the production of a single model—

the Model T—to supply cheap, efficient automobile transportation. He bent his efforts solely toward improving production so as to increase speed and lower costs of output. He achieved this end by completing one of the largest industrial establishments in the world. The giant plant that rose on the banks of the River Rouge after World War I became a superb example of modern integrated production. Here Ford produced nearly all the parts that went into the T and even made his own glass and steel. Into the Rouge poured a ceaseless stream of Ford-owned ore, coal, and lumber. Every minute or so out came a completed car. A brilliant technological achievement, the Rouge was far less impressive as a business venture. Huge capital investment brought inflexibility and high fixed costs. The whole complex was set up to build a product that was more than fifteen years old. Even small changes in design could come only at great expense.

And after 1924 the demand for the Model T began to drop. By 1926 leading automobile and financial journals were pointing out that the Ford Motor Company was having its troubles. For the first time it was meeting real competition. Profits were melting away. Dealers were growing dissatisfied. Industrial analysts and the industry as a whole wondered how Ford would respond. What would he do next?

The Challenge of General Motors

Ford's difficulties came partly from a failure to appreciate the changing nature of demand and its implications for management as well as marketing. But they came just as much from the swiftness with which the administrators of General Motors understood and adjusted to the new situation. By 1925 General Motors had fully recovered from the earlier crisis. From 1921 on, its new managers had been experimenting as ceaselessly and vigorously to perfect techniques of marketing and management as Ford had experimented to perfect methods of production during the previous decade.

The results were impressive. By 1927 competition had forced Ford to abandon the T and to shut down for months before coming out with his new product, the A. Even in 1929, the year of the A, Ford took only 31.3 per cent of the market while General Motors kept 32.3 per cent (see Table 1). As Ford's profits dropped, those of General Motors rose. In 1928 the latter reported a profit of $296,256,203—one of the largest ever made by an American business corporation up to this time. During the decade between 1927 and 1937, which included the darkest days of the great depression, General Motors averaged an annual profit of $173.2 million, the highest of any large corporation in the United States. In these same ten years Ford averaged an annual net loss of $1.4 million (see Table 5).

General Motors' Innovations in Management

In its innovations in management, General Motors pioneered beyond the automobile industry. Its decentralized form of administrative organization, for example, became a model not only for Ford and Chrysler in later years, but for much of the rest of American industry. This type of structure had been initially proposed to Durant by Alfred P. Sloan, Jr., the president of one of the parts firms that Durant had purchased in 1916. One of Pierre du Pont's first acts on becoming president was to put Sloan's plan into effect. Under his proposal the operating units—the car, truck, parts, and accessories divisions— retained their full autonomy. As under Durant, their managers continued to control their own production, marketing, purchasing, and engineering. What was new, however, was the creation of a general office, consisting of general executives and advisory staff specialists, to assure over-all coordination, control, and planning.

After 1921 President Pierre du Pont, assisted by Alfred Sloan (who succeeded Du Pont to the presidency in 1923) and two or three other able senior officers, worked hard to transform Sloan's plan into an effective working organization. They carefully defined and redefined the roles of the general and staff executives in the general office as well as those of the senior executives in the operating divisions; they also set up or clarified the lines of authority and communications running between the many offices. Secondly, they labored at developing a mass of statistical information to flow through these channels to provide the general staff and operating officers with a clear and continuous picture of the performance of the many divisions and of the corporation as a whole. Increasingly, this information and the action taken on it came to depend on the annual forecast of the market. By 1925 this forecast helped to determine costs, prices, production schedules, purchasing, employment, and the over-all allocation of the corporation's resources. It served as a yardstick against which current performance, as recorded in ten-day and monthly reports from all operating divisions and their dealers, could be checked.

By 1925 General Motors' innovations in management had produced a new decentralized type of organization for the large industrial enterprise. It became a model for much of American industry because it supplied a viable alternative to the centralized, functionally departmentalized structure (that is, a department for each major function—production, sales, purchasing, research, and so forth) that had been developed in the second part of the nineteenth century first by the railroads and then by the early large integrated industrial enterprises. It provided as well a more effective administrative form than did the loosely controlled holding company in which only financial ties connected the several operating subsidiaries with each other and with the general office.

To Henry Ford, such a careful articulation of the channels of communication and authority and such reliance on statistical analyses were meaningless. As he stressed in 1922, "The Ford factories and enterprises have no organization, no specific duties attaching to any position, no line of succession or of authority, very few titles, and no conferences." He firmly believed that in his company work was done more efficiently and abilities were more quickly recognized than in enterprises like General Motors. In these very same years, ironically, his more competent executives were leaving in droves—with the best of them, such as William S. Knudsen in production and Norval Hawkins in sales, going directly to General Motors. Soon authority at Ford had become concentrated in the hands of a few tough, unscrupulous, hard-headed, and hard-handed favorites.

General Motors' Innovations in Marketing

Henry Ford's failure to come to terms with the administrative needs of a great modern business enterprise was possibly less disastrous for his company during the 1920's than his refusal to acknowledge his competitor's innovations in modern mass marketing. Besides reshaping their administrative organization, the new managers at General Motors paid serious attention to long-term business strategy and tactics. Early in 1921 the Executive Committee decided to abandon Durant's policy of extended vertical integration by owning or controlling sources of basic supplies and raw materials. Instead, they would only stay in businesses "that relate directly to the construction of the car, truck or tractor." Secondly, they began to design a product line to carry out a new fundamental marketing policy—"a car for every purse and purpose." Their aim was to reach all sectors of the market. By using some of the same parts and supplies in the models for the different markets they hoped to achieve further economies of scale. Thus while Ford was building the Rouge, General Motors was turning more to outside suppliers, and while Ford continued to concentrate on one model, General Motors began to produce the largest array of products in the industry.

With the creation of the Pontiac in 1925, the General Motors car line was practically completed. The Executive Committee and the newly formed Interdivisional Sales Committee then began to concentrate on expanding their share of the market. They did this by steadily improving the performance and regularly changing the appearance of their many models. Charles P. Kettering's Research Staff improved axles, transmissions, crankshafts, and the like in order to make General Motors' cars easier and more comfortable to drive, and Harley Earl's new Styling Section made their lines and color more pleasing to the customer's eye. Nor did the senior executives forget advertising, as the handsome budget of the new Institutional Advertising Committee indicated.

General Motors paid as much attention to dealer relations as to product development and product differentiation. By the 1920's nearly all automobile companies retailed their cars through local dealers who were usually tied by contract exclusively to one company, but who still operated more as independent merchants than manufacturers' agents. The companies' distribution network of branch sales offices, warehouses, and assembly plants provided the dealer with a steady flow of cars but left to him the final selling of the product to the customer. During the years of expansion dealers enjoyed a highly profitable business, but as the market leveled off and competition stiffened, they were among the first to feel the pinch. With the onslaught of the depression after 1929 and the cruel and insistent shrinkage of demand, the pinch became a relentless squeeze.

In defining their relationships with the dealers during the 1920's, Ford and General Motors often developed diametrically opposite policies. Alfred Sloan showed his awareness of the dealers' changing needs. He and his associates rejected Ford's policy of insisting that the dealers make 20 per cent on the sale of each used car. On new cars they raised the dealers' margin substantially above that of Ford's to 24 per cent of list price. They helped the dealers install modern accounting procedures and did their best to keep them from becoming overstocked. General Motors also pioneered in financing both dealers and customers. As early as 1919 John J. Raskob, treasurer at General Motors, had formed the General Motors Acceptance Corporation. Strengthened by Donaldson Brown during the 1920's, its purpose remained the enlargement of the market for General Motors products. Ford did not embark on a comparable program until 1928.

With the demise of the Model T, the Ford Motor Company gradually did begin to adjust its policies to the realities of the changing market and competition. But neither the new models nor the modified policies were effective enough to meet the General Motors challenge. Ford expected to make the Model A for as long a period as he had manufactured the T. It sold very well in 1929. But by 1932 the competition forced Ford to bring out a new model, the V-8. Like its two predecessors, it was an excellently engineered car; but Ford had not yet improved his marketing policies and dealer relationships enough to regain leadership in the industry. Nor did attempts to enlarge his line by paying more attention to the Lincoln, which he had purchased in 1922, bear fruit. Even the development of a new model, the Mercury, failed to better his situation. Not only did Ford continue to fall far behind General Motors in profits and share of the market, but he also lost out to Walter Chrysler (see Tables 1 and 5). The latter, by imitating the General Motors strategy of the full line and product differentiation and by concentrating his production and marketing talents on the low-price Plymouth, had 25.4 per cent of the market by 1937 as compared to Ford's 21.4 per cent, and by 1940 23.7 per cent to Ford's 18.9 per cent.

The Challenge of Labor

In the 1930's Ford and his two great competitors were troubled by more than a loss of customers. A still greater challenge came from the demands of their working force and from organized labor. Modern mass production, particularly the assembly line, had created a new type of working force. In the huge new automobile factories the clear distinction between highly skilled shop labor and unskilled heavy manual labor was becoming increasingly blurred. By far the largest number of employees had routine, repetitive jobs as machine tenders and assemblers. These monotonous, fatiguing operations did not require strenuous exertion but did call for considerable alertness, dexterity, and judgment. This new type of labor force brought new challenges to both management and organized labor.

Of all the leaders in the automobile industry, Henry Ford paid the closest attention to the needs and requirements of the new type of labor force. As the industry's largest employer, his personnel problems were the most complex. To meet them he fashioned one of the first modern employee-relations departments. Under the guidance of that staff office, the workers at Ford came to enjoy working conditions as safe, clean, and healthy as any in the nation. The new department also reorganized and systematized the chaotic wage structure and employment practices then existing in the rapidly expanding Ford plants. General Motors and others of the larger automobile companies soon adopted similar wage and employment classifications and procedures. They were slower, however, in taking on Ford's most famous labor innovation, the five-dollar day. As part of his program for better personnel relations Ford lowered the time of the working day to eight hours, and in January 1914 he raised the average daily wage to five dollars, which was then about twice the normal wage for automobile production workers.

The trade-union movement responded more slowly to the requirements of the new labor force. This was partly because Ford's innovations and their adoption by others helped keep the workers temporarily satisfied with their condition. It was also because there was very little place for the new mass-production worker in unions that were made up largely of skilled men. The new worker was not trained in any existing trade, nor did the tasks of assemblers or machine tenders fall clearly under the jurisdiction of the craft unions that dominated the American Federation of Labor. Therefore, when Ford dropped many of his earlier liberal personnel policies and began exploiting his workers, the AF of L was still unable to organize his or any other major automobile company.

Even after the economic and political consequences of the great depression of the early 1930's created a situation favorable to the expansion of unionism, the AF of L failed to move into the automobile or other mass-production industries. From the mid-1920's on, labor leaders like William Green and John L. Lewis were insisting that only unions built along industrial rather than craft lines could meet the needs and demands of the new worker. Only unions that included every worker in an industry—the skilled, the semiskilled and the unskilled—could become powerful enough to overcome the solid opposition of the great corporations to organized labor. Yet the skilled workers who made up most of the AF of L unions distrusted the industrial type of structure. They were afraid of being outvoted. They saw themselves competing with new organizations for potential members, and they maintained that the large size of these new groups would make the industrial union unstable and unmanageable.

The controversy over the industrial union split the ranks of labor asunder. The result was not a modification of the older craft union but rather the widespread formation of new industrial unions joined together under a brand new national federation, the CIO. Formed as the Committee for Industrial Organization in 1935 by the eight industrial unions then associated with the AF of L, the new alliance took the name of the Congress for Industrial Organization after its unions had been suspended from the older federation. By 1938 the fledgling CIO was rapidly organizing the automobile, rubber, steel, and other mass-production industries.

Within the automobile industry the victory of the new industrial union, the United Automobile Workers, came only after a series of hard-fought battles. General Motors, Ford, Chrysler, and the smaller firms had adamantly refused to deal with the UAW or to consider the possibility of any one union acting as the sole spokesman for their working forces. To ward off the UAW they turned to time-honored practices of employing labor spies to ferret out union organizers or even sympathizers and to prevent them from entering their plants. Nevertheless, with effective and enthusiastic CIO leadership, particularly from John L. Lewis, and the use of an unconventional—indeed illegal—weapon, the sitdown strike, the United Automobile Workers wrung recognition from General Motors and Chrysler early in 1937. Ford held out until the spring of 1941, as Harry Bennett, the toughest and most powerful of Henry Ford's lieutenants, was much less hesitant about using force than were the executives of the other two companies.

Conclusion

By World War II the pattern of labor relations, marketing, management, and production in the automobile industry had been pretty well systematized. Not only did both Ford and General Motors follow the same policies of production and labor relations, but after Henry Ford II took over his grandfather's company, he adopted lock, stock, and barrel the techniques of management and marketing developed earlier by General Motors. The great challenges of the war and immediate postwar years were the conversion to defense needs and then the reconversion to peacetime production. But while highly significant, conversion and reconversion did not have the lasting impact on the industry that the strategy of growth after 1908, the strategy of competition in the 1920's, and the challenge of labor of the 1930's had had.

Because of the high prosperity resulting from the postwar boom and continuing through the Korean War, methods of action devised before 1941 became increasingly routinized. Then as the market leveled off after 1955 and as competition, including that from abroad, increased, the industry was again under pressure to work out improvements in production, management, and marketing. The outlines of these new developments are just beginning to emerge. Yet they can be essentially little more than modifications of the pioneering achievements of Henry Ford, William C. Durant, Alfred P. Sloan,

Jr., Richard C. Grant, and John L. Lewis. The creative work of these men had an impact far beyond the limits of the automobile business. For during the generation between 1910 and 1940, the automobile industry had become one of the most significant in the nation's economy, and its leaders had altered existing ways and fashioned new ones for carrying on the basic economic functions of production, finance, marketing, management, and labor relations. An inside look at how these innovators viewed and met their challenges should therefore be of interest to both students and practitioners of American business.

PART I

The Strategy of Growth, 1908–1920

Innovations in Modern Production and Finance

INTRODUCTION

As the nation's economy quickly recovered from the short but sharp financial panic of 1907, the fledgling automobile industry began to reach in earnest for the national market. In 1908, as production doubled, each of the two dominant leaders in the industry made decisive steps to meet the potential demand. On October 1, 1908, the first examples of Henry Ford's superb utility car, the Model T, were ready for delivery. Two weeks earlier, the president of the country's largest automobile producer, the Buick Motor Company, chartered the General Motors Company.

During the industry's period of swift growth from 1908 until the early 1920's, production remained the industry's paramount challenge. Second only to production was the need for capital. Until the initial demand for this new type of transportation was met, the rewards went to those who were the swiftest and most efficient in turning out cars. The higher the volume of production, the lower the cost of making each individual automobile. Thus increasing volume made it possible to lower the price and still maintain high profits and wages. Yet rapid expansion of production required the building and purchasing of vast manufacturing and distribution facilities. Most automobile makers were able to finance such expansion out of profits. Others, anxious to exploit the new opportunities as quickly as possible, turned to outside investors for the essential capital.

Expansion of the automobile industry and of its individual enterprises was in no sense an automatic process. To be successful, the new automobile companies had to meet a number of basic conditions. Their product had to be reliable and simplified enough to be used by all kinds of people. They had to provide an effective distribution network of branch offices and dealers to assure their customers prompt delivery and to provide regular and efficient service and repair (including the replacement of parts and accessories). If these two conditions were successfully met, then the resulting call for their product usually required an extensive expansion of production facilities. It also led to obtaining hitherto independent companies that made parts, accessories, and other supplies. A manufacturer could not risk having to stop his whole production line merely because a supplier had been unable to deliver spark plugs, flywheels, or roller bearings at the promised time. It was the cost of constructing these new production facilities and of carrying out a policy of *vertical integration (that is, the policy of manufacturing one's own parts and supplies) that raised problems of finance.*

As the histories of Ford and General Motors clearly reveal, there was more than one way of meeting these requirements for success. William C. Durant of General Motors sought to obtain his assembly, manufacturing, supply, and distribution facilities through the purchase of existing automobile companies. His course put a premium on financial skills and the developing of new financial techniques. Henry Ford preferred to concentrate on designing the most suitable product for the mass market and then on producing it in the largest possible volume. Because of his brilliant success in achieving this goal, Ford was rarely troubled by financial problems. Profits easily paid for growth and integration. While Durant's policy of expansion through purchasing and combination ultimately brought him personal financial disaster, Ford's policy of expansion through improved mass production brought astonishing financial success and made his company the largest and most efficient automobile producer in the world.

Ford—Expansion Through Mass Production

❨ To MEET the still relatively new mass market, Henry Ford had to pioneer in the ways of modern mass production. This able innovator was not, as legend sometimes has it, an untutored farm boy. Although he was raised on a farm, he received an apprenticeship as a machinist at James Flower & Brothers Machine Shop in Detroit and then worked at the Detroit Drydock Company. He next tried his hand at farming. Finding it unrewarding, Ford returned to the city in 1891 to work as an engineer at the Edison Illuminating Company. The lighting of homes with electricity was still a brand-new business and one that was as technologically complex as any in the country. Ford proved himself so competent in this demanding job that in 1893 he became the company's chief engineer.

He then began to spend his spare time experimenting with building the new horseless carriage recently developed in Europe. At first he tested the results of his work and made a reputation for himself making and driving racing cars. By 1903 he was ready to move into the manufacturing of automobiles for the commercial market. In June of that year he formed the Ford Motor Company. Alexander Y. Malcolmson, a Detroit coal dealer, and John Gray, a Detroit banker, provided most of the small amount of capital needed ($28,000 in cash). Other stockholders included James Couzens, Malcolmson's secretary, who would soon become the business brain of the Ford Motor Company, and two brothers, John F. and Horace E. Dodge, well-trained machinists who at first built engines and chassis for Ford and then later headed a major automobile company of their own.

Before long a critical controversy shook the new Ford Motor Company. Malcolmson wanted the firm to devote its energies to its high-priced, six-cylinder Model K, while Ford insisted that they concentrate on the development of a reliable, low-priced car. This issue was finally resolved when Ford, supported by Couzens and the Dodge brothers, bought Malcolmson out for $175,000 in July 1906. This move gave Ford control of over 50 per cent of the company's stock.

Ford then turned to bringing out a product for the mass market. First came the Model N. This car, built of tough vanadium steel, was light but still rugged enough to stand up under the difficult driving conditions in the United States before the day of the paved highway. The N was mechanically simple enough to be driven and even repaired by people without mechanical skills or training in working with machines. The excellent profits coming from the N encouraged Ford to improve it on the basis of two years' experience. The new model, the T, first appeared for sale in the autumn of 1908. By that time Ford's closest associate, Couzens, had made an ambitious start in setting up a network of branch offices and dealers. Once the product had been developed and the sales organization devised, the basic challenge facing the Ford Motor Company became one of production.

In his constant quest for ways to improve and to speed up the manufacturing and assembly processes, it became Ford's basic principle to take "the work to the man" instead of "the man to the work." First he and his associates devised a "line-production system"—that is, the placing of machines and men in a carefully planned sequence of operations. Next came the development of conveyors, rollways, and gravity slides to bring materials regularly and smoothly to the assemblers. Finally, in the summer of 1913, the Ford engineers began to work out a moving assembly line. Instead of having a group of workers assemble a flywheel magneto, an engine, or a chassis at a single location, they decided to move the individual parts past each worker. That worker carried out a single step in the assembly operation. In October 1913 the moving assembly line had its first test run in putting together a chassis. By the end of the year it had reduced the average labor time expended on a single Model T chassis from twelve hours and twenty-

eight minutes to two hours and thirty-eight minutes. By spring of 1914 the Highland Park plant was turning out over 1,000 vehicles a day, and the average labor time for assembling a chassis had dropped to one hour and thirty-three minutes. To increase output still further and to lower costs, Ford had begun earlier to set up branch assembly plants. By August 1913 thirteen of these were in operation in the United States and one was under way at Manchester, England.

The following three selections indicate how Ford met the challenge of demand and how his responses led to the innovation of the moving assembly line and other methods of modern mass production. The first selection comes from the Federal Trade Commission's *Report on the Motor Vehicle Industry*, published in the late 1930's as the result of the first major investigation of the automobile industry by a government agency. The investigators, among the first outsiders to have access to automobile company records, provide a useful brief description of Ford's strategy of growth through product improvement, mass production, and vertical integration. The next selection is taken from Ford's own book, *My Life and Work*, and gives the innovator's views (as of 1922) of what he did and why. Although the words of the book were written by a collaborator, Samuel Crowther, the ideas presented were, according to historian Allan Nevins, "unquestionably Ford's." The third item is taken from the writings of two prominent professional engineers, Horace L. Arnold and Fay L. Faurote, who spent several months at the Highland Park plant in 1914 studying Ford's brilliant technological contributions to modern production. Because their book, *Ford Methods and the Ford Shops*, viewed these achievements through expert eyes, it played an important role in spreading the knowledge of Ford's innovations throughout American industry. The excerpts describing the assembling of the chassis and the painting, japanning, and upholstering of the body were chosen because they demonstrate both the extent and the limits of the new mass-production techniques.

In examining these three quite different sources, the reader should consider the different emphases given the events and developments by the government report, the autobiography, and the professional analysis. He should also keep in mind the following questions: Why did the Model T sell so well? Why did it become so quickly the cheapest car on the market and the

one which gave the customer the most value for his dollar? What precisely were Ford's innovations? What did Ford consider the basic ingredients of mass production? Why did the improvement of product precede the improvement in process? Could it possibly have been the other way around—that is, could the assembly line have come before the development of the T? What besides the moving assembly line does modern mass production require? Why did mass production encourage vertical integration? If Ford was able to sell automobiles at a lower price than any competitor and to offer the highest wages in the industry while still making enormous profits, who or what was being exploited?

THE BROAD STRATEGY

1] The Federal Trade Commission Reviews Ford's Experience

Model T, the Universal Car

WHATEVER the facts about model K, the manufacture and distribution of the 6-cylinder car as well as of the 2-cylinder car was discontinued; and during a period of 18 years commencing in 1908, Ford Motor Co. manufactured and offered for sale only one basic model of passenger automobile, although this was offered in several styles of body. This was model T.

In model T, Ford realized his ideals and embodied his ideas with reference to a "universal car." One of these ideas was that of standardization of the design of the vehicle and of the parts thereof and of the manufacture of these parts with such precision that any part could be replaced from stock with another part so exactly like it that the replacement part would fit exactly into the mechanism, notwithstanding any changes that may have been made in the car design. The idea of interchangeable parts as applied to a specific

FROM Federal Trade Commission, *Report on the Motor Vehicle Industry* (Washington, D.C., U.S. Government Printing Office, 1939), pp. 627–33.

model of machine was standard practice long before this in some industries, but it had not been fully applied in the automobile industry; and the development of it in this industry, especially as applied to improvements in structural design, was apparently largely due to Ford.

It is said that in 1903, Ford said to John W. Anderson,[1] "The way to make automobiles is to make one automobile like another automobile, to make them all alike, to make them come through the factory just alike—just like one pin is like another pin when it comes from a pin factory, or one match is like another match when it comes from a match factory." [2] By such standardization and such precision in manufacture it would be possible to manufacture the parts in quantity production in different factories, located in different communities, and yet have these parts fit together perfectly in the process of assembling them into completed automobiles. If, in the operation of such a motor vehicle, a part should fail, this part could be replaced by its exact duplicate from a conveniently located stock of repair parts. A part of the idea was to manufacture parts and completed automobiles in large quantities so as to reduce cost, reduce the price to the ultimate purchaser, and to stimulate demand. An important idea was that of lightness of the motor vehicle, bringing about economy in operation by the owner. Analysis of a light but strong valve strip stem taken from a wrecked French racer in 1905 resulted in discovery that the material contained vanadium. No steel maker in America at that time knew how to make vanadium steel and a man with such knowledge was imported from England. The process was difficult, because it required a temperature of 3,000 degrees Fahrenheit whereas ordinary furnaces did not go beyond 2,700 degrees. A small steel company made trials under a guaranty against loss and was successful. The result was steel with a tensile strength of 170,000 pounds as compared with 60,000 to 70,000 pounds for ordinary steels.[3] With steel of such tensile strength, parts could be made lighter and yet be sturdier than parts made out of ordinary steel. Simplicity of design and accessibility of the engine, frame, axles, etc., were important for the purpose of minimizing repair costs when repairs should be necessary. Sturdiness of design resulting in durability, so as to assure a long useful life and to economize first cost, was an important part of the idea. Ford's policy and practice was to carry on research for the purpose of improving the structure of the product and the processes in fabricating it so as to increase the economy to the owner and to reduce the price. Price reductions, Ford stated, should be made because of the economies achieved in manufacture, not because of public dissatisfaction with the product.

. . . The principal distinguishing features were a planetary transmission, a rear axle of unusual design, a magneto built into the flywheel as an integral part of the motor, the use of vanadium steel, and relative lightness and power. Incorporation of the magneto as a part of the flywheel reduced the weight of the car. Vanadium steel was used in the car to make it stronger

1 [John W. Anderson was a Detroit lawyer who received 5 per cent interest in the Ford Motor Company as payment for drawing up the company's papers of incorporation. In 1919 Ford purchased Anderson's share in the company for $12.5 million.]

2 Ford, *My Life and Work*, p. 59.

3 Ford, *My Life and Work*, p. 66.

and lighter, increasing the ratio of the horsepower to the weight and making the car cheaper to operate. The car was simple of design, making it easy to operate and easy to maintain and repair. The parts were so precisely manufactured that a number of cars could be disassembled, the parts mixed, and the same number of cars rebuilt from the parts. It is said that this could not be done with any other car in the low-priced field as late as 1913.[4]

Speaking of this car in 1928, the United States Board of Tax Appeals stated:

Model T was a utility car. It was a good car. It had a good reputation and a thoroughly accepted standing in 1913. It was used by all classes of people. It was the cheapest car on the market and was a greater value for its price than any other car. Because of its low price it had a much larger field of demand than any other car. It was within the purchasing power of the greatest number of people and they were rapidly availing themselves of it. There was a greater demand for it than for the car of any other company.[5]

In order to manufacture model T cars with the maximum production economy, Ford Motor Co. built a plant at Highland Park, Mich. (just outside of Detroit), designed and laid out specially for the production of this car. Construction of this plant was begun in 1909; and the plant was completed, occupied, and placed in operation near the end of 1910. A noteworthy feature of the construction of this plant was that it was designed and laid out on what has come to be known as the "line production system." In the plant previously used, as in other ordinary factories, machines, such as drill presses, milling machines, lathes, boring mills, planers, etc., were located in groups according to the type or class of operation; and the material in the process of manufacture was conveyed from group to group according to the sequence of operations. This resulted in a large amount of crisscrossing of the lines of progress and a large amount of shop transportation. The Highland Park plant was designed to avoid this by having the machines and the employees operating them placed in such sequence that the material would move in a predetermined line of production without interruption or loss of time in transporting material from the place of one operation to the place of the next. This means a production line for each part that is to be processed within the factory. For example, in the connecting rod production line, a babbitting operation occurred between two machine tool operations; and a babbitting furnace was placed between the two machine tools, so that the part, after passing through the first of the two machining operations, moved only a few feet to the place of the babbitting operation, and, after the completion of this operation, moved only a few feet to the place of the next machining operation. While similar methods of mechanical handling and economical operation were used before this in some other industries, such as the steel industry, Ford seems to have taken the lead in this matter in the manufacture of such complex mechanisms as automobiles. It reduced inventories, eliminated storage rooms and eliminated the transportation of materials from one department to another—materially

4 U.S. Board of Tax Appeals Report, vol. 11, pp. 1095, 1096.
5 Ibid., p. 1117.

lowering the cost of production. It is said that Ford Motor Co. was the first company to use conveyors to bring material to workmen instead of having the workmen go after the material. This conveyor system was designed so as to keep the material 3 feet off the floor at all times.

An important idea in the design and the subsequent improvements of the Highland Park plant, and of later plants, was the development of specialized machinery designed to perform specific operations in the process of making the respective parts of this car. Each manufacturing operation was studied, and special machinery was designed to perform the operation. Research was carried on for the purpose of improving machine design and of developing new machines so as to reduce the operations to the smallest possible unit. After such a machine was developed, the operation was performed by unskilled labor which could be trained in a few days. New improvements and developments that reduced costs were installed every year. In this manner production costs were lowered progressively.

It is said that in 1913, this plant was equipped with a large number of very expensive single-purpose machines and unique manufacturing contrivances and fixtures. Among these special machines were multiple drilling machines, which drilled simultaneously 45 holes in one cylinder block from four directions in $1\frac{1}{2}$ minutes. With these machines, it was not necessary to take a casting out and turn it bottom side up or around in order to continue the drilling process, as would be required if a standard general-purpose drill press were used. The use of these machines secured accuracy in drilling, avoided loss of castings, minimized the time of operation, and economized floor space. This particular machine as built could be used only on model T motors. Another specialized machine was a milling machine that permitted the milling of 12 cylinder blocks in one operation. A special radiator assembly machine inserted many tubes through a large number of punched sheets in one stroke of a press. Special machines were used for painting wheels, the entire wheel being immersed in the paint and being dried by spinning, the excess paint being thrown off by centrifugal force. Bliss presses were used to press the forms of crank cases out of flat steel plates in one operation; these were also used to form, in one operation, fender plates from rectangular pieces of steel. It is said that these were the first steel crank cases to be used on motor cars; and by making the crank cases of sheet steel, the weight of the car was reduced and its efficiency was increased.

Experiments were also carried on in a research department for the purpose of improving the steels used in making high-speed tools and in treating these high-speed tools so as to improve the quality of red-hardness and increase the speed at which these tools could do their work of drilling, turning, boring, milling, and planing metal parts.[6]

The United States Board of Tax Appeals stated, in 1928, with reference to this Highland Park factory:

All machines were grouped more closely together in the Ford plant than in the ordinary factory. In many instances to accomplish this the beds of lathes and of milling machines were cut off. This close grouping economized operation.

6 Ibid., pp. 1096 and 1098.

In every detail the factory was laid out on a large-production scale. It had been tooled regardless of cost, having in mind only the greatest efficiency, and was laid out with the idea of taking advantage of every possible economy and of producing the quantity desired at the lowest possible price. At that time no other company was able to tool in the same manner or manufacture as cheaply. The plant was recognized as the greatest advance in manufacturing methods in the country at that time, and was the best automobile producing layout in the United States.[7]

It is said that in 1910, Ford Motor Co. was purchasing its bodies, wheels, and radiators from other manufacturers. In June 1912, plans were started for buildings known as W and X, to be erected at Highland Park. Construction was started in May 1913. In preparation for this construction, railroad tracks were rearranged so as to provide shipping facilities for the proposed buildings. Each of these buildings was a 6-story structure, 840 feet long by 60 feet in width, and each having a floor space of 348,800 square feet. They were separated by a craneway that was 800 feet long, 40 feet wide, and that was roofed with glass. This provided a light well throughout the length of the buildings. The craneway side of each building was left open without a wall. Heating plants and air washers were installed on the roofs and the heated or washed air was forced through the buildings by means of hollow columns, the buildings being thus ventilated and the temperature regulated. As air escaped from the open sides of the buildings, it automatically provided heat and ventilation for the craneway without extra expense. It is said that in these respects, these buildings were unique in factory construction. A railroad track entered the craneway, and projecting platforms were built at several places in each floor of these buildings in such manner that materials could be loaded or unloaded at any point on any floor in either building by means of a crane. The buildings were designed so that material could be hoisted as near to the roof as possible and would progress downward from floor to floor during the manufacturing operation. Holes were cut through the floors, and parts that started in rough at the top floor could pass by gravity down through chutes, conveyors or tubes, emerging as finished articles on the ground floor.

Assembly Plants

ANOTHER idea adopted, developed and put into practice by the Ford management was that of decentralization of manufacture, using specialized plants in the vicinity of Detroit as plants in which to manufacture parts, much of the assembling of these parts into the completed automobiles taking place in branch assembly plants located in various parts of the United States. Time was required for the purpose of giving full effect to this plan. Eventually, assembly plants were put into operation in the following cities: Kansas City, Mo., in October, 1910; Long Island, N.Y., in July 1911; Chicago and San Francisco in October 1913; Memphis, Los Angeles, and Denver in November 1913; Detroit and Portland (Oreg.) in January 1914; Seattle in February, 1914; Cambridge (Mass.) and St. Louis in April 1914; Columbus in June 1914; Dallas and Houston in July 1914; Minneapolis in December

7 Ibid., p. 1099.

1914; Indianapolis and Pittsburgh in February 1915; Atlanta in March 1915; Cincinnati in April 1915; Cleveland in August 1915; Louisville in October 1915; Buffalo during November 1915; and Milwaukee, Washington, Oklahoma City, and Omaha at dates not specified but not earlier than 1915.

Parts were manufactured in the factories in the vicinity of Detroit, or were purchased from factories located at other points, were shipped to these assembly points and were there assembled into the completed automobiles. Several economies are claimed for this system of branch assembly plants. Transportation costs were economized by shipping parts instead of completed automobiles to these assembly plants because the freight cars could be more heavily laden, the straight carloads of parts took lower class rates, and ordinary freight cars could be used instead of special cars. Loading and handling costs were minimized; and diversion and reconsignment were made more practicable and available. Parts made by other manufacturers could be shipped directly to the assembly plants instead of to Detroit; thereby minimizing the freight charges and handling costs. Another advantage was that stocks of parts could be accumulated at the various assembly plants, economizing storage space at the Detroit factories and permitting production of the parts in those portions of the year in which business was slow, thus eliminating the sharp curves of production. The assembly plants also established immediate sources of supply in the regions in which they were located. Dealers were furnished with stocks of parts from these assembly plants; and in many cases were able to drive the cars from the assembly plants to their places of business instead of having them transported by rail.

Also with the establishment of these branches, supervision of dealers was taken over by branch managers. It is said that very close supervision was maintained over the dealer, the control extending even to the appearance of the dealers' salesrooms. Dealers were also required to carry adequate stocks of those parts that were most in demand, thus enabling prompt service and prompt repairs to the car owners.[8]

Models in 1908–09

PURSUANT to this policy of concentrating on the production of one model of car, Ford Motor Co. offered this model in five styles of body during the fiscal year 1908–09; namely, a touring car retailing at $850, a town car at $1,000, a roadster at $825, a coupe at $950, and a landaulet at $950, these prices being f.o.b. Detroit. All of these were merely style variations of model T. The sales during the first year of model T production amounted to 10,607 cars.

Price Policy and Prices of Model T Cars

AS BEFORE stated, the policy of Ford Motor Co. was to manufacture a car of such design and in such manner that it could be offered to the public at a low price and also to reduce prices in line with reduced costs as production economies were achieved through improvement in the structure of the product and in processes of manufacture and through attained volume. Table 1 shows the prices, f.o.b. Detroit, of the model T runabout and the

8 Ibid., pp. 1104 to 1106.

model T touring car as of various dates from October 1, 1908, to February 11, 1926.

TABLE 1. PRICES OF MODEL T RUNABOUTS AND TOURING CARS, BY DATES, OCT. 1, 1908, TO FEB. 11, 1926 [a]

DATE	RUNABOUT	TOURING	DATE	RUNABOUT	TOURING
Oct. 1, 1908		$850	Aug. 16, 1918	$500	$525
Oct. 1, 1909		950	Mar. 4, 1920	550	575
Oct. 1, 1910		780	Sept. 22, 1920	395	440
Oct. 1, 1911	$590	690	June 7, 1921	370	415
Oct. 1, 1912	525	600	Sept. 2, 1921	325	355
Aug. 1, 1913	500	550	Sept. 16, 1922	319	348
Aug. 1, 1914	440	490	Oct. 17, 1922	269	298
Aug. 1, 1915	390	440	Oct. 2, 1923	265	295
Aug. 1, 1916	345	360	Dec. 2, 1924	260	290
Feb. 21, 1918	435	450	Feb. 11, 1926	290	310

[a] U.S. Board of Tax Appeals Reports, vol. 11, p. 1116.

It will be observed from the foregoing table that the price of the touring car on October 1, 1908, was $850, and that it was increased to $950 on October 1, 1909. From that date there was a progressive reduction of the price of this car until it reached a low of $360 on August 1, 1916. During the period of rising wage rates and prices of materials in the latter part of the war period and the immediate post-war period, the prices were increased from time to time to a maximum of $575 on March 4, 1920. After that date, prices were again reduced progressively and reached a new low of $290 on December 2, 1924. There was an increase of $20 on February 11, 1926. Commencing with a price of $590 on October 1, 1911, the prices of the runabout followed a course paralleling that of the prices of the touring car. A minimum of $345 was reached on August 1, 1916, after which the prices were increased progressively to $550 on March 4, 1920, and again were progressively decreased thereafter to a new low of $260 on December 2, 1924. The price of the runabout was increased $30 on February 11, 1926.

With these progressively diminishing prices, the sales of model T cars increased by leaps and bounds. The aggregate sales during the calendar year 1908 amounted to 5,986 cars. The sales during the succeeding calendar years up to 1919 were as follows: 1909, 12,292 cars; 1910, 19,293 cars; 1911, 40,402 cars; 1912, 78,611 cars; 1913, 182,809 cars; 1914, 260,720 cars; 1915, 355,276 cars; 1916, 577,036 cars; 1917, 802,771 cars; 1918, 402,908 cars; and 1919, 777,694 cars. During a considerable portion of 1918, the factories of Ford Motor Co. were engaged in the manufacture of Liberty motors and submarine chasers, and the production and sale of automobiles were greatly reduced, pursuant to the policy of the United States Government to limit the production of commodities that were not deemed necessaries of life in order to concentrate as much of the productive resources as practicable in the production of war materials and munitions. This explains the reduction of the company's sales by approximately one-half in 1918 as compared with 1917.

During the same period sales increased in invoice value from a little over $4,700,000 during the year ended September 30, 1908, to more than $24,656,-000 in 1911, to nearly $89,109,000 in 1913, to more than $206,867,000 during the year ended July 3, 1916, and to approximately $305,637,000 in the year ended July 31, 1919.

.   .   .   .

IMPLEMENTING THE STRATEGY

2] Ford Recalls His Accomplishments

W E HAD been through an experimenting period of five years. The cars were beginning to be sold in Europe. The business, as an automobile business then went, was considered extraordinarily prosperous. We had plenty of money. Since the first year we have practically always had plenty of money. We sold for cash, we did not borrow money, and we sold directly to the purchaser. We had no bad debts and we kept within ourselves on every move. I have always kept well within my resources. I have never found it necessary to strain them, because, inevitably, if you give attention to work and service, the resources will increase more rapidly than you can devise ways and means of disposing of them.

We were careful in the selection of our salesmen. At first there was great difficulty in getting good salesmen because the automobile trade was not supposed to be stable. It was supposed to be dealing in a luxury—in pleasure vehicles. We eventually appointed agents, selecting the very best men we could find, and then paying to them a salary larger than they could possibly earn in business for themselves. In the beginning we had not paid much in the way of salaries. We were feeling our way, but when we knew what our way was, we adopted the policy of paying the very highest reward for service and then insisting upon getting the highest service. Among the requirements for an agent we laid down the following:

1. A progressive, up-to-date man keenly alive to the possibilities of business.

2. A suitable place of business clean and dignified in appearance.

3. A stock of parts sufficient to make prompt replacements and keep in active service every Ford car in his territory.

4. An adequately equipped repair shop which has in it the right machinery for every necessary repair and adjustment.

FROM Henry Ford in collaboration with Samuel Crowther, *My Life and Work* (New York, 1922), pp. 59–60, 67–74, 79–86.

5. Mechanics who are thoroughly familiar with the construction and operation of Ford cars.

6. A comprehensive bookkeeping system and a follow-up sales system, so that it may be instantly apparent what is the financial status of the various departments of his business, the condition and size of his stock, the present owners of cars, and the future prospects.

7. Absolute cleanliness throughout every department. There must be no unwashed windows, dusty furniture, dirty floors.

8. A suitable display sign.

9. The adoption of policies which will ensure absolutely square dealing and the highest character of business ethics.

And this is the general instruction that was issued:

A dealer or a salesman ought to have the name of every possible automobile buyer in his territory, including all those who have never given the matter a thought. He should then personally solicit by visitation if possible—by correspondence at the least—every man on that list and then making necessary memoranda, know the automobile situation as related to every resident so solicited. If your territory is too large to permit this, you have too much territory.

[Ford next stresses the importance of light vanadium steel in manufacturing his product.]

The vanadium steel disposed of much of the weight. The other requisites of a universal car I had already worked out and many of them were in practice. The design had to balance. Men die because a part gives out. Machines wreck themselves because some parts are weaker than others. Therefore, a part of the problem in designing a universal car was to have as nearly as possible all parts of equal strength considering their purpose— to put a motor in a one-horse shay. Also it had to be fool proof. This was difficult because a gasoline motor is essentially a delicate instrument and there is a wonderful opportunity for any one who has a mind that way to mess it up. I adopted this slogan:

"When one of my cars breaks down I know I am to blame."

From the day the first motor car appeared on the streets it had to me appeared to be a necessity. It was this knowledge and assurance that led me to build to the one end—a car that would meet the wants of the multitudes. All my efforts were then and still are turned to the production of one car—one model. And, year following year, the pressure was, and still is, to improve and refine and make better, with an increasing reduction in price. The universal car had to have these attributes:

1. Quality in material to give service in use. Vanadium steel is the strongest, toughest, and most lasting of steels. It forms the foundation and super-structure of the cars. It is the highest quality steel in this respect in the world, regardless of price.

2. Simplicity in operation—because the masses are not mechanics.

3. Power in sufficient quantity.

4. Absolute reliability—because of the varied uses to which the cars would be put and the variety of roads over which they would travel.

5. Lightness. With the Ford there are only 7.95 pounds to be carried by each cubic inch of piston displacement. This is one of the reasons why Ford cars are "always going," wherever and whenever you see them—through sand and mud, through slush, snow, and water, up hills, across fields and roadless plains.

6. Control—to hold its speed always in hand, calmly and safely meeting every emergency and contingency either in the crowded streets of the city or on dangerous roads. The planetary transmission of the Ford gave this control and anybody could work it. That is the "why" of the saying: "Anybody can drive a Ford." It can turn around almost anywhere.

7. The more a motor car weighs, naturally the more fuel and lubricants are used in the driving; the lighter the weight, the lighter the expense of operation. The light weight of the Ford car in its early years was used as an argument against it. Now that is all changed.

The design which I settled upon was called "Model T." The important feature of the new model—which, if it were accepted, as I thought it would be, I intended to make the only model and then start into real production—was its simplicity. There were but four constructional units in the car—the power plant, the frame, the front axle, and the rear axle. All of these were easily accessible and they were designed so that no special skill would be required for their repair or replacement. I believed then, although I said very little about it because of the novelty of the idea, that it ought to be possible to have parts so simple and so inexpensive that the menace of expensive hand repair work would be entirely eliminated. The parts could be made so cheaply that it would be less expensive to buy new ones than to have old ones repaired. They could be carried in hardware shops just as nails or bolts are carried. I thought that it was up to me as the designer to make the car so completely simple that no one could fail to understand it.

That works both ways and applies to everything. The less complex an article, the easier it is to make, the cheaper it may be sold, and therefore the greater number may be sold.

· · · · · · · · · · · · ·

I designed eight models in all before "Model T." . . .

The "Model T" had practically no features which were not contained in some one or other of the previous models. Every detail had been fully tested in practice. There was no guessing as to whether or not it would be a successful model. It had to be. There was no way it could escape being so, for it had not been made in a day. It contained all that I was then able to put into a motor car plus the material, which for the first time I was able to obtain. We put out "Model T" for the season 1908–1909.

The company was then five years old. The original factory space had been .28 acre. We had employed an average of 311 people in the first year, built 1,708 cars, and had one branch house. In 1908, the factory space had increased to 2.65 acres and we owned the building. The average number of employees had increased to 1,908. We built 6,181 cars and had fourteen branch houses. It was a prosperous business.

. . . .

Therefore in 1909 I announced one morning, without any previous warning, that in the future we were going to build only one model, that the model was going to be "Model T," and that the chassis would be exactly the same for all cars, and I remarked:

"Any customer can have a car painted any colour that he wants so long as it is black."

I cannot say that any one agreed with me. The selling people could not of course see the advantages that a single model would bring about in production. More than that, they did not particularly care. They thought that our production was good enough as it was and there was a very decided opinion that lowering the sales price would hurt sales, that the people who wanted quality would be driven away and that there would be none to replace them. There was very little conception of the motor industry. A motor car was still regarded as something in the way of a luxury. The manufacturers did a good deal to spread this idea. Some clever persons invented the name "pleasure car" and the advertising emphasized the pleasure features. The sales people had ground for their objections and particularly when I made the following announcement:

I will build a motor car for the great multitude. It will be large enough for the family but small enough for the individual to run and care for. It will be constructed of the best materials, by the best men to be hired, after the simplest designs that modern engineering can devise. But it will be so low in price that no man making a good salary will be unable to own one—and enjoy with his family the blessing of hours of pleasure in God's great open spaces.

This announcement was received not without pleasure. The general comment was:

"If Ford does that he will be out of business in six months."

The impression was that a good car could not be built at a low price, and that, anyhow, there was no use in building a low-priced car because only wealthy people were in the market for cars. The 1908–1909 sales of more than ten thousand cars had convinced me that we needed a new factory. We already had a big modern factory—the Piquette Street plant. It was as good as, perhaps a little better than, any automobile factory in the country. But I did not see how it was going to care for the sales and production that were inevitable. So I bought sixty acres at Highland Park, which was then considered away out in the country from Detroit. The amount of ground bought and the plans for a bigger factory than the world has ever seen were opposed. The question was already being asked:

"How soon will Ford blow up?"

Nobody knows how many thousand times it has been asked since. It is asked only because of the failure to grasp that a principle rather than an individual is at work, and the principle is so simple that it seems mysterious.

. . . .

Contrast the year 1908 with the year 1911. The factory space increased from 2.65 to 32 acres. The average number of employees from 1,908 to 4,110, and the cars built from a little over six thousand to nearly thirty-five thousand. You will note that men were not employed in proportion to the output.

We were, almost overnight it seems, in great production.

.   .   .   .

The more economical methods of production did not begin all at once. They began gradually—just as we began gradually to make our own parts. "Model T" was the first motor that we made ourselves. The great economies began in assembling and then extended to other sections so that, while to-day we have skilled mechanics in plenty, they do not produce automobiles—they make it easy for others to produce them. Our skilled men are the tool makers, the experimental workmen, the machinists, and the pattern makers. They are as good as any men in the world—so good, indeed, that they should not be wasted in doing that which the machines they contrive can do better. The rank and file of men come to us unskilled; they learn their jobs within a few hours or a few days. If they do not learn within that time they will never be of any use to us. These men are, many of them, foreigners, and all that is required before they are taken on is that they should be potentially able to do enough work to pay the overhead charges on the floor space they occupy. They do not have to be able-bodied men. We have jobs that require great physical strength—although they are rapidly lessening; we have other jobs that require no strength whatsoever— jobs which, as far as strength is concerned, might be attended to by a child of three.

.   .   .   .

A Ford car contains about five thousand parts—that is counting screws, nuts, and all. Some of the parts are fairly bulky and others are almost the size of watch parts. In our first assembling we simply started to put a car together at a spot on the floor and workmen brought to it the parts as they were needed in exactly the same way that one builds a house. When we started to make parts it was natural to create a single department of the factory to make that part, but usually one workman performed all of the operations necessary on a small part. The rapid press of production made it necessary to devise plans of production that would avoid having the workers falling over one another. The undirected worker spends more of his time walking about for materials and tools than he does in working; he gets small pay because pedestrianism is not a highly paid line.

The first step forward in assembly came when we began taking the work to the men instead of the men to the work. We now have two general principles in all operations—that a man shall never have to take more than one step, if possibly it can be avoided, and that no man need ever stoop over.

The principles of assembly are these:

1. Place the tools and the men in the sequence of the operation so that each component part shall travel the least possible distance while in the process of finishing.

2. Use work slides or some other form of carrier so that when a workman completes his operation, he drops the part always in the same place—which place must always be the most convenient place to his hand—and if possible have gravity carry the part to the next workman for his operation.

3. Use sliding assembling lines by which the parts to be assembled are delivered at convenient distances.

The net result of the application of these principles is the reduction of the necessity for thought on the part of the worker and the reduction of his movements to a minimum. He does as nearly as possibly only one thing with only one movement.

The assembling of the chassis is, from the point of view of the non-mechanical mind, our most interesting and perhaps best known operation, and at one time it was an exceedingly important operation. We now [1922] ship out the parts for assembly at the point of distribution.

Along about April 1, 1913, we first tried the experiment of an assembly line. We tried it on assembling the fly-wheel magneto. We try everything in a little way first—we will rip out anything once we discover a better way, but we have to know absolutely that the new way is going to be better than the old before we do anything drastic.

I believe that this was the first moving line ever installed. The idea came in a general way from the overhead trolley that the Chicago packers use in dressing beef. We had previously assembled the fly-wheel magneto in the usual method. With one workman doing a complete job he could turn out from thirty-five to forty pieces in a nine-hour day, or about twenty minutes to an assembly. What he did alone was then spread into twenty-nine operations; that cut down the assembly time to thirteen minutes, ten seconds. Then we raised the height of the line eight inches—this was in 1914—and cut the time to seven minutes. Further experimenting with the speed that the work should move at cut the time down to five minutes. In short, the result is this: by the aid of scientific study one man is now able to do somewhat more than four did only a comparatively few years ago. That line established the efficiency of the method and we now use it everywhere. The assembling of the motor, formerly done by one man, is now divided into eighty-four operations—those men do the work that three times their number formerly did. In a short time we tried out the plan on the chassis.

About the best we had done in stationary chassis assembling was an average of twelve hours and twenty-eight minutes per chassis. We tried the experiment of drawing the chassis with a rope and windlass down a line two hundred fifty feet long. Six assemblers travelled with the chassis and picked up the parts from piles placed along the line. This rough experiment reduced the time to five hours fifty minutes per chassis. In the early part of 1914 we elevated the assembly line. We had adopted the policy of "man-high" work; we had one line twenty-six and three quarter inches and another twenty-four and one half inches from the floor—to suit squads of different heights. The waist-high arrangement and a further subdivision of work so that each man had fewer movements cut down the labour time per chassis to one hour thirty-three minutes. Only the chassis was then assembled in the line. The body was placed on in "John R. Street"—the famous street that runs through our Highland Park factories. Now the line assembles the whole car.

It must not be imagined, however, that all this worked out as quickly as it sounds. The speed of the moving work had to be carefully tried out; in the fly-wheel magneto we first had a speed of sixty inches per minute. That was too fast. Then we tried eighteen inches per minute. That was too slow. Finally we settled on forty-four inches per minute. The idea is that a man must not be hurried in his work—he must have every second necessary but not a single unnecessary second. We have worked out speeds for each assembly, for the success of the chassis assembly caused us gradually to overhaul our entire method of manufacturing and to put all assembling in mechanically driven lines. The chassis assembling line, for instance, goes at a pace of six feet per minute; the front axle assembly line goes at one hundred eighty-nine inches per minute. In the chassis assembling are forty-five separate operations or stations. The first men fasten four mud-guard brackets to the chassis frame; the motor arrives on the tenth operation and so on in detail. Some men do only one or two small operations, others do more. The man who places a part does not fasten it—the part may not be fully in place until after several operations later. The man who puts in a bolt does not put on the nut; the man who puts on the nut does not tighten it. On operation number thirty-four the budding motor gets its gasoline; it has previously received lubrication; on operation number forty-four the radiator is filled with water, and on operation number forty-five the car drives out onto John R. Street.

Essentially the same ideas have been applied to the assembling of the motor. In October, 1913, it required nine hours and fifty-four minutes of labour time to assemble one motor; six months later, by the moving assembly method, this time had been reduced to five hours and fifty-six minutes. Every piece of work in the shops moves; it may move on hooks on overhead chains going to assembly in the exact order in which the parts are required; it may travel on a moving platform, or it may go by gravity, but the point is that there is no lifting or trucking of anything other than materials. Materials are brought in on small trucks or trailers operated by cut-down Ford chassis, which are sufficiently mobile and quick to get in and out of any aisle where they may be required to go. No workman has anything to do with moving or lifting anything. That is all in a separate department—the department of transportation.

We started assembling a motor car in a single factory. Then as we began to make parts, we began to departmentalize so that each department would do only one thing. As the factory is now organized each department makes only a single part or assembles a part. A department is a little factory in itself. The part comes into it as raw material or as a casting, goes through the sequence of machines and heat treatments, or whatever may be required, and leaves that department finished. It was only because of transport ease that the departments were grouped together when we started to manufacture. I did not know that such minute divisions would be possible; but as our production grew and departments multiplied, we actually changed from making automobiles to making parts. . . .

Highland Park now has five hundred departments. Down at our Piquette plant we had only eighteen departments, and formerly at Highland Park we had only one hundred and fifty departments. This illustrates how far we are going in the manufacture of parts.

.   .   .   .

The factory keeps no record of experiments. The foremen and superintendents remember what has been done. If a certain method has formerly been tried and failed, somebody will remember it—but I am not particularly anxious for the men to remember what someone else has tried to do in the past, for then we might quickly accumulate far too many things that could not be done. That is one of the troubles with extensive records. If you keep on recording all of your failures you will shortly have a list showing that there is nothing left for you to try—whereas it by no means follows because one man has failed in a certain method that another man will not succeed.

.   .   .   .

3] Two Professional Engineers Analyze Ford's Innovations

THE FORD engineers certainly do make great labor reductions in the foundry, the machine shop, and in body-upholstering by simple endless-chain installations, because in all assembling operations it costs much less in labor-time expenditure to move an assembly in progress past fixed points of component supply than it costs to hold the assembly in progress stationary and bring the components to the one assembling location, and because the moving assembly gives more floor space for assemblers and hence permits the more minute subdividing of assembling operations.

.   .   .   .

Ford Chassis Assembling

THE Ford chassis assembling in moving lines affords a highly impressive spectacle to beholders of every class, technical or non-technical. Long lines of slowly moving assemblies in progress, busy groups of successive operators, the rapid growth of the chassis as component after component is added from the overhead sources of supply, and, finally the instant start into self-moving power—these excite the liveliest interest and admiration in all who witness for the first time this operation of bringing together the varied elements of the new and seemingly vivified creation, on the three Ford chassis assem-

FROM Horace L. Arnold and Fay L. Faurote, Ford Methods and the Ford Shops (New York, 1915), pp. 129–40, 360–70.

bling lines where over 1,200 have been put together and driven out of doors into John R Street in one single 8-hour day.

. . . Up to August, 1913, the Ford chassis was assembled in one location. First the front and rear axles were laid on the floor, then the chassis frame with springs in place was assembled with the axles, next the wheels were placed on the axles, and the remaining components were successively added to complete the chassis. All components needed to make up one chassis had to be brought by hand to each chassis-assembling location. This routine of stationary chassis assembling was, in September, 1913, worked with two lines of assembling-floor space, 600 feet long, 12 feet chassis-to-chassis centers, 50 assembling locations in each 600-foot line, 100 cars in process of assembling in the two lines. Working in this routine 600 men were employed, 500 being assemblers who were supplied with components by 100 men acting as component carriers.

About April 1, 1913, the first sliding assembling line, used for assembling the Ford fly-wheel magneto, was placed in work and immediately showed a large reduction in assembling labor-cost. Consequently, the possibility of lowering chassis-assembling costs by introducing the moving assembling line for chassis assembling became a matter of discussion among the Ford engineers.

In the month of August, 1913 (the dull season), 250 assemblers, with a stationary assembling location for each chassis, the assemblers being served by 80 component carriers, worked 9 hours per day for 26 days to turn out 6,182 chassis assemblies. Total labor hours $330 \times 9 \times 26 = 77,220$ hours, giving 12 hours and 28 minutes for labor time on each chassis, about as good as was ever done with stationary chassis assembling.

The assembling line was long—600 feet—but even at that did not give room enough, and 12½ hours of labor time seemed altogether too much for one chassis. It was in the dull season, and an experiment was made with rope and windlass traction on a moving assembly line 250 feet long. Six assemblers traveled with the chassis as it was slowly pulled along the floor by the rope and windlass past stationary means of component supply, and the chassis-assembling time was reduced to 5 hours and 50 minutes of one man's time, over 50 per cent saving.

October 7, 1913, on a moving-assembly line 150 feet long, with no helpers, components being piled at suitable locations, 140 assemblers in the line completed 435 chassis assemblies in one 9-hour day, 2 hours and 57 minutes of one man's time for each chassis assembling.

The assembling line was lengthened by degrees to 300 feet, giving the men more room, and on December 1, 1913, 177 assemblers working 9 hours turned out 606 completed chassis assemblies, about 2 hours 38 minutes of one man's time to each chassis.

December 30, 1913, working two assembling lines, 191 men completed 642 chassis assemblies in one 9-hour day, a little less than 2 hours 40 minutes of one man's time for each chassis, the cars being pushed along by hand.

January 14, 1914, one assembling line was endless-chain driven, with favorable results.

January 19, four chassis-assembling lines were worked, only one line being chain-driven. The wheels were put on as soon as the axles and the chassis frames were assembled, and the assemblies in progress ran with their front wheels on the floor and their hind wheels carried in 3-wheeled cradlcs, used to give easy placing of the rear wheels on the motor-starting drive at the end of the line.

February 27, 1914, the first high line of rails with chain drive was used. The chassis slid on its axles as pulled by the chain, and the wheels were applied only a short distance before the motor-starting was reached. This first high line was made with rails 26¾ inches above the shop floor, and at once showed great advantages, the best time for one chassis assembling being only 84 minutes, while the worst time was 2 hours. Two other high lines were soon installed, 24½ inches high, with chain drives; tall men worked on the line 26¾ inches high, and short men on the other two lines, 24½ inches high.

The Ford engineers make a point of "man-high" work placing, having learned that any stooping position greatly reduces the workman's efficiency. The differing heights of the chassis-assembling high lines are believed to be decidedly advantageous.

On these three high lines, on April 30, 1914, 1,212 chassis assemblies were completed in one 8-hour day, each chassis being assembled in 1 hour 33 minutes of one man's time, as against 12 hours 28 minutes, the best time with stationary chassis assembling, September, 1913—93 minutes as against 728 minutes—and it must be borne in mind that the September, 1913, Ford practice in chassis assembling was fully abreast of the best known in the trade. Very naturally this unbelievable reduction in chassis-assembling labor costs gave pause to the Ford engineering staff, and led to serious search for other labor-reduction opportunities in the Ford shops, regardless of precedents and traditions of the trade at large.

The chassis was not completed when it ran out into John R Street, and the first practice was to let the driver run the chassis up and down until he thought best to abandon it to the motor inspector and the rear-axle inspector, and to return to the end of the assembling lines for another chassis to drive out into John R Street. The bodies were allowed to slide down an incline from the second floor, and were then dragged along the pavement by one man and stood on end in a bunch south of the chute.

When the assembly was completed on the John R pavement, and had been inspected by the motor inspector and the rear-axle inspector, it was again boarded by a driver and taken to the bunch of bodies, where four men lifted a body into place on the chassis, and the completed automobile assembly was then driven to the shipping-clerk's office, between the railway tracks, ready for shipment.

This procedure afforded plenty of gaps and vacancies for discretionary proceedings on the part of all the men working outside under the head assembler. The next radical improvement was made by laying down the angle-iron John R street track, running southward from the exit door, under the body-chute and something more than a chassis length to the south of the

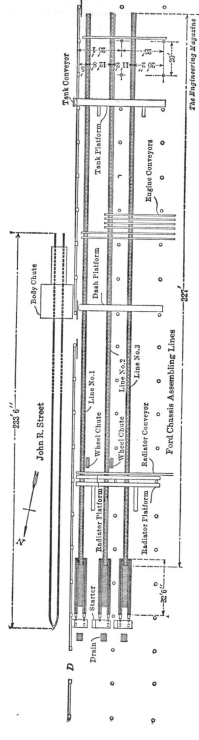

FIGURE 1. PLAN OF CHASSIS-ASSEMBLING LINES
The chassis assemblies begin at the south (right-hand) end, and move to the north (left-hand) end, under the overhead gasoline-tank platform, the motor-carrying chain-hoist tracks, the dash assembly platform and the radiator platform. They then take the wheels, run on the wheels on roller frames over the pit where a workman caps the front-axle bracing globe, and then down a short incline onto the motor-starting drive for the rear wheels. Then the chassis is driven under its own power, through the door, *D*, and on the John R street track to the southward.

chute; and the chute itself was presently equipped with a car-body handling rig, not regarded as the final thing, but serving to place a body on the chassis with one handling only.

· · · · · · · · · · · · ·

How the Ford Bodies Are Finished: Painting, Upholstering, Japanning and Baking

PAINTING needs plenty of room and time; furthermore, it must be done by skilled men. At least, that was my belief until I saw the way that it was done in the Ford plant. But here again, one is obliged to alter preconceived conceptions and acknowledge that Ford ingenuity has triumphed.

As in the chassis assembly, . . . the bodies are painted and upholstered, topped and trimmed complete, on an endless-chain track conveyor. This system of finishing has been but recently introduced.

Following one after another like the successive negatives on a motion-picture film, the bodies may be seen in every stage of completion.

Like a railroad system with its stations, side-tracks, depots, and terminals, the body-painting and upholstering process line wends its way over three successive floors of the new, big, six-story building on Manchester Avenue, now running straight for 850 feet at a time, turning right-angled corners—now going down-grade to the floor below, back and across, until finally the terminal is reached—the "chassis-body assembly bridge" outside.

Starting in the east end of the fifth floor, to which the rough product is raised by means of an inclined conveyer, . . . the bodies are thrown onto the endless-chain track and given a thorough sanding and cleaning inside and out. As now arranged, it is necessary to truck the bodies from the head of the inclined conveyer to the end of the track, but it is proposed to put in a short conveyer running crosswise of the building, which will do this work, and on this the preliminary cleaning can be done, thereby giving room on the main track (which runs a distance of 850 feet parallel with Manchester Avenue) for the first priming operation, now done in separate rooms off the line.

Driven at a speed of about 25 feet per minute the bodies soon reach the point where this first "priming" operation takes place. This is the only operation, with the exception of drying, which necessitates the removal of the bodies from the track, and in all probability as soon as the cross conveyer has been put in this method of priming will be displaced by one identical with that used for the second and succeeding coats. At the present time, however, the body is removed from the track, slid onto a truck, and shoved into one of the small painting rooms just north of the track. Here a workman wearing a mask and equipped with a giant atomizer, behind which there is a pressure of 80 pounds per square inch, gives the body a thorough spraying with a brown body metal primer which dries very rapidly. The entire surface is covered in a surprisingly short time, and with a shove, the body is sent rolling across the floor to another man who with a critical eye goes over it and with a hand brush smooths out or touches up any points which, in his judgment, need further attention.

The body is then allowed to dry thoroughly before it is placed back on the track. After being sanded, it is ready for its second priming; a blue-black coat which is "flowed on" in the following manner: standing on opposite sides of the track are two men equipped with hoses, the nozzles of which remind one of fanlike vacuum-cleaner nozzles, except that the ends, instead of being entirely open, are perforated, the holes extending in a line at right angles to the direction of the flow. A large tank mounted on the floor above, and connected to the hose by means of a system of pipes, furnishes a constant stream of paint. The system is operated entirely by gravity, but by the elevation of the tank to the floor above a sufficient head is secured to insure a flow of about 6 gallons a minute.

When the body has progressed to the point where it is opposite these men, they completely shower the surface with the protecting liquid, starting at the top and working down. This they do in an incredibly short time. Some points on the back of the front seat and on the dash, which they are unable to reach easily, are afterwards done by hand, with a brush. The rear end of the body is slightly elevated by a "shield block" which prevents the paint from dripping into the track and also helps to drain the excess liquid back into the system.

On both sides of the track, and directly under the sprayers, are large galvanized-iron drip tanks which drain into a central catch tank below. Surplus paint, therefore, drips into these pans and finds its way back, after passing through screens, into the paint-supply system again. A smaller gear pump, located in the pipe line about 6 feet from the track, returns the liquid to the tank above, so that a sufficient amount can be used at all times to do the job properly, without fear of wasting it. . . . About 200 feet of the track are required for each painting operation. The "color varnish" coats and "finishing" coats are flowed on in the same manner. After the body has traveled about 200 feet, it is sufficiently dry to be removed and stacked for drying, which requires about 24 hours.

It is then placed back on the track and "mossed"; that is, rubbed lightly with curled hair and prepared for its first color varnish. This operation is performed on a cross track running from the finish end of the priming track to the starting end of the color-varnish line, which runs back from the west to the east end of the same building, parallel with the priming track.

A similar system of tanks, piping, draining trays and strainers is utilized for this operation. About 200 feet of draining tank is here required to carry off the surplus color varnish. The body is also slightly elevated at the rear, by a cross drain board, as before.

After being allowed to drip for a time which experience has shown to be sufficient, it is removed and stacked for drying. At the end of this drying, it is again "mossed," given a second coat of color varnish in the same manner as before, and stacked to dry.

At this point the upholstering operation begins. Sets of back springs are put on the seat backs, materials needed for upholstering, including partially finished "back assemblies," a big bag of hair, trimming strips, etc., are dumped into the inside of the body, just as it is shoved onto an inclined belt-conveyer which takes it to the floor below.

Here it is deposited on a metal-topped table, turned through an angle of 180 degrees, and pushed onto the "rubbing deck," where the exterior surface is given a thorough rubbing with pumice and water. The same type of track conveyer system is employed here to keep the work in progress. Instead of utilizing an ordinary "rubbing deck" where the bodies are turned up at various angles and must be handled by hand, with much labor and inconvenience, the Ford engineers, with their common-sense way of doing things, have mounted the track in the center of a concrete gutter, along which are placed, at regular intervals, water outlets and pans of powdered pumice. So conveniently arranged is everything that after the body starts on its journey across the deck, there is nothing but rubbing, washing, and polishing to be done. This work is accomplished under the most favorable conditions. The bodies are always at the proper height and in the proper position so that the work can be done without stooping or manual handling.

The pumice and water can be used freely and the work done well, in the time allowed for progress across the deck.

When it arrives at the other end, at the beginning of the two parallel upholstering lines, it is smooth and dry. At this point the work is turned through an angle of 90 degrees, divided, and started down two parallel tracks running the full length of the fourth floor.

Already provided with materials, and starting with the foundation of springs previously fastened in place at the end of the color-varnish operation on the upper floor, the upholsterers now proceed to fasten the made-up "cushion backs" to the body, by tacking the material firmly to the bottom of the back of the seat, finishing it up with a strip of welt and black-headed upholsterers' tacks.

The sides are treated in a like manner, being built out by constantly introducing curled hair taken from the large bag of hair with which each body is supplied. The burlap is tacked to the edge of the top of the seat, stuffed, and sewed in place. More hair is then forced in and a big roll made by pulling the leather over it. It is finished with the welt, securely tacked in place.

A number of men work on the same body at the same time; some walking along the outside and some riding inside. Each man does his job and then turns it over to the next man, so that the process is a continuous one. The body, all this time, is moving toward the "finish varnish" room.

Finally, when the main part of the upholstering is finished, holes are drilled in the door frame and door, and the door straps put on. The body is then ready to be cleaned, preparatory to receiving its final varnish coat. This cleaning is done by two giant vacuum cleaners, which remove all the hair, bits of leather, threads, and dirt, from the interior. The exterior, in the meantime, is being wiped carefully and thoroughly by hand.

In its progress the body has, by this time, started to enter the final varnish room, through an opening in the partition extending well into the final finishing room.

Here the "finishing varnish" is "flowed on" in the same manner as the other coats, and then carefully retouched by hand, in order to insure a perfect surface free from air bubbles, dry spots, bits of hair, and dust.

A metal cap is placed over the dash, so that when the body is handled it can be set upon this end without injury to the finish.

Individual trucks, fitted with draining troughs running around all four sides, are lined up along the side of the track. When a body comes to the end, it is slid off onto a truck, shoved over to a man who acts in a dual capacity of inspector and final finisher. He looks the job over carefully, touches it up slightly, if it needs it, and then turns it over to a man who pushes it back into the dark part of the room, where the bodies are allowed to stand until dry.

Now comes the only real break in the finishing-process line. There is, as yet, no chute or conveyer down which the bodies go after being varnished. The next operations—putting on of the windshield, top, and other equipment—are performed on the third floor, to which the bodies, therefore, are transferred as soon as they are sufficiently dry to permit of handling without damage.

In the Top Department is to be found a very interesting feature of Ford construction, because it is one of the few places where individual fitting seems to be necessary. Each Ford windshield and top is fitted to its special body. The putting on of the top and curtains is a real "custom-tailored" job.

Starting on the third floor, at the east end of the building, the bodies are again put on the conveyer track, and the windshields, which have previously been made up in the Windshield Department, and transferred in a finished condition to their proper position in the line, are now put on. Each windshield is specially fitted to an individual body.

By this time, the body has reached a point where it is ready for the top. Top bows are made in a department near by and delivered in a finished condition at proper points along the track for attachment as the body reaches that stage of completion.

From four to six workmen now begin to work on the job. One puts on the rear bows, another the front, another adjusts the brace rods which hold the bows in their proper position.

While the top bolts are being tightened up and truss rods and spreaders adjusted to proper position, the side pads are thrown over the top and nailed on; other men put on the roof of the top, which is composed of the "deck" and "quarters." The "back stays" and "back curtain" are soon added. This material is thrown on as fast as possible, waiting operators step up to the framework, quickly tack the top material into place; the back curtains and side stays are nailed to the body and to the top of the back bow; the "quarters" and "deck" are then stretched tightly over the framework, drawn down, tacked and finished with a "welt" strip.

The cushions, horn, and pasteboard for the bottom of the rear seat, the mats and footboard, are then thrown in by a man who does nothing else but make up these things in a package and pass one into each body as it goes along.

Other men are engaged in fitting the side curtains, which is another job requiring special care, because each set of curtains is cut to fit a particular body and top. The eyelets are put in, and after curtains have been "tried on" a second time, the whole job is inspected. The top is folded down and securely tied, all loose articles secured, the doors tied shut, a box of tools thrown in, after which it is given a shove onto a roller platform. This is set at right angles to the conveyer track, and carries the body to the top of the incline leading to the "chassis-body assembly bridge"—the end of the process.

This, then, is the story of the finishing of the Ford body.

* * * * * * * * * * * * * *

General Motors— Expansion Through Financial Combination

❲ THE FINANCING of the initial expansion of plant and facilities in the automobile industry differed radically from that used by the earlier railroad and the contemporary electrical businesses. Far smaller amounts of capital were needed to start an automobile company, for its organizers could purchase parts, accessories, and other supplies on credit and sell their finished product quickly for cash. The money from the resulting sales met operating costs, and profits were used to pay for the expansion of factories and equipment. Since initial investment was small, the early automobile manufacturers had far less need to rely on the bankers and the nation's money markets than had the builders of the railroads, the electric-power producers, and

many of the manufacturers in American heavy industry. As Henry Ford was to demonstrate dramatically, an automobile company could grow huge through self-financing.

But to the ambitious William C. Durant, the president of the Buick Motor Company, self-financing was too slow. By 1908 Durant had become, like Ford, convinced of the potential mass market for automobiles. If he was to win his share of a possible 500,000-a-year car market, Durant decided he must combine the producing, assembly, and distribution facilities of many existing concerns. To achieve his ends he had to rely on business and financial rather than on technical and engineering abilities and know-how. His experience, therefore, provides as significant a study of modern industrial finance as Ford's does of twentieth-century production.

The differences in the strategies of expansion used by Ford and Durant may have reflected their very different backgrounds, experience, and personalities. Ford's parents were farmers; Durant came from a prominent family in Flint, Michigan. His grandfather had been Michigan's Civil War governor. Ford had been a machinist; Durant had started early in life building great business enterprises. While Ford had a somewhat narrow, introspective personality, Durant was a warm, outgoing man. Nearly all his associates agreed that Billy Durant could charm the birds right out of the trees.

At the age of twenty-five, Durant began to carve out his first business empire in his home town's major industry, carriage making. In 1885 he joined with J. Dallas Dort, a young hardware salesman, to form the Durant-Dort Carriage Company. Within a short time the partners had built their nationwide distribution organization, had constructed a large factory to assemble carriages, and had purchased or set up a number of specialized works in Flint to make bodies, wheels, axles, upholstery, springs, and even whip sockets. By the turn of the century Durant's company was the largest carriage maker in the nation and its president was already a millionaire.

The coming of the horseless carriage presented both a threat and a challenge. In the autumn of 1904 Durant moved into the new industry by purchasing a tiny bankrupt Flint automobile-manufacturing firm, the Buick Motor Company. By pursuing the same strategy of expansion that he had used in the carriage company, Durant made Buick the largest automobile-manufacturing firm in the United States within less than four years. He redesigned the car and constructed large assembly plants in Flint and nearby Jackson. He encouraged the building of parts-and-accessories factories, bringing to Flint such able industrialists as Charles S. Mott, a leading axle maker, and Albert C. Champion, manufacturer of the best-known spark plugs in the country. At the same time he set up a national distribution organization, relying heavily (as he did in manufacturing) on his existing carriage-company personnel and facilities. Thus Buick, which had produced 28 cars in 1904, sold 8,847 vehicles in 1908. Ford, the nation's second largest producer, turned out 6,181 in that same year.

It was then that Durant began to predict sales for the industry of 500,000 cars a year, of which he expected Buick to take 10 per cent. To meet this objective, Durant conceived and carried out a plan to combine the resources of the most efficient car producers with those of Buick. Initial negotiations with Ford, Willys-Overland, and the E. R. Thomas Company of Buffalo failed. Then in the fall of 1908 Durant joined Buick, Cadillac, and Oldsmobile to form the General Motors Company. This holding company quickly came to control ten automobile, three truck-making, and ten parts-and-accessories firms.

The basic units of the new combination were automobile companies with national sales organizations. Besides Buick, these included Olds, Oakland, Cadillac, and the McLaughlin Motor Car Company, Limited, in Canada. No man knew better than Durant that to buy a company without a distribution network was only to buy a factory or a patent. More important for the new company's future growth than the purchases of minor car companies were those of the firms making bodies, engines, gears, transmission systems, lamps, rims, steering mechanisms, and similar products.

Durant required little actual cash to finance this combination. The great advantage of the holding-company device was that purchases could be made through exchange of stock. The stockholders of the companies selling out to General Motors received stock of the holding company rather than cash for their securities. The reason Durant's negotiations with Ford and some of the others fell through was not because they asked too high a price for their enterprises, but because they demanded to be paid largely in cash rather than in General Motors stock. Also, whatever Durant's motives were in engineering this combination, they could hardly have been to control the whole automobile industry: in 1908 the total output of all the producers he tried to combine, including Ford, was only a little over one-third of the output of automobiles produced in that year.

In carrying out his policy of expansion, Durant never anticipated a temporary decline in demand. Therefore he did not bother to build up cash reserves. Nor did he make any attempt to form the organizational structure essential to control his new industrial empire and help him achieve the potential economies of integration and combination. He continued to rely on cash received for his cars to pay for materials and labor, even though he had greatly expanded output. In the two years after the formation of General Motors, income from sales, still largely from Buick, almost doubled, rising from $29 million to $49 million. Then a slight business recession in 1910 brought an unexpected drop in sales and Durant was suddenly caught short of funds to pay suppliers and his working force. To meet the emergency he was forced

to borrow $12,750,000 from a group of bankers including Lee, Higginson & Company of Boston, and J. & W. Seligman & Company and the Central Trust Company, both of New York. In return he signed a five-year voting-trust agreement giving the bankers control of General Motors.

The bankers, more interested in current profits than in future expansion, paid much closer attention than Durant had to internal efficiency and organization. James J. Storrow, a senior partner of Lee, Higginson, became chairman of the General Motors Finance Committee. He appointed as president Charles W. Nash, a capable production man whom Durant had put in charge of first the Durant-Dort Carriage Company and then Buick. To replace Nash at Buick, Storrow brought in Walter P. Chrysler, a well-trained, highly competent engineer from the American Locomotive Company. In rationalizing their production methods, Storrow, Nash, and Chrysler borrowed much from Henry Ford. But they began to give more thought than Ford to costs and to providing for systematic improvement of product and process.

In the meantime Durant had not been idle. He had built himself another large automotive enterprise by acquiring another small company, Chevrolet, and by applying the same methods of expansion that he had used at Durant-Dort Company and Buick. Furthermore he had convinced Pierre du Pont and Du Pont's closest business associate, John J. Raskob, to invest personal funds in Chevrolet. Durant's profits from Chevrolet and his backing from the Du Ponts permitted him to buy General Motors stock secretly. When the voting-trust agreement expired in 1915, Durant was once again in control.

Back in the saddle, Durant immediately embarked on his old strategy of expansion through combination. He moved first toward integration rather than expanding production facilities. In 1916 General Motors purchased (largely through the exchange of stock, as before) makers of roller bearings, rims, radiators, horns, and starting, ignition, and lighting systems. Durant combined these enterprises into the United Motors Company and placed at its head Alfred P. Sloan, Jr., the former owner and manager of a subsidiary producing roller bearings. During this continuing expansion Durant failed, as before, to concern himself with over-all administration. He did transform General Motors (now entitled Corporation rather than Company) from a holding into an operating firm, with the subsidiaries becoming divisions. In actual fact the divisions remained almost completely independent units, with Durant himself the only link holding them together.

The nation's entry into World War I temporarily held up the execution of Durant's plans. Even so, during this hiatus he purchased enterprises making tractors which would be allowed, indeed encouraged, to continue production when war needs brought about curtailment of passenger-car output. He also bought a refrigerator company in order to give his dealers something to sell if car production was halted.

When the armistice of November 1918 unexpectedly brought peace, Durant was ready to move into one of the most ambitious expansion programs ever proposed in American industry. The huge automobile market had become a reality, and the capital required to meet it was now more readily available than it had been earlier. In addition to the personal investments by individual Du Ponts and their associates, the Du Pont Company itself purchased $42.6 million worth of General Motors' stock

in 1918 from the profits it had made from the sale of explosives to European powers. In making this investment Du Pont Company executives agreed to watch General Motors' financial affairs but to allow Durant a free hand in operating matters. John J. Raskob left his position as treasurer at Du Pont to take over the same role at General Motors. Raskob quickly became as enthusiastic as Durant about the abundant prospects for profit in the automobile industry.

The postwar program included the purchase of new facilities and the expansion of existing ones. New automobile companies, including Scripps-Booth and Sheridan, were purchased. The assembly plants, as well as the factories making parts and accessories, were enlarged, while Cadillac obtained a large new plant. A fifteen-story office building and a large laboratory were started in Detroit. Credit and insurance companies were formed. This expansion, which would double General Motors' output, increased the need for assured supplies of tires, leather, aluminum, gears, castings, and machine tools. Durant, therefore, made a $500,000 investment in the Goodyear Tire and Rubber Company and even larger investments in Doehler Die Casting Company, General Leather Company, and Brown-Lipe-Chapin Company, makers of gears. Thus the vast expansion program of 1919 and 1920 was the grand culmination of a strategy of growth that Durant had first devised for Durant-Dort and then executed successfully at Buick and at Chevrolet.

The selections on Durant's strategy of expansion are somewhat parallel to those on Ford's. The Federal Trade Commission's *Report on the Motor Vehicle Industry* reviews General Motors' growth from 1908 to 1920. Then comes the closest thing to an autobiography available on Durant. Durant provided W. A. P. John with much of the information used in an article written in 1922, entitled *"That* Man Durant," and then read and approved the manuscript before publication. Both the government report and the authorized biography include the salient facts about Durant's strategy of expansion (though neither selection is quite accurate), but each has a very different approach to the events. The second set of readings, which includes the corporation's annual report for 1919 and internal memoranda from John J. Raskob, indicates the scope of the postwar expansion program as well as the methods of financing it.

In evaluating each selection the posi-tion and motives of its writer should always be kept in mind. The following questions are pertinent: How may the differences in personality, training, and early industrial experience of their leaders have affected the strategy of growth at Ford and General Motors? What were the major defects of Durant's strategy, and what were its greatest advantages? What were Durant's own greatest talents and his greatest weaknesses? What in reality were Durant's major sources of capital? Was Durant a manufacturer or a financier or neither? What accounts for Durant's bitter attitude toward "the bankers"? What exactly were the sources of his own personal fortune? (In the spring of 1920 he was worth $90 million.)

THE BROAD STRATEGY

1] The Federal Trade Commission Reviews General Motors' Experience

General Motors Co., Predecessor to General Motors Corporation

GENERAL MOTORS CO., the predecessor to General Motors Corporation, was organized under the laws of the State of New Jersey on September 16, 1908. The organization of this company was promoted by William C. Durant who had previously associated himself with the Buick Motor Co. of Flint, Mich. Soon after he reorganized Buick and increased its output, Durant seems to have visioned the possibilities of the motor-vehicle industry and to have foreseen the profits to be garnered by a large motor-vehicle corporation.

Immediately after organization General Motors Co. began acquiring the capital stocks of Buick Motor Co. and before the end of 1908 it had acquired all but a comparatively few of its outstanding common shares. Of the shares

FROM Federal Trade Commission, *Report on the Motor Vehicle Industry* (Washington, D.C., U.S. Government Printing Office, 1939), pp. 421–26.

purchased, 18,870 shares of common and 1,130 shares of preferred were bought from William C. Durant at $150 per share payable two-thirds in General Motors preferred and one-third in its common stock. General Motors Co. then proceeded to purchase all of the stock, or a substantial interest, in other motor-vehicle or motor-parts companies. By the end of 1909 General Motors had acquired, or substantially controlled, more than 20 automobile and accessory companies, including Buick, Cadillac, Oldsmobile, and Oakland.

Soon after William C. Durant became associated with Buick Motor Co. he moved the Buick assembly to Jackson, Mich.,[1] and then later organized the Janney Motor Co., also located at Jackson. He realized that axles were almost as important as motors in the manufacture of motor vehicles and therefore he induced the Weston-Mott Co. to move from Utica, N.Y., to Flint, Mich., and allotted this company a strategic site in the new industrial area next to Buick. With the Weston-Mott Co. came C. S. Mott who later became a director and vice president of the General Motors Corporation. Mr. Durant also brought Albert Champion, a Frenchman, to Flint, and induced him to locate there, the manufacture of the famous AC spark plug.

Proposed Acquisition of Ford Motor Co., Willys-Overland Co., and E. R. Thomas Co.

IT IS apparent that William C. Durant intended to gain control of the entire motor-vehicle industry. This observation is substantiated by the fact that in 1908, negotiations were carried on looking toward the acquisition of the Ford Motor Co., the Willys-Overland Co., and the E. R. Thomas Co. of Buffalo, maker of the "Thomas Flyer." Except for the lack of cash which was demanded first by Henry Ford and then by R. E. Olds it is most likely that these companies would have been purchased. In *Men, Money and Motors,* Theodore F. McMannus gives the following account of the negotiations:

The automobile business was a hazardous business. Durant appreciated this. His azure dreams of power were often disturbed by nightmare flashes. Fly-by-night concerns with no objective save a skimming of the market and immediate profits for their promoters were everywhere. Durant realized there had to be stabilization. Early in 1908 he proposed to Ford, Couzens, Briscoe, and Olds a consolidation of Ford, Maxwell-Briscoe, Reo, and Buick.

Ford and Couzens played with the idea, matched wits against the wits of the others, and when Durant appeared more hopeful they tossed in this stipulation: "We will go in only on condition that we receive $3,000,000 in cash."

Not to be outdone by the Ford and Couzens ultimatum, R. E. Olds got to his feet and pronounced sentence on the consolidation: "If you do that for Ford you have got to do likewise by Reo. We will expect three millions in cash also." Durant waved his hands. The meeting ended. The project was abandoned.

Durant, however, was not easily discouraged. Calling aside Benjamin Briscoe, he said, "Let's go it alone, we two."

Briscoe was willing and the two men went to see George W. Perkins of J. P. Morgan & Co. The banker agreed to underwrite $500,000 of the new $1,500,000

[1] Assembly later moved back to Flint, Mich.

capital required. A charter was tentatively drawn up and the consolidation was to be called the International Motors Co.

Again in 1909, Durant tried to obtain Ford Motor Co., for on October 26, 1909, the board of directors of General Motors authorized the purchase of the entire capital stock of Ford Motor Co. for $8,000,000. The proposed term of purchase provided that $2,000,000 was to be paid immediately in cash and the balance in 1 or 2 years if arrangements could be made to finance the deal. It appears that arrangements could not be made to finance the Ford purchase. Henry Ford held out for cash and the new holding company did not have the cash and bankers could not be found who would finance the acquisition. Likewise it is apparent that arrangements could not be made to finance the purchase of the entire capital stock of the E. R. Thomas Co. of Buffalo or of Willys-Overland Co. of Toledo, Ohio.

Early Activities of William C. Durant in the Motor-Vehicle Industry

BUICK MOTOR CO. was the nucleus around which William C. Durant laid the foundation of what was to become the present immense General Motors Corporation. The Buick Motor Co. was organized by David D. Buick, a member of the firm of Buick & Sherwood, manufacturers of plumbers' supplies, located in Detroit, Mich. Mr. Buick had been experimenting with motor vehicles and in the early part of 1903 put on the market a small single-cylinder car. In order to finance the subsequent experiments in automobiles the Buick Co. borrowed considerable sums from the Briscoe brothers, then manufacturing sheet metal in Detroit, Mich. Subsequently the Briscoe brothers took an interest in the Buick Manufacturing Co., changed the name to Buick Motor Car Co., and later assumed charge of its finances, to protect their loans to the Buick Manufacturing Co. After reorganization the Briscoe holdings represented $99,700 out of the total $100,000.

The Briscoes were unable to carry their load and determined to sell their interest in the Buick Co. A purchaser was found in James H. Whiting, president of the Flint Wagon Works of Flint, Mich. Mr. Whiting was one of the first to realize that the automobile would largely supplant the horse and thereby horse-drawn vehicles. Faced with the eventual loss of the wagon business, Mr. Whiting began to look for an automobile which would become the basis for an industry to use part of his plant. The manufacture and sale of Buick cars was not an immediate financial success and Mr. Whiting decided that he needed a young man to master the new business and one who would think in terms of profits rather than in mechanics. He discussed this subject with F. A. Aldridge of the Durant-Dort Carriage Co. during a meeting of carriage manufacturers in Chicago. Mr. Aldridge advised him that the man he should interest, the one man who fitted the specifications and who was immediately available, was William C. Durant. Mr. Durant already was considered a leader among his associates in the wagon business.

By November 1, 1904, the deal with Durant was complete and on that day the capital of Buick Motor Car Co. was increased from $75,000 to

$300,000, divided into shares of $100 each. Holders of the old stock agreed to accept for each share a share of 7-per cent preferred stock with a 25-per cent bonus of common stock. With Buick prospering in 1907 and beginning 1908 at a pace that promised a strong financial position at the end of the year, Durant was ready to attempt a merger of the principal motor-vehicle manufacturing concerns. He planned the formation of a corporation which would operate as a holding company of which there were many examples among the "trusts" of the period. Subsequently it will be shown that General Motors changed from being essentially a holding to principally an operating company. After acquiring Buick, the General Motors Co. continued to acquire other companies in the motor-vehicle field and to construct additions to the acquired plants. This development continued at such a fast rate that by 1910 the company was hard pressed for funds to continue its expansion. William C. Durant put forth great effort to find funds and save the enterprise. In fact he dropped everything else to search for money. After many disappointments in his search for capital Durant was faced with the situation that only by stepping out of the management could he interest the bankers in making a loan to the company. He, therefore, resigned as president and J. & W. Seligman & Co., of New York, and Lee, Higginson & Co., of Boston, arranged to make a loan of $12,750,000 in cash. As security for this loan the company executed a blanket mortgage on all of its Michigan property which had just previously been transferred to the General Motors Co. of Michigan, a corporation set up to hold title for purposes of securing the loan. The latter company held title to the properties and leased them to the manufacturing companies. For the amount of cash stated, General Motors Co. issued $15,000,000 of 6-per cent notes secured by the mortgage. In consideration for making the loan the company delivered to the bankers $4,169,200 in preferred stock and $2,000,000 in common stock, both at par. In total, therefore, the bankers received $8,419,200 in par value of stock and discount on notes for a loan that netted the company $12,750,-000 in cash.

Coincident with the loan and the resignation of William C. Durant, the bankers took control of the company. Most of the old directors resigned and new ones were elected. However, Durant maintained his place as a director of the company. . . .

Durant Organizes Chevrolet

AFTER William C. Durant lost control of General Motors the company followed a policy of retrenchment. In the retrenchments which followed, Buick's No. 2 plant was abandoned and motor operations moved to the north end of Flint.

The Flint Wagon Works had discontinued manufacturing the Whiting car and the carriage business had showed a steady decline from the rising competition of the automobile trade. The Flint Wagon Works, therefore, was anxious to liquidate. Durant bought the wagon-works property, plant, and contents and organized the Little Motor Car Co. to occupy the property. The company was named for William H. Little, who had been general manager of Buick under Durant. The Little Co. at first built only one model, a small 4-cylinder runabout, selling [at] around $650, which placed it in competition with Ford.

During the same time Louis Chevrolet, a member of the famous Buick racing team, was engaged in designing and experimenting with a light car similar to those manufactured in France. It was his idea to combine beauty of design with power and sell at a moderate price. The idea appealed to William C. Durant, who accordingly backed Chevrolet's experiments in Detroit. In November 1911 the Chevrolet Motor Co. of Michigan was incorporated. Up to this time Chevrolet had built only four or five experimental cars.

In July 1911 the Mason Motor Co. was incorporated. Immediately it started producing motors in the old Buick No. 2 plant, which was rented for this purpose. There, as contracted for, the motors for both the Little and Chevrolet cars were built by the Mason Motor Co. Chevrolet was getting into small production and Chevrolet sales offices were opened in Chicago, Philadelphia, and Boston. It was offering a large six-cylinder car priced at $2,500 and upward.

The production at the Little plant in Flint far exceeded what had been done by Chevrolet in Detroit. The Flint enterprise actually was making money while the Detroit operation was losing. Consequently, Durant planned a much heavier schedule for Flint during 1913, but this schedule was considerably reduced. The fact that Flint was operating at a profit suggested the advisability of concentrating all manufacturing at Flint. Consequently, the Chevrolet Motor Co. discontinued operations in Detroit and moved to Flint in August 1913. For a time Chevrolet occupied the old Imperial Wheel Co. plant on property now owned by Buick. Soon thereafter Durant further consolidated his Flint position by extending his interest in the allied Mason Motor Co.

The year 1914 which witnessed the revival of general business activities in the United States found both the Little and Chevrolet cars in production at Flint. Chevrolet introduced its famous Baby Grand touring car and Royal Mail roadster. The organization had apparently become highly efficient through the necessity of making its own way on very little capital. The used-car problem had not developed and installment selling was still in the future. Chevrolet Co. sold for cash every car it produced. So great was the demand that if a shipment was not taken off the railroad track promptly by the consignee, someone else in the community could be depended upon to lift it without delay. As the money rolled in Durant transferred his offices from Detroit to New York in order to extend the sales from that center and also to work out a plan which he had formed for recovering control of General Motors Co. The latter had prospered under the Nash management and its profits were large. Payment had been promptly made on its funded debt and large reserves accumulated. Even then the eastern bankers apparently failed to appreciate the full possibilities of General Motors as thoroughly as Durant.

Chevrolet expansion went on at top speed during 1915. The Little car discontinued production and following an exchange of real estate all of

Chevrolet's operations were concentrated in the western part of Flint. The Baby Grand and Royal Mail cars continued to be produced in volume and demand ran into large production.

In 1915 Chevrolet Motor Co. of Delaware was incorporated with a capital of $20,000,000 which was increased to $80,000,000 in December. This corporation acquired all of the stock of Chevrolet Motor Co. of New York, Chevrolet Motor Co. of Michigan, Chevrolet Motor Co. of Bay City, Chevrolet Motor Co. of Toledo, Ohio, Mason Motor Co. of Flint, and contract interests in Chevrolet Motor Co. of Canada, Ltd., and Chevrolet Motor Co. of St. Louis.

·   ·   ·   ·   ·   ·   ·   ·   ·   ·   ·   ·   ·

Durant Regains Control of General Motors

WITH the organization of Chevrolet Motor Co. of Delaware, Durant contemplated offering Chevrolet stock in exchange for General Motors stock. The word went out that Chevrolet would trade five shares of Chevrolet stock for each share of General Motors common. Those who had followed Durant by investing early in Buick and General Motors began to send in or bring in their stock for exchange. It is related that one man brought in a large brief case of General Motors certificates to the Chevrolet headquarters in New York for exchange. The original offer held until January 25, 1916, when a change was made by which four shares of Chevrolet common stock were offered in exchange for one share of General Motors common stock. Through this offer William C. Durant regained control of a majority of the outstanding common stock of General Motors Co. Before demonstrating his control of General Motors through Chevrolet, however, Durant offered to have Chevrolet taken into the General Motors organization. This offer was declined and then his control was publicly announced and exercised.

The certificates of stock establishing control of General Motors by Durant were brought in in baskets at the stockholders' meeting of September 16, 1915. Thus on the seventh anniversary of the incorporation Durant was again complete master of the situation. A dividend of $50 per share on the common stock was declared at this meeting and paid on October 15, 1916. The advantages of this disbursement for the victors were evident when consideration is given to the cost of acquiring the control. Borrowed money had gone into the stock as well as Chevrolet earnings. The treasury of Chevrolet received a huge sum and was thereby partially reimbursed.

On November 16, 1915, the following directors were elected representing the Du Pont interests, namely, F. L. Belin, Pierre S. Du Pont, J. Amory [Haskell], and John J. Raskob. Other new directors were Arthur G. Bishop and Louis G. Kaufman. Messrs. Strauss and Storrow, perhaps reading the handwriting on the wall, had retired from the board in the preceding June. Pierre S. Du Pont was elected chairman of the board, a position he held for over 13 years. L. G. Kaufman took Mr. Storrow's place as chairman of the finance committee, and Charles Nash continued as president. The Du Ponts were first interested by Durant in taking a flyer with him in Chevrolet during his drive for control of General Motors. This interest was immediately recognized by recognition on the board of directors.

The fact that Chevrolet, the smaller company, controlled General Motors, a much larger company, called for a reorganization. This was effected by the organization of the General Motors Corporation of Delaware, the dissolution of the New Jersey company and the acquisition by the Delaware company of the Chevrolet Motor Co. Just prior to obtaining control of General Motors, Durant started assembling various accessory and parts companies into a corporation called United Motors Corporation. Subsequently General Motors Corporation of Delaware acquired this corporation.

. . . During the period 1916 to 1920 General Motors continued with its program of expansion through both acquisition and the extension of existing facilities. It was first organized on the basis of a holding company but in 1916 it dissolved the Buick, Oldsmobile, Cadillac, Oakland, Jackson-Church-Wilcox, General Motors Truck, Northway, and Weston-Mott corporations. From that point the corporation became essentially an operating company instead of a holding company as originally planned in 1908.

.   .   .   .

2] Durant Describes the Same Events to a Journalist

WHILE this article was being written, I telegraphed one of his old lieutenants, a man I interviewed months ago, and asked him to point out if he could, the great fundamental of W. C. Durant's unmatched ability to carry his visions to successful completion. And the answer contained only ten words: *He knows men. The right kind and the other kind.* Just ten words. Remember them. And you will understand why W. C. Durant has done what no other man dares attempt.

One day an acquaintance hailed him as he was driving down one of Flint's streets, and gave him a lift in a two-wheeled road cart. The cart was of patented construction and had several unusual features. Upon learning that it was being built in the city of Coldwater, Michigan, the future builder of Flint's industrial greatness promptly boarded a train for that city. Within twenty-four hours he had contracted to purchase the entire business, patents and all, and was on his way back to Flint to raise the money he had agreed to pay—some $2,000. Hardly had he taken off his hat in his office when in came his good friend, J. Dallas Dort, then clerking in the town's leading hardware store across the street. Dort inquired as to his whereabouts for the past few days. Durant explained what he had done in Coldwater, and announced that he was going into the business of building road carts. Immediately sensing the possibilities of the venture—for he had ridden in the

FROM W. A. P. John, "*That* Man Durant," *Motor* (January 1923), pp. 244–48. Reproduced from *Motor* magazine. Copyright 1923 The Hearst Corporation.

cart himself—Dort suggested that they become partners. And the upshot was that Dort received half interest in the company for $1,000. And with that $2,000, the Durant-Dort Carriage Company commenced operations in 1886, the senior partner aged twenty-five in charge of sales and finance, the junior partner, one year younger, responsible for production.

For a few months small numbers of carts were tediously built by hand labor. Then came the rush of orders that swelled into a flood tide. In a few years the company, having built up a complete line of vehicles with amazing rapidity, became the largest (watch how often that word occurs in describing the creations of W. C. Durant) builders in the world, operating fourteen plants in the United States and Canada, and marketing 150,000 vehicles a year. Back of that characteristic success was characteristically broad vision in financing, sales, manufacturing, selection of men, and characteristic adherence to the Durant precept of business success (the same today as it was in 1886): that increased production and production facilities would while reducing costs, give a better product and permit a greater number of people to enjoy it—and at the same time pay increased profits.

Here must be interspersed several incidents whose influence will be later recognizable. At one time the Durant-Dort Carriage Company went into the bicycle business—organizing a separate company and placing some of the stock with the citizens of Flint. As a result of the decline of the bicycle fad, the venture proved a failure—so much so that the stockholders stood to lose practically all they had invested.

The amount invested by outside stockholders was large. But Durant went to his partner and said substantially this: "Dallas, that money was invested by our friends because they had confidence in you and me. No human power or skill could have saved that business. General conditions, not mismanagement, were responsible. Our friends trusted us and relied upon our judgment. I think you and I should make good their loss." Dort agreed, and their investment was returned.

Later, a well-known Flint citizen approached Durant with the purpose of investing a considerable sum in the Durant-Dort Carriage Company. Durant advised him that no Durant-Dort stock was for sale, but he did say that the organization of an accessory company was being considered in which the money could be invested with potential profit. The money was invested, but the proposition failed to produce the expected profits. When the capital invested was practically dissipated, Durant called in that well-known Flint citizen, and said: "You went into this on my recommendation. The money is gone. Here is my note at 6 per cent, for your investment. I'll take it off your hands."

Remember that trait of protecting those who believe in him and his works. It will recur again.

It was in 1903 that those incidents first bore fruit. The Flint Wagon Works, the oldest and largest factory in Flint, had taken up as a side line venture the manufacture of gasoline engines, gradually veering into the production of an automobile. That automobile was the Buick. Sixteen had been built. A succession of mistakes in judgment had not only thrown the affairs of the company into a deplorable state, but had involved three of

Flint's financial institutions. Not to mince the words, the situation was grave; the prosperity of Flint itself was tottering. It was to Mr. Durant that the head of the company turned—turned for assistance in reorganizing, stabilizing, and reclaiming what had been dissipated. After two conferences, Durant agreed to reorganize the company. And in forty-eight hours he had, by personal solicitation, raised in the village of Flint, no less than $500,000 cash—raised it simply because the people of that city had abiding faith in his integrity and ability! It was a marvelous—and a moving—demonstration of man's confidence in his fellow man. Old residents of Flint are still discussing it.

With the money in hand he went to the officers of the company and said: "You may retain all titles and offices—all directorates. But before this money is placed in the business I must have absolute control. This fortune comes from my friends—men and women who trust me—who gave it because I asked for it. If the venture fails I will be responsible. If it succeeds, the credit must be mine. Unless I have absolute control I cannot turn over the money for any purpose." He was given absolute authority over every phase and detail of the business.

In the reorganization, $303,000 worth of common stock had been set aside for promotion purposes, the investors having purchased 7% preferred stock with a 25% bonus of common stock. Of the $303,000, $202,000 was transferred to Durant for his work. And Durant, instead of keeping it as he was legally and morally entitled to, immediately transferred it to the Durant-Dort Carriage Company, for which he was working as president at a salary of $25 a week, asserting that he had used the company's time, and as such his associates were entitled to share in the fruits of his labors. That stock, utterly worthless unless W. C. Durant gave it value, grew to be worth millions. And every man participating in the earnings of Durant-Dort benefited thereby in proportion.

Becoming chief executive of Buick, Durant's first step was to cut away the tangled skeins of mismanagement. When the banks were extricated and all obligations settled, only $75,000 of the $500,000 remained. And it was from this specific picayune sum that the whole of General Motors, with its countless millions, sprang.

In his new work he immersed himself with characteristically joyous vigor and with characteristic results. Almost a whole year was consumed in making the elementary Buick an automobile. Only twenty-eight cars were sold in 1904, because Durant, always master salesman, knew that a permanent foundation of success lay only in a product that was right. The next year 627 Buicks were built and sold; the next 2,295; the next—it was 1907, with its panic—Buick not only increased its business by 50%, but its president announced that but a few years hence the company would be building 50,000 cars a year. The bankers laughed. And his rivals in trade called him a "Merry Andrew." Shortly afterward he again made a prediction that by 1917 America would require 1,000,000 motor cars a year. And they cried: "This man is mad."

But Durant, unperturbed, smiling and confident, kept on rushing additions to the Buick Plant at such a speed that for over two years more than

2,200 men were employed on construction work alone—building additions that cost millions—and which were paid for wholly out of profits, and without the increase of outside capitalization. When what is practically the vast Buick plant of today was completed, even in Flint, where his most intense admirers and ardent friends are legion, they sometimes wondered if he were not compromising the future. They wondered. But Durant knew.

Ever the builder and ever the dreamer, he shortly thereafter startled the whole world with the crystallization of the project that only W. C. Durant could conceive and carry to completion. Out of the profits of Buick, he acquired control of Cadillac, then only a fraction of what it is today; and Oldsmobile, which had been earning scarcely any profits at all; and Oakland, then practically bankrupt; and other companies of lesser importance. Of these he created in October, 1908, the General Motors Corporation, with a capitalization of $10,000,000.

Financiers who toyed with millions gasped at the magnitude of the project. Skeptics, uninformed, and utterly devoid of vision, they asserted that it was too big—although it was only a fraction of what it was when he finally relinquished control twelve years later. They protested that it would be unwieldy—that it would be top-heavy. They predicted that even the most auspicious conditions could not produce sufficient sales to justify the $10,-000,000 capitalization.

The following year the gross sale of General Motors products exceeded $34,000,000. Net profits, according to audit, exceeded $10,500,000—a sum larger than the combined profits of all divisions' best previous years. The following year, when the total business leaped to $50,000,000, net profits exceeding $11,500,000 were earned, even after almost $1,000,000 had been set aside for a special contingency fund. Other units were being acquired. The business was being rounded out. The Durant principle of mass production, lower costs, lower prices, wider distribution, and increased profits was being carried out to an ever increasing degree.

From the outset, the price of General Motors stock had been rising—because its value was increasing in proportion to its earnings. It would not be hard to imagine that certain envious eyes were turned upon the controlling interest. For even the most unimaginative person could sense that General Motors was basically sound—that as the years passed it would produce a steady stream of profits. Control could not be bought—for control rested in the hands of one man who cared not one whit for money. And who spent eighteen hours a day at his task purely for the exhilaration of accomplishment. No, control could not be bought—then. But later—?

Credit the fox with cunning. By it he acquires those things otherwise to be gained only by the industry of the beaver or the fierce buccaneering of the timber wolf.

Credit those who watched and waited for their patience—for the soundness of their reasoning that every mortal will sooner or later be caught napping in his judgments.

When the first rumblings of the panic of 1910 were being sensed, some banking zealot whose name is unimportant, but who should be immortal for the narrowness of his vision, publicly stated that conservative bankers were viewing the motor car industry with skepticism; that no one knew whether it had an economic foundation, or whether it was merely another "bicycle craze." One statement brought on another. Bankers' heads came together. They decided to curtail their co-operation with the industry—to protect themselves at any cost.

Into this panicky situation General Motors moved under conditions that seem unbelievable to us who are not forced to bank for a living. Having earned exceedingly large profits since its organization, and because of that fact never having had to complete its working capital by the sale of stocks, General Motors had been carrying on its vast operations by using a line of credit that was practically unlimited. So, as intrinsically sound as the Bank of England, General Motors suddenly found its bankers changing over night—refusing for no reason other than an unfounded fear for the future, to continue to extend the credit that the company required to continue operations. Banks with which the company had been carrying balances as high as $1,000,000, and which a few months previous had urged the company to increase the credits they were using, refused to continue their co-operation. Instead of coming to the assistance of a valued and profitable client—instead of complying with a fundamental law of good business, their answer was, when translated into common English, "We regret that we cannot continue your line of credit. Please make other arrangements. We are not sure that the automobile business is sound or here to stay. Your loans must be paid at maturity."

Fifteen million dollars was the minimum amount required to carry on the business and prevent a receivership. And at this psychological moment certain powerful interests interceded. They would advance the $15,000,000. In return—strike down your Jolly Roger, Captain Kidd!—they demanded absolute control of a voting trust of the common stock for a period of five years ending September 18, 1915. So pressing was the need for a working capital that the offer was accepted. Durant, bereft of his unfettered freedom in the management of every phase of the business by the practically confiscatory terms, stepped down to an inactive directorship.

In his place was elected, at his suggestion, Charles W. Nash, one of Durant's strongest lieutenants—and a man whom his chief had described as the ablest production executive and soundest business man in the organization. Once more credit the fox for his cunning. Bankers cannot produce. They hoard. And acquire. And control. And not infrequently choose able men to produce the profits. In this instance, they did not err.

For the subsequent five years no dividends were paid on General Motors stock—despite the fact that after a quick post-panic recovery, the company's volume increased and profits were accumulating. Perhaps—mind you I merely state an amateur's hypothesis—it was understood that a stock which pays no dividends declines in market value; and that such a stock can be picked up casually at bargain prices. A few shares here today, a few there tomorrow, and presto! someone owns 51 per cent. At any rate, General Motors, with a par value of $100, sagged away until it kicked about the corners at $24 a share.

While General Motors was making profits and paying no dividends, and the stock was falling in price, W. C. Durant was not content with an inactive directorship in the company he had created. Hardly had he relinquished control when he, with a few associates, organized the Chevrolet Motor Company back in Flint, the birthplace of most of Durant's conceptions. And what follows, gentle reader, will whisk you off to the deepest purple of high romance, and make you wonder at the elemental bigness of the quiet smiling man.

When the company was ready to commence operations, there was in the treasury only $275,000. Truthfully a pittance, according to the standards of financing of the industry. For a year or so the Chevrolet Motor Company remained an inconsequential factor. Then in a gradually increasing stream, Chevrolet cars began to roll from the factory shipping docks. Even then no one paid much attention to Flint's newest motor company—although knowing the past, they should have sensed that something unordinary was bound to happen.

Along toward 1915, an awakening interest was noticed in General Motors stock. Some person or persons, as unknown as they were persistent, began buying here, there, and everywhere—in little driblets—in big lots. It began to rise point by point and approach in price its intrinsic level. As the 18th of September, 1915, approached, Wall Street, Flint, and the entire industry began first to simmer and then to seethe. Up—up—up—up—climbed General Motors. Shares that once went begging for buyers at $24 finally traded hands at $264. Someone—someone with faith in General Motors and faith in the automotive industry—was buying. Came the day of the meeting. Into it walked W. C. Durant—this comes from a financial writer who knows—quiet, calm, and smiling. And later out of it walked a group of bankers utterly beside themselves with amazement. For it developed that the Chevrolet Motor Company, which in some fifteen months had grown to a colossus with assets of $94,000,000, held in its treasury enough General Motors stock to control the meeting! And W. C. Durant was president of the Chevrolet Motor Company.

The voting trust was dissolved. The certain interests received their $15,-000,000—which was merely withdrawn from the untouched surplus that had been piling up for the five years. A cash dividend of $50 a share was declared, to make up for the dividendless years preceding. And Durant, the conceiver and the builder, was back at the helm, having as his associates a new and tremendously wealthy group whose financial aid had enabled him to regain control, and who immediately were given important duties in the conduct of the business.

For several weeks the country was treated to some fascinating financial adjustments. The ludicrous situation of Chevrolet owning General Motors —of the garden snake having swallowed the bull frog, was solved by exchanging Chevrolet stock for General Motors, whereby the former became a division of the latter. And incidentally, those canny or lucky persons who purchased General Motors in 1912, when it was selling for $24, and hung on to it, could have sold their holdings in 1918, receiving $2,100 for each $24 invested.

Rescued from the galling halter of banker control, and restored to the guidance of the man who was almost wholly responsible for its being, General Motors passed into a new and even more auspicious era. The magic formula of greater production was again promulgated throughout the entire fabric of the great institution. Greater production—lower costs—greater value—greater profits: That was the creed that came straight from the directing head.

To protect his sources of material supply, Mr. Durant had brought a group of parts makers and engineering companies into a consolidated corporation, financially strong. They became the United Motors. For this bit of financing Durant received a stock bonus amounting to $9,000,000. And just as he had done in the instance of the Buick and Durant-Dort, he refused to accept this money for himself. Though in this case he was working without a salary, he turned the $9,000,000 into the treasury of the Chevrolet Motor Company, retaining nothing for himself.

Three years passed. Years that successfully established new records of earnings and a more comprehensive service to the motor-buying public. I saw a letter dated January 21, 1920, from an important member of the finance committee, commenting upon the company's growth through the year 1919. Two sentences are worthy of exact transcription, "In other words, General Motors today is eight times as large as the company the bankers were managing. This is a fine tribute to your foresight."

. . . .

IMPLEMENTING THE STRATEGY

3] The Annual Report for 1919 Outlines the Postwar Expansion Program

Expansion of Manufacturing Facilities

THE EXPANSION of manufacturing facilities at your plants, which was necessarily interrupted during the war, has been resumed. The more important projects during the year are stated briefly as follows:

Passenger Car, Truck and Tractor Plants

Buick Motor Division, Flint, Michigan. During the year the capacity of this Division was increased from a production of 350 passenger cars per day during January to 500 per day during the last quarter. Construction now

FROM *Annual Report of the General Motors Corporation for 1919* (April 9, 1920), pp. 8–14.

under way at Flint and St. Louis will bring the total productive capacity for Buick cars to more than 700 per day. The capital expenditure during 1919 was $5,018,660.88.

Cadillac Motor Car Division, Detroit, Michigan.   Construction was started on a new factory for the Cadillac Division early in 1919. Rapid progress is being made on this plant, which will embody the very best and latest ideas for economical manufacture, and when completed this factory will have a capacity of approximately 30,000 passenger cars per annum. New construction by this Division required $4,937,160.81 during the year. The rapidly growing business also required the erection of a new sales and service building in Detroit and a service building in Chicago.

Chevrolet Group.   During 1919, the productive capacity of the plants at Flint, Tarrytown, Fort Worth, and St. Louis was increased to 800 cars and trucks per day; additional construction under way will, when completed, permit the production of 900 passenger cars and 50 trucks per day. Capital expenditures by this Division during the year required $7,420,460.19.

General Motors Truck Division, Pontiac, Michigan.   Rearrangement of the plant in Pontiac and additions to present buildings will permit the production of 20,000 trucks per annum. Congestion at the Pontiac plant will be largely relieved by the establishment of an assembly plant in Eastern territory during 1920.

Oakland Motor Car Division, Pontiac, Michigan.   With the completion of new construction started in 1919 the capacity of this Division will be increased to 350 passenger cars per day. A number of new departments will be established, making the plant more nearly self-contained, and insuring uninterrupted supply of the principal units.

Olds Motor Works Division, Lansing, Michigan.   At a cost of $2,552,-090.44, the capacity of the Olds Motor Works was increased to 300 passenger cars and trucks per day, and the plant put on a much more independent basis than it formerly enjoyed by the addition of facilities to manufacture some of the more important units formerly supplied by other Divisions.

Scripps-Booth Corporation, Detroit, Michigan.   This Company was recently removed to a modern factory where its product can be built under much more efficient conditions. The new facilities will make possible the production of 100 Scripps-Booth cars per day.

Samson Tractor Division, Janesville, Wisconsin.   Your Corporation has been proceeding actively with the manufacture of the Samson line of farm tractors, implements, and trucks. New facilities, which are practically complete, provide for the manufacture of 100,000 tractors per year.

Fisher Body Corporation Investment

YOUR Corporation was fortunate in assuring an enlarged supply of bodies through the acquisition of a majority interest in the Fisher Body Corporation, Detroit, Michigan, the largest builder of automobile bodies in the world. The Fisher Body Corporation is expanding its Detroit facilities, thereby assuring your Corporation an adequate supply of bodies, particularly of the closed type, demand for which is increasing rapidly. The item "Notes Payable Account Fisher Body Corporation Stock Purchase," shown on the Balance Sheet, represents the balance due on account of this purchase and matures over a period of five years. The total cost ($27,600,000) of the above stock is included in Investments.

.   .   .   .

General Motors Export Company

THE cessation of hostilities in Europe, after the production of motor cars for civilian purposes had been suspended for practically four years, provided an unusually active market, and the export business of your Corporation made notable strides during the year. A largely increased allotment of production for export has been made in order to more nearly meet the pressing foreign demand for your products.

General Motors Acceptance Corporation

EARLY in the year the General Motors Acceptance Corporation was organized to assist dealers in financing their purchase of General Motors' products, and also to finance, to some extent, retail sales. The gross business done by this Corporation in 1919 exceeded $20,000,000.00.

Housing Facilities for Employes

THE extension of manufacturing facilities entailed a large increase in the number of employes, and at those points where it was impossible to provide housing facilities to meet this increase by any other means, the Corporation erected a large number of houses, which were sold to employes at cost, less a liberal allowance in recognition of present inflated construction cost.

Administration Building

THE rapid growth of your Corporation made it necessary to provide suitable executive quarters in Detroit. There was begun the construction of an office building which will furnish ample accommodations for the needs of the Corporation and its allied interests for many years. Up to December 31st, the sum of $4,219,313.24 had been expended on account of this project, and is shown in Investments.

4] Financing of the Postwar Expansion Program at General Motors

a] J. J. RASKOB TO GENERAL MOTORS FINANCE COMMITTEE

December 12th, 1918.

To: FINANCE COMMITTEE
FROM: CHAIRMAN

AFTER talking with Mr. Durant regarding the probable expansion program which the General Motors Corporation should adopt as quickly as possible, I have prepared the following estimate of capital expenditures, provision to finance which should be considered by the Finance Committee. The program cannot be completed in less than twelve months and the following estimates are quite liberal:

United Motors Corporation loans at banks	$ 2,000,000.00*
United Motors Corporation expansion excluding houses	2,000,000.00
United Motors Corporation subsidiary preferred stocks	1,300,000.00*
Purchase of Chevrolet-California stock to give us complete ownership	1,200,000.00*
Purchase of McLaughlin-Buick-Canadian property	6,500,000.00*
Walkerville Motor and Tractor plant	1,000,000.00*
Tractor development including working capital requirements	6,000,000.00*
Office building	4,000,000.00*
Proposed credit and insurance companies	4,000,000.00*
St. Louis assembly plant	2,500,000.00*
Other assembly plants	2,000,000.00
Light axle plant	1,500,000.00
Frame plant	1,500,000.00
Forge plant	500,000.00
Scripps-Booth plant	750,000.00
Scripps-Booth notes outstanding	750,000.00*
Scripps-Booth additional working capital	500,000.00
Scripps-Booth—purchase of outstanding stock	400,000.00*
Truck plant	3,000,000.00
Truck axle plant	500,000.00
Differential gear plant	1,500,000.00
New Cadillac plant	3,000,000.00
Houses	2,500,000.00*
Experimental laboratory	1,000,000.00*
Central Foundry plant	1,200,000.00*
Miscellaneous appropriations	1,000,000.00*
TOTAL	$52,800,000.00

FROM Du Pont-General Motors Anti-trust Case, Government Trial Exhibit, No. 134.

Although it is not certain that this total amount will be required within the next twelve months, the items marked with a star totaling $36,150,000.00 should be arranged for immediately; the other items cover an expansion program which should be adopted and work started as soon as it is physically possible to do so after giving careful consideration and study to the details of each particular case. It must be understood that the figures shown opposite the respective items are very rough estimates, are not made from any carefully worked out plans and are given merely to arrive at a total which will indicate to the Finance Committee the probable financial needs of the Company during the next twelve or fifteen months.

After talking with Mr. Durant and Mr. Haskell I am confident in my opinion that if the Finance Committee will provide $52,800,000.00 for expansion during the next twelve or fifteen months we will have amply provided for financing all of the construction work the Executive Committee can possibly accomplish in that period.

My recommendation for providing this money is as follows:

To be provided out of earnings after taxation and dividends	$24,700,000.00
To be provided through sale of $18,000,000.00 par value common stock at $120.00 per share, which stock will be offered to a Syndicate in which all of the common stockholders of the Company will have opportunity of participating	21,600,000.00
To be provided through issuing common stock in payment for the McLaughlin-Buick properties instead of paying for these properties in cash	6,500,000.00
TOTAL	$52,800,000.00

To accomplish the above it will be necessary to authorize the sale of an amount of stock equal to say, 15%, of the total stock outstanding after our acquisition of the United Motors and McLaughlin-Buick properties—this stock to be offered to a Syndicate at $120.00 per share, in which Syndicate all common stockholders of the Company shall have opportunity of participating pro rata.

If the foregoing recommendation meets with the approval of the Finance Committee, the Board of Directors should be called immediately together for the purpose of passing such resolutions as are necessary to consummate the transaction.

b] J. J. RASKOB TO DU PONT FINANCE COMMITTEE

March 19th, 1920.

To: FINANCE COMMITTEE
        DU PONT COMPANY
FROM: J. J. RASKOB

THE GENERAL MOTORS CORPORATION, in order to carry out a development program which has been reduced to the greatest degree possible without sacrificing its position in the industry, will need $60,000,000.00 of new capital. Due to the investment conditions existing in the world and particularly in this country it is felt impossible to raise this new capital through the sale of debenture stock and as the capital will be permanently required in the business it is felt that it should not be secured through the issue of short term notes so that it becomes necessary for the common stockholders to supply the money themselves or to interest new partners.

The development of the industry during the past four years has been such as to increase the assets employed from $58,000,000. in 1915 to $452,-000,000. in 1919, an increase of approximately $400,000,000. in four years or at the rate of $100,000,000. per year. There is every reason to believe that there will be ample opportunity afforded for expansion at a very rapid rate during the next few years and this affords splendid opportunity to interest new partners without the present partners sacrificing anything. In other words if the present partners have $400,000,000. employed earning 30% and the industry can employ $60,000,000. additional which will also earn 30% then there is no sacrifice in having the $60,000,000. additional supplied by others provided they are satisfactory partners.

We are in the fortunate position of having Nobels keenly interested in the matter. Sir Harry McGowan [1] is here now and we have discussed this situation very thoroughly with him with the result that we have tentatively suggested that the General Motors Corporation which has approximately $150,000,000. of common stock outstanding make an offer of 20% additional common stock to its stockholders aggregating $30,000,000. of new common stock to be issued at $200.00 per share thus supplying the $60,000,000. required. Of this $30,000,000. of new common stock the rights accruing to the duPont-Durant stockholdings will be approximately 60% or $18,000,-000. par value which at $200.00 per share will cost $36,000,000.

Mr. Durant has consented to turn his rights over to Nobels provided duPont will do likewise with the understanding that Nobels will purchase the stock and hold it as an investment and not purchase it as a speculation.

My recommendation is that Finance Committee approve the principle enunciated herein and request the DuPont American Industries, Inc. to

---

1 [A senior executive in Nobel's Explosives Company, Limited, which became part of Imperial Chemical Industries, Limited, the giant British chemical enterprise.]

FROM Du Pont-General Motors Anti-trust Case, Government Trial Exhibit, No. 140.

surrender its rights to Nobels provided this arrangement can be carried through.

There is attached hereto a memorandum showing how the price of $200.00 per share is justified as a proper price for a partnership basis.

J. J. RASKOB

The Crisis of 1920–21

❰ THE PLANS of Durant and Raskob, as well as those of Henry Ford, were predicated on an ever expanding market. Then suddenly in the late summer of 1920 the market vanished. The automobile industry was struck by the first major economic depression to occur since its founding. The challenge facing those larger automobile companies that had so recently and greatly expanded their output was no longer one of production or even of effective reduction of operations. Overnight it became one of financial survival.

In this last of its financial crises General Motors survived primarily because it had the backing of one of the nation's wealthiest families, the Du Ponts, and one of its most powerful banking houses, J. P. Morgan and Company. The preceding two selections indicated the size of the financial operations carried on in 1920 and the ways in which they were handled. General Motors was fortunate indeed that Raskob's request for $64 million had been proposed and acted upon before the depression struck in full force. Funds raised for expansion were used to tide the cor-

poration through a period of tight money and few sales. Even so, General Motors had to borrow over $80 million in short-term notes in the fall and winter of 1920.

Although Raskob had planned on raising more than half of the $64 million abroad, only $15 million was obtained in England, and $6 million more came from Canada. The remaining $15 million of the Nobels' share was temporarily acquired by Chevrolet and Canadian Explosives, Limited. In June Durant and the Du Ponts agreed that the remaining $28 million of the issue should be sold by a syndicate headed by J. P. Morgan and Company. On July 17 Morgan announced that 99 per cent of this amount had been spoken for.

The money came just in time. Owing to Durant's personal, haphazard methods of management and over-all control, the operating divisions continued to spend large sums for supplies and equipment during the spring and summer of 1920, even after the general office, through an Inventory Allotment Committee, had specifically ordered the curtailment of such expenditures. The division managers continued to buy because they—not the general office—controlled their funds. When the market for automobiles collapsed, they found themselves without money to pay their suppliers or even to meet their payrolls. The general office provided the necessary cash out of the funds raised from the earlier stock issue and short-term loans. At the same time it worked to restore control over divisional spending. Even so, by the time the depression was over General Motors had to write off over $100 million as dead loss.

Durant's departure from General Motors resulted less from financial mismanagement within the corporation than from his own personal financial difficulties. In the late spring and early summer of 1920 he began buying General Motors stock in large quantities. Whatever his reason, the purchases apparently complicated the Morgan Company's delicate task of placing $28 million worth of new securities in a generally falling stock market without a loss. Even after the syndicate had completed its task Durant continued to buy. Finally in November he had reached the limits of his resources in his efforts to keep up the price of General Motors stock. His large personal fortune was gone, and he owed over $30 million to his brokers.

Durant then turned to the Du Ponts for aid. Pierre du Pont feared that the dumping of the financier's huge holdings on the market during the severest onslaught of the depression could threaten General Motors' already shaky credit. It might even stimulate financial panic on Wall Street. So he joined with the house of Morgan to form a company in which Durant had a share in order to take over Durant's stock and pay off his debts. No longer directly a major stock-holder in General Motors, Durant then resigned from the presidency and ended all connections with the corporation he had founded. Pierre du Pont—the only man who could command "the respect and cooperation of the banks, the investing public and the General Motors Corporation personnel"—took his place. Du Pont at once began a thorough reorganization of the corporation's management structure and its production, marketing, and financial policies. Only after this drastic reformation had been completed was General Motors in a position to challenge seriously Ford's dominance of the industry.

Even Henry Ford felt the depression of 1920. In the fall of that year his company had to face financial problems for the first time. In July 1919 Ford had issued a $20-million dividend for which the Dodge brothers had successfully sued in court. In the same month Ford completed arrangements to buy out his minority stockholders at the enormous sum of $105 million. For this he arranged to borrow $75 million. Expansion created even more serious problems for Ford in 1920 than did these other commitments. To meet the postwar demand he determined to double his output. So he enlarged his plans for a huge new plant on the River Rouge, spending over $60 million on it in three years. He went even further than Durant in carrying out a policy of integration, paying close to $20 million for timber, ore and coal lands, and even a railroad.

Ford's response to the sharp drop in the demand for cars in the late summer of 1920 was to slash his prices, institute rigorous economies, and shift to his suppliers and dealers part of the financial burden of carrying the company through the storm. As a result he lost little but good will by the crisis. When the demand for cars revived in 1922, Ford was better equipped to meet it than any of his competitors. He had far greater resources and held over 50 per cent of the market. Yet within less than a decade he was struggling desperately to maintain a much smaller share of the market and to make any profit at all.

The following selections indicate how General Motors and Ford weathered the industry's sharpest crisis. In the first selection a financial expert, Lawrence Seltzer, writing in 1928, analyzes the developments at General Motors during the months of crisis. The second selection presents Durant's version of these events. The third selection gives Pierre du Pont's account of Durant's personal financial crisis and the resulting changes in a letter to his brother written a few days after the happenings. The Ford experience is reviewed briefly in another selection by Seltzer. This is followed by a brief summary of Ford's position as seen by a contemporary business writer in the fall of 1922.

Rather lengthy selections have been included on Durant's difficulties and his departure from General Motors because this is one of the few events in American business history where it is possible to obtain in detail differing versions of what happened by the insiders involved. Whose account, Durant's or Du Pont's, appears to be closer to reality? On which points do they agree and on which do they disagree? Who was largely responsible for the expansion program? Was that expansion program, as Durant suggests, the basic cause of General Motors' difficulties in 1920? Is John's presentation of Durant's motives convincing? What motives other than the ones they indicate might he or Du Pont have had? Did Durant receive equitable treatment from the Du Ponts and Morgan? What other alternatives were open to the three parties involved? How wisely did Ford handle the crisis of the postwar recession? What were possible serious long-range costs of his actions? What other alternatives might he have chosen?

DURANT'S DISASTER

1] A Financial Expert Analyzes the Crisis at General Motors

The Post-War Crisis

THE PROCEEDS of the sale of common stock netted the General Motors Corporation about $60,000,000 by December 31, 1920 (254,764 shares having not been fully paid for at that time); and the funds and financial backing thus acquired were of tremendous aid to the Corporation in meeting the emergency created by the sudden curtailment of the demand for its products that set in in August and September, 1920.

FROM Lawrence H. Seltzer, *A Financial History of the American Automobile Industry* (New York, 1928), pp. 197–202.

The year 1920 had begun very auspiciously. The Corporation had just completed the most successful year in its history. The demand for its cars had continued at a high level throughout the closing quarter of the year just ended; and this demand increased afresh in the early months of 1920. Both volume of sales and net profits promised to exceed the record-breaking volume of 1919; and indeed, this promise was realized for financial volume of sales. . . .

The early promise and actuality of an increased volume of business, however, led to heavy increases in the volume of inventories. Starting at the beginning of the year at $128,696,652 (as compared with $91,137,513 at the opening of 1919), the inventories mounted rapidly, reaching a total of $167,-965,641 on April 30, and $209,000,000 by the end of October, when a tremendous decline in the demand for the Corporation's products had already set in.[1]

The large increase in the financial volume of inventories occasioned concern as early as the month of March, 1920; and at that time, the Executive Committee approved a definite program of production with a view toward minimizing the inventory requirements.[2] The administrative organization of the Corporation, however, made it extremely difficult to enforce the rulings of the Executive Committee. While the Corporation had become chiefly an operating company, the actual administration of its plants was in the hands of divisional managements, each concerned with the expanded production of its own product. In May, 1920, a special Inventory Allotment Committee was appointed to establish a more effective control over the inventory demands of the various divisions; but the rulings of this committee obtained no more adherence on the part of the operating divisions than had the more general injunctions of two months previous. Thus, in his annual report for 1922, President Du Pont declared:

The report of the Inventory Allotment Committee was presented and approved before June 1, 1920. It was unfortunate that the rulings of the Executive and Finance Committees and their cautions remained unheeded. As a result, inventories reached a total of $209,000,000 at the end of October, 1920, exceeding by $60,000,000 the allotments of the Executive and Finance Committees and by $100,000,000 the amount in actual use during the active summer of 1922. This excess accounted for about 70 per cent of the borrowings at that time.

It was doubly unfortunate that the spirit of the committee rulings was totally disregarded by a few of the Divisions, the losses of which, due to expanded inventories and commitments for the future, amounted to $48,579,872, or much more than the total operating deficit of the whole corporation during the year 1921. The operating losses of these Divisions during the liquidation and reconstruction period of 1921 added $15,330,938, making a total of $63,910,810 on their account.

Not only was the Corporation called upon to finance its growing volume of inventories, however, but the fulfillment of its program of fixed-plant expansion, involving the completion of construction projects already under way, entailed a capital expenditure of approximately $79,161,951 in 1920, nearly $15,000,000 of which was required merely for its new office and ad-

---

1 Annual report for 1922.   2 Ibid.

ministration building in Detroit.[3] A sudden decline in sales in the late summer and fall of 1920, therefore, created an exceedingly embarrassing situation. The extent of this decline and its effect, in view of the Corporation's greatly expanded investment in fixed plant and inventories, may be seen from Table 1, in which the Corporation's sales of cars and trucks are presented by months for 1919 and 1920.[4]

TABLE 1. GENERAL MOTORS SALES OF CARS
AND TRUCKS BY MONTHS, 1919 AND 1920

MONTH	1919	1920
January	25,039	34,313
February	25,936	33,864
March	29,844	42,504
April	32,991	42,183
May	39,130	42,653
June	34,710	46,852
July	31,720	45,479
August	31,986	32,899
September	33,437	28,796
October	41,847	18,302
November	36,329	12,798
December	28,770	12,432
	391,738	393,075

On its face, the ability of the General Motors Corporation to weather this storm, the results of which were seriously aggravated by the obsolescence and decline in value of inventories, plant, and equipment purchased or constructed at 'boom' prices, was fairly remarkable. More than $100,000,000 was written off the books of the Corporation between 1920 and 1922 for the devaluation of plant, equipment, and inventories, and for operating and liquidation losses.[5] In the three years ended in 1920, the Corporation's fixed capital expenditures had aggregated $281,556,104; and in a period of pronounced distress in the money markets and in general business, it found itself in possession of more than $200,000,000 of depreciating inventories, with further commitments already made.[6] On the other hand, the following favoring factors may be noted and emphasized:

1. The Corporation's program of fixed-capital expansion had been soundly financed: it had not entailed the flagrant absorption of working capital in fixed assets nor the use of short-term obligations for such additions. Indeed, except for purchase-money obligations and small mortgages assumed, it had not involved the creation of any funded debt whatever. The financial sources of the expansion program are summarized in Table 2.[7]

2. While the Corporation's program of fixed-capital expansion had not

3 Annual reports of 1920 and 1921.
4 From the records of the General Motors Corporation.
5 Annual reports for 1920, 1921, 1922.

6 *Ibid.*, 1922.
7 *Ibid.*

Table 2. Financial Sources of Fixed Capital Expansion of General
Motors Corporation, 1918–20

From net earnings reinvested:

Net earned income, 1918, 1919, 1920, exclusive of extraordinary write-offs of 1920	$193,801,804	
Less federal taxes $47,274,750		
Less dividends paid $57,386,370		$ 89,140,684

From sale of securities (cash):

Common stock	98,494,835
Six per cent debenture stock	25,425,000
Seven per cent debenture stock	6,906,800 [a]
Employees' bonus, deducted from income but paid in newly issued stock	13,569,144

                                                    134,395,779

Securities issued for properties:

Debenture and common stock	122,141,520
Fisher Body purchase-money notes (net outstanding)	9,840,000
Mortgages assumed	1,629,070

                                                    133,610,590

                                                  $357,147,053

[a] Represents actual cash received from $10,998,700 par value of this stock issued; the remainder ($4,091,900), was paid in six per cent debenture stock.

provided for commensurate additions to its working capital, the previous strength of its working-capital condition permitted considerable extension without serious jeopardy. The ratio of current assets to current liabilities at the end of 1918 was 5.5 to 1; at the end of 1919, 3.84 to 1; at the end of 1920, 2.24 to 1. The last-named ratio reflects large 'write-offs' for inventory depreciation, and, like the others, allows for accruals of interest and of preferred and debenture dividends. We have several times observed, moreover, that the working-capital requirements of automobile producers were minimized by various practices peculiar to the industry. Finally, we may note that the new capital investment in the Corporation between 1918 and 1920 exceeded the total of fixed-capital expenditures by more than $75,000,000. (See Table 2.)

3. The ability of the General Motors Corporation to withstand the situation occasioned by the sharp slump in its sales in the latter part of 1920 is not adequately explained, however, by reference to the fact that its current assets at the worst were approximately two and one-quarter times the amount of its current liabilities. To the extent that these assets consisted of inventories that could not be liquidated presently, the working capital ratio is misleading. The actual cash position of the Corporation and its ability to borrow were, in fact, of far greater importance. In these emergency essentials, the Corporation was fortunate indeed. The net earnings of 1920,

before special 'write-offs' and before the setting-up of a 'reserve for unforeseen contingencies,' but after all other operating and income charges save dividends, had aggregated $67,273,313; the Corporation had realized approximately $60,000,000 in cash from the sale of common stock in July, 1920; and, with the support of the powerful financial group that had become identified with its financial management in connection with this stock issue, it was able to borrow a maximum (on October 13, 1920) of $82,784,824 on its short-term notes in the midst of the acute financial situation of late 1920. By reason, most immediately, of these financial operations, the Corporation was able not only to maintain its solvency, but to pay full dividends on its debenture and preferred stocks, totaling $5,620,246, in 1920, and to disburse quarterly in 1921, from the earnings of 1920, a total of $17,893,288 in cash dividends on common stock.

2] Durant Recalls the Story of His Financial Difficulties and His Departure From General Motors

THREE days after my manuscript was mailed to Mr. Durant, a long distance call asked me to come to New York at once. Mr. Durant wished to place before me, for the first time any writer had seen them, the facts of the General Motors stock "crash." Would I come? Would I!

Ensued perhaps the most hectic three days I have ever spent since my earliest newspaper work. I have been to New York—these words are being scribbled on my knees in an upper berth of the west-bound Wolverine— where I had placed before me a staggering mass of documentary evidence which threw a startling, new light upon the situation; and which, if properly used, not only will establish W. C. Durant in the public mind as the most commanding figure the entire automotive industry has ever known, but will reveal him to be utterly worthy of that high place and of the trust that countless thousands place in him.

But I must write with the utmost care. Irreparable hurt could be done by careless use of what I have been privileged to know. There is much I cannot even mention—since the time for its publication in this magazine is not yet ripe. Yet believe me when I write that what follows is not based upon the word of W. C. Durant (although that is good enough for me), but upon documentary proof of the most positive and incontrovertible sort.

To place the cart before the horse for the moment, let me explain that by an amazingly successful campaign of propaganda, W. C. Durant has been saddled with the blame for a series of errors in judgment that seriously embarrassed General Motors late in 1920. I believed it; almost every one believed it—because Durant did not care to reveal the truth when the truth

FROM W. A. P. John, "*That* Man Durant," *Motor* (January 1923), pp. 248–52. Reproduced from *Motor* magazine. Copyright 1923 The Hearst Corporation.

might have been taken as an alibi. He chose first to come back with Durant Motors, Inc.[1] He has come back. A balance sheet showed me that. And now he has chosen to talk.

The errors of judgment are well known. Earning at the rate of twelve and one-half to thirteen millions of dollars a month, General Motors went into a scheme of expansion the like of which has never been attempted in the automotive or any other industry. The corporation's capital was voted up to more than one billion dollars. Fifty million shares of no par value stock were authorized. Stock dividends were voted that would release five hundred thousand shares of common each quarter. A housing and dormitory program involving over 33 millions was set under way. An office building to cost over $20,000,000 was begun in Detroit. Various factories were radically expanded. New and very costly plants were constructed at peak prices. United Motors Corporation was absorbed and other divisions were acquired for cash or by stock exchange. All this called for untold millions—for so many, many millions that the corporation, instead of having a cash surplus of 106 millions of dollars in the banks, as at the first of the year, owed its banks 80 millions and was obligated in other ways for an additional 120 millions. In other words, the execution of the expansion plan had required over 300 millions of dollars—had drastically reduced the liquid working capital and had tied up a vast sum in fixed investments—all because the company was earning at the rate of over 12 millions of dollars a month. In other words, it was what is called "expansion against prospective earnings" and that, according to good business, is bad judgment, because you are borrowing on the hope that profits will continue.

As I pointed out previously, when Durant had regained control from the bankers in 1915, it had been made possible by the generous financial aid of an immensely wealthy group, who had become associated with him. Representatives of this group were placed on important committees of the Corporation—such as the executive and finance committees. Before I attempt to show who was responsible for the almost fatal expansion program, I ask you to bear these two facts in mind: (1) W. C. Durant had up to 1919 enjoyed supreme, final and unfettered authority over every phase of the business. He had established policies and saw that they were executed; (2) he had with him a powerful group to whom he owed his regain of control and whose presence in the Corporation gratified him and his associates.

Although I am in possession of the facts, I am not permitted (either by my judgment or that of the editor) to reveal who was responsible for the fatal expansion program. All that I can do here is to establish the fact that W. C. Durant *was not responsible,* either directly or indirectly. For one solid hour I read document after document, bearing the signatures of over twenty men, stating that Mr. Durant had not only *not inaugurated the program,* but had emphatically cautioned against it in meeting after meeting. And not all those men are "Durant men" either!

At this point I overcame my amazement to ask the quiet, smiling Titan

1 [Durant formed this company six weeks after he left General Motors. He manufactured the Durant, the Star, the Flint, and the Locomobile before it failed in the early 1930's.]

why, as chairman of the executive committee, he had permitted the program to be carried out against his repeated warnings. And his answer was characteristic: He owed them much for their aid (although by permitting him to handle for them a single investment of $24,000,000 they had made over 70 millions of dollars); they had a reputation for being conservative business men; and they were supremely confident. That they were supremely confident I know. I saw a most comprehensive chart prepared not by Mr. Durant, but by his associates, covering a period of eight future years, and setting forth the results of the plan, year by year. And the last year, according to the estimate, would see the company using over one billion dollars liquid capital, earning 142 per cent on its outstanding common stock, which would have a market value of $1,000 a share! Oh, the figures were impressive. So impressive that Mr. Durant smiled, and I giggled. Well, anyhow, the 300 millions were spent and the 106 million dollar cash surplus was replaced by 200 millions of obligations.

Then came the post-war reaction—swift and deadly. An economic depression seized the country. Money became tight. Security prices collapsed over night. Factories shut down. Unemployment spread, bringing with it much genuine, though perhaps temporary, poverty. Bankruptcies increased at a sickening pace. People stopped buying all but the necessities of life. They stopped buying motor cars. They kept—if they could—what cars they had and waited for better times.

Even such soundly entrenched concerns as Ford and Dodge Brothers felt the pinch and shut their gates for varying periods. General Motors was not immune. Its sales dropped away. One by one the various divisions curtailed production and began to operate at decelerating momentum. Without sales and with large inventories to be liquidated, profits declined. Dividends became impossible. The stock began to drop in price. And General Motors, like thousands of other American business institutions, large and small, found itself face to face with the task of weathering the storm.

The public had been in no mood to absorb a previously offered issue of 7% debenture stock (which is a preferred stock, you understand), but with its working capital dissipated as a result of its great expansion program, the company, in urgent need of funds, decided upon an underwriting of 64 million dollars' worth of common stock at a most favorable price of $20 a share. At the time the issue was contemplated the market price of General Motors common was $38.50 a share. It being an unusually attractive investment, a syndicate of English-Canadian interests underwrote 36 of the 64 millions of stock at that price. On account of the exchange situation, they arranged to pay 10% of the purchase price in June, 1920, and the balance on December 1st that same year.

Before the balance of the issue (28 millions) could be offered for sale, a very serious market situation developed. Large holders of General Motors stock, not in sympathy with the expansion program, decided to sell. Associates of W. C. Durant, previously content to leave their large investments in his hands, went to him frankly and said they were unwilling to continue as stockholders under the new order of things. The public, in the grip of the post-war depression, which was heightened by the effect of the railroad strike, was in no mood to purchase securities, regardless of their intrinsic value. This was especially so with General Motors, because the company's temporary embarrassment had become known and the report was, as was to be expected, distorted as the news spread. Briefly, it was a very poor market for the sale of securities by individuals or by corporations.

Knowing the value of General Motors stock, spurred by his sublime faith in the Corporation he had conceived and created, remembering that 28 millions of the 64 million dollar issue had yet to be sold, bearing in mind that 90% of the English money would not become due until December 1st, and holding uppermost in his thoughts the trust that had been placed in him by thousands of stockholders who had invested in General Motors because of their faith in him, Durant's conception of his responsibility made him feel that it was his duty to protect against the slaughter of General Motors stock. For the manipulators were kicking it about relentlessly, since the market was favorable for such buccaneering operations.

So whenever large blocks of General Motors were offered for sale, he, knowing their value and the earning power of the company, purchased them privately. In one instance he and his associates arranged the purchase of 150,000 shares from a western group for a consideration of $4,500,000, secured by abundant collateral supplied by the Chevrolet division of the General Motors Corporation, but the notes were acceptable only after Mr. Durant personally had endorsed them.

Still the price dropped—to 32. Feeling that the market had to be supported for the reasons previously enumerated, he organized a buying syndicate with his associates to purchase the stock as offered on the market, and to thus protect its price. To the members of that syndicate he gave a personal guarantee against loss. The stock dropped to 30. Another syndicate was formed to purchase down as low as 28.

About this time the balance of the 64 million common stock issue (the 28 million that the English syndicate had not absorbed) was underwritten by certain Wall Street representatives. And although they were assuming only very slight obligations, due to the fact that the company's stockholders had the right to purchase the stock at the $20 figure (when the market was $28) and would snap up almost the entire amount, the Wall Street crew demanded a staggering bonus. That bonus was the right to purchase 200,000 shares at $10 a share, when the market was $28! The stock was to be taken from the treasury of the Chevrolet Motor Company, the underwriters fearing criticism if it were to be taken from General Motors. Durant objected—strenuously and bitterly, by letter and in person. Faced by the refusal of the Wall Street representatives to underwrite the issue unless their demands were complied with, he finally gave in, exacting a promise that the stock was later to be returned to Chevrolet by General Motors.

And that compromise caused his destruction!

Remember the last syndicate, according to its articles of agreement, was purchasing General Motors down to 28. Remember that W. C. Durant was pouring out his fortune in a sublime and unselfish endeavor to maintain the price against conditions that were being artificially created. Remember that he *believed* in General Motors; that his friends believed in him; and that he was keenly conscious of their faith in him. (Do not forget those two incidents back in Flint where he reimbursed those who had lost through faith in his judgment.)

One day—it was July 27, 1920—one hundred thousand shares of General Motors stock were suddenly dumped into the market. The market was demoralized. General Motors stock broke to 20½. Durant—caring not one whit for money, and caring everything for the thousands who believed in him— bought that stock. More came into the market, at a lower price. He bought that, too. Then more and more and more—always at decreasing prices, which made all his previously acquired holdings worth just so much less. Alone, unsupported, single-handed, and smiling—he fought the battle, purchasing the stock down to $12 a share, endeavoring to save General Motors for those who had made it possible more than ten years previous.

Finally the odds became too great, even for Durant's great courage and greater faith. His friends had been extricated without loss. But his entire personal fortune had been sacrificed. In a few short months he had turned himself from a man worth 90 millions of dollars to one owing two millions. And after making this great sacrifice; after standing in the breach that a receivership might be avoided, protecting with his fortune the interests of every stockholder of General Motors—what then? He was forced to sell his holdings at a price that would not pay his debts, and this having been accomplished he was *asked to resign.*

On December 1, 1920, he appeared in his office for the last time as president of General Motors. About him his men were working with tears welling in their eyes and their throats filled with a strange thickness. He entered— quiet, unperturbed, and smiling. He signed a few papers, attended to a few details, and then put on his hat and coat.

"Well," he said, without a trace of rancor or regret, as he glanced about the room, "May first is usually national moving day. But we seem to be moving on December first." That was the exit line of the man who has been called the "soul of General Motors." O'Neill has never written a finer one.

.   .   .   .

3] Pierre du Pont Gives His Story of the Same Events

Dear Sir:

Recent developments in General Motors Corporation's affairs make it necessary to record developments of the past two weeks, which I do from notes made by me from circumstances that are still clearly in mind. Before dealing with this part of the history I should like to record a few words

LETTER FROM Pierre du Pont to Irénée du Pont, President, E. I. du Pont de Nemours & Company, November 26, 1920. Du Pont-General Motors Anti-trust Case, Defendants' Trial Exhibit, No. DP50.

in regard to my previous understanding of Mr. Durant's personal affairs.

Since my first acquaintance with Mr. Durant some years ago he had never up to Thursday, November 11th, 1920, said anything to me concerning his personal affairs. When the du Pont interests bought into the General Motors Company and acquired an investment of $25,000,000 worth of stock at slightly above par, it was understood from Mr. Durant that he, possibly together with his immediate family, held a similar amount of stock (including his holdings in the Chevrolet Company, which was then, as now, a holding company of General Motors Common Stock). It was known to us at that time that the larger part of Mr. Durant's stock stood in the name of brokers, but this was supposed to be a matter of convenience. I am quite sure that if Mr. Durant was a borrower on this stock at the time, nothing was said about it. During the months that followed our acquisition of stock up to last spring I knew at times that Mr. Durant had permitted his stock to be lent in the street [Wall Street; that is, on the stock and money markets]. I also knew that he was at times [a] purchaser of stock, both directly and through advising people to buy. I had never supposed that he purchased other than by payment outright or in amount within his ability to carry, in view of his seemingly large fortune. I do not remember his mentioning any case in which he was a seller of stock, nor does it appear now that he has ever been other than a purchaser. I have never abetted Mr. Durant in any thoughts of stock and market control which he mentioned to me; in fact, what little has been said would tend to discourage market operations rather than to encourage them; but, as I said before, Mr. Durant has never spoken to me about personal affairs and it has never appeared that the stock operations were anything but personal. I have a strong impression, which Mr. Raskob confirms, that Mr. Durant was entirely out of the stock market in the spring of 1920. I have supposed that he owed no money, particularly on brokers' accounts. When syndicates were formed in recent months by Morgan & Company, it was my understanding that Mr. Durant would not operate in the stock market in any way, as it is impossible for two parties to act independently in a satisfactory way. I have been disappointed during recent weeks to hear Mr. Durant mention supporting the market, in view of the fact that the Morgan syndicate was not doing so properly. My judgment has been against this independent action, but I am not sure that the subject has been discussed in a way that has indicated to Mr. Durant any clearcut ideas on my part; in fact, I have pictured his purchases to sustain the market as being limited to a number of shares well within his supposed purchasing power and that of his immediate friends who might have helped him in placing the stock. I have felt quite certain up to November 11th that Mr. Durant was not operating in the stock market and was not a borrower of money.

Notwithstanding the above opinions that were quite firmly fixed in my mind, there have been rumors of Durant's speculations. Both Mr. Raskob and I have felt that Morgan & Company have been ignorant of the extent of Mr. Durant's operations since they became purchasers of General Motors Common Stock. Morgan & Company have had every opportunity to question Mr. Durant on the subject and I have not felt it my duty to pry into

Durant's affairs. Some time within the past six weeks Mr. Morrow [1] of Morgan & Company asked Mr. Raskob and me some questions regarding Mr. Durant's personal affairs, particularly as to his possible stock market operations. To this we replied that we knew nothing of his personal affairs and that he had never confided in us. I advised Mr. Morrow that he question Mr. Durant personally, as we felt sure that he would be candid in his answers. This led to a meeting in Mr. Morrow's office in November, 1920, at which he, Mr. Durant, Mr. Raskob and I were present. During that meeting I stated that it was fair that the partners in ownership of General Motors' stock should know each other's position and informed the meeting on the part of the du Pont interests that all of our stock, both General Motors and Chevrolet, was held by the company, unpledged, and that we were not buyers or sellers of stock in any amount. I also stated that I, personally, was not a borrower of money on the stock; that my shares were held by me, and that I had not bought or sold stock recently. I stated that so far as I knew, none of the individuals in the du Pont group were borrowers on General Motor's stock or operating in any way. Mr. Morrow stated that the shares purchased by Morgan & Company and their friends were still held and that there was no intention to sell. I do not remember that Mr. Durant made as positive a statement on his part, but he did not give any intimation that he was a borrower on the stock or operating in the market in any way. Mr. Morrow asked him the direct question whether he knew of any weak accounts in the market, to which Durant replied "no." He left us with the impression that his holdings were as clear as our own. Knowing Mr. Durant and the peculiarities of his makeup, I do not think that he intended to deceive us in any way; but Mr. Morrow, who was not inclined to be as generous, I think censures Mr. Durant severely for his failure to be frank with us.

We now come to Thursday, November 11th, 1920. Without any idea in the heads of Mr. Raskob or the writer that Mr. Durant was involved in any way, on the date above mentioned Mr. Durant asked me to lunch with him. At the meeting he stated that he had been informed that "the bankers" had demanded his resignation as President of the General Motors Company, to which demand he was ready to accede, as he was determined to "play the game," for the reason that the company as well as he, personally, "was in the hands of the bankers" and must act accordingly. I immediately took exception to his statement about the company, explaining that our borrowings were not greater than could be prudently carried in view of our large working capital and other assets and in view of the cash balance carried by the company and the forecasts of our financial affairs. I explained that our banking partners concurred in this opinion and saw no difficulty in carrying our loans until liquidation through the operations of the business could be accomplished. Mr. Durant stated that he was worried about his personal accounts but made no definite explanation, and no opportunity was presented for an inquiry, which did not seem necessary at the time.

1 [Dwight W. Morrow, who joined J. P. Morgan and Company in 1914 and retired in 1927 to become Ambassador to Mexico.]

However, after leaving this meeting, Mr. Raskob speculated on the probable meaning of Mr. Durant's words. In answer to Mr. Raskob's question the next day as to the condition of Mr. Durant's affairs and particularly as to whether his indebtedness amounted to "six or twenty-six million dollars," Mr. Durant replied that he would have to look up the matter. Mr. Raskob and I left New York on Friday (12th) and did not return until the following Tuesday, November 16th, at which time we went to Mr. Durant's office in the morning, with the determination to endeavor to find out his true position, as we had agreed in conversation that Durant's personal affairs, if seriously involved, might indirectly affect the credit of General Motors Company. Mr. Durant was very busy that day, seeing people, rushing to the telephone, and in and out of his room, so that although we waited patiently for several hours, interrupted only by lunch time, it was not until four o'clock that afternoon that Mr. Durant began to give us figures indicating his situation. He had pencil memoranda of the number of loans at banks. The total memoranda, as written down by us from what he said, showed an indebtedness of twenty million dollars, all presumably on brokers' accounts and supported by 1,300,000 shares of stock owned by others and by an unknown amount of collateral belonging to Durant; also, $14,190,000 which Durant estimated he owed personally to banks and brokers, against which he held three million shares of General Motors stock, this, of course, exclusive of the 1,300,000 shares owned by others. Mr. Durant stated that he had no personal books or accounts and was wholly unable to give definite statements as to the total indebtedness; what part of it was his personal and what part was the indebtedness of others on which he had lent collateral without other commitment. Apparently, he had no summary of brokers' accounts in hand. However, the whole situation, besides being very involved, seemed very serious. Mr. Durant promised to ask his brokers for accounts in order to make a more positive statement.

On Tuesday evening (Nov. 16th) Mr. Durant had a call from McClure, Jones & Reed, brokers, for $150,000, to support his account. This account was fixed up in some way.

On Wednesday (Nov. 17th) we inquired for the brokers' accounts and found that directions had been given to make the statement as of the close of business Wednesday, November 17th, so that nothing could be done that day. Meantime, the statements already given appeared so indefinite that Mr. Raskob and I were loath to believe the accounts in any way accurate. However, the situation seemed serious enough to warrant speculating on a plan for relief. We decided that, in order to avert a crisis, it might be possible to organize a company to take over Mr. Durant's holdings, issuing $20,000,000 of notes, which would be offered as collateral to the holder of obligations, and that the du Pont interests might invest $7,000,000 or even $10,000,000 in securities of the Company in order to furnish cash to liquidate pressing accounts and make payments, in part, of others.

On Thursday, November 18th, the broker accounts started to come in, and it required all of that day to get the statement in [a] shape that was agreed upon by Mr. Durant as correct. The statement, however, was not capable of accurate checking, excepting from the broker accounts presented. There was nothing to show that these covered all the broker accounts, and there was nothing very definite in regard to bank loans, nor to the syndicate accounts in which Mr. Durant was involved as lender of collateral. However, a summary sheet was made up from the data and given to the typist for copying late Thursday afternoon. About that time Mr. Durant called Mr. Raskob and me to his office, stating that some of the Morgan partners were to call upon him shortly and asked us to be present at the meeting. We told him that his position differed so entirely from that represented to us and to Morgan & Co. that it was impossible for us to sit in a meeting with him and the Morgan partners, unless he agreed to make a complete statement to them. He did not agree to this point and we left the room. About 6:30 p.m. we started to leave for the hotel and met Messrs. Morrow, Cochran,[2] and Whitney,[3] who had met Mr. Durant, with a promise on the part of Mr. Whitney to return at nine o'clock that evening. Mr. Morrow called me aside and stated that they wanted to get in touch with me for a few minutes' interview. He and his associates and I then repaired to Mr. Raskob's room and, after a few preliminaries, I asked whether Mr. Durant had made a complete statement to them. To this Mr. Morrow replied "yes," and produced a copy of the typed summary which I had prepared but which I had not yet myself seen in finished form. Then ensued a discussion of the whole subject, in which the Morgan partners outlined their opinion of the extreme seriousness of the situation and the panic that might result, in the event of Mr. Durant's failure, which might possibly involve the failure of several brokers and some of the banks, particularly as there were two large and critically weak accounts in the street. Mr. Morrow stated that he would give up an engagement and return at nine o'clock and I agreed to break an engagement and do likewise. Our conversation occupied not much more than a half hour. I returned to the hotel and, together with Mr. Raskob, went to the office at the appointed time, where three Morgan partners had assembled. Mr. Raskob outlined to Mr. Morrow our rough plan of giving assistance in which it appeared that, we, representing the du Pont interest, were willing to help materially in this very desperate situation. Mr. Morrow stated that he thought the plan impossible of execution because of the very critical condition in the market and recommended that we endeavor to place a loan of $20,000,000.00, among the banks, in order that an offer of cash for all Mr. Durant's indebtedness might be made. Mr. Raskob and I agreed on [the] part of the du Pont interests that we would furnish $7,000,000.00, and sufficient additional collateral toward the project. The Morgan partners were very complimentary as to the willingness of du Pont to help in the situation, Mr. Cochran using the expression that "there are two firms in this country who are real sports, viz., du Pont and Morgan."

Discussion ensued as to the treatment of Mr. Durant, Mr. Morrow mak-

2 [Thomas Cochran had become a partner in J. P. Morgan and Company in 1917.]

3 [George Whitney remained a director of J. P. Morgan and Company until 1955 and served for many years as a director of General Motors.]

ing the suggestion that one-fourth of the equity in the shares should remain with Durant and that some portion of this equity might have to be used in order to help place the notes. He stated in the beginning that Morgan & Company would ask no commission or payment of any kind for their services in the deal. This division of equity was discussed with careful consideration of justice to Mr. Durant and these carrying the load. After this preliminary discussion, the Morgan partners stated that they must go as carefully as possible into Mr. Durant's accounts before any attempt was made to float a loan. This investigation they proposed to start upon immediately and, therefore, went to Mr. Durant's room, and checking of the accounts was carried forward and the proposition of relief presented to Mr. Durant by Mr. Morrow. Mr. Durant thought that one-fourth of the equity returned to him was harsh. Mr. Morrow then moved to one-third. Mr. Durant suggested to me that 40% to him and 60% to the du Pont interests would be more nearly fair. This part of the negotiations was all in good spirit and with apparent endeavor on all sides to be just in a difficult situation. Checking of accounts and discussion of the subject continued without interruption until about 5:30 o'clock Friday morning, about which time Mr. Durant and I signed a memorandum, agreeing to the general proposition of the $20,000,000 note issue and issue of stock to support the $7,000,000 furnished by the du Pont interests; also, the loan of additional collateral, estimated at 1,300,000 shares. Memorandum also agreed that the equity in the stock representing the selling price above $9.50 per share, plus costs and interests, should be divided one-third to Durant and two-thirds to du Pont. Even at this date the total indebtedness was uncertain and the syndicate accounts still involved.

After a hurried breakfast we all retired for a couple hours' sleep and returned to business at 9:30 o'clock that morning. Messrs. Morgan & Co. arranged a loan of $20,000,000 with the principal banks in New York before five o'clock that evening (Nov. 19th). In the meantime, the plan was suggested that the du Pont interests take 8% Preferred stock for their cash, and for the loan of collateral, 80% of the Common stock, the latter representing the equity in the selling price of the stock above $9.50, plus costs and interest. Twenty per cent of this Common stock was set aside for the bank interests furnishing the loan of $20,000,000. On that day the du Pont Finance Committee met and agreed to divide the 80% Common stock equally with Mr. Durant, leaving the proportions 40% Durant, 40% du Pont and 20% bankers. This is the plan that has been finally consummated. While rumors of the deal were active on Saturday (Nov. 20th), announcement was not made until Monday (Nov. 22nd), when Morgan & Company started to gather in the stock. Throughout the whole transaction the Morgan partners have appeared to greatest advantage. They threw themselves into the situation wholeheartedly, stating at the start that they asked no compensation. They have acted with remarkable speed and success, the whole deal involving $60,000,000 or more, having been planned and practically completed in less than four days, in which are included a Saturday and a Sunday.

FORD'S SUCCESS

4] The Financial Expert Analyzes the Crisis at Ford

The Crisis of 1920–21

IT WAS during this year that the Ford Motor Company was faced with the greatest, and, so far as the records disclose, the only, financial crisis in its history.

The post-war boom in general business had shown signs of imminent collapse early in 1920, and, as summer came, the automobile business experienced a marked slackening in sales. The business of the Ford Motor Company slumped with that of others. On September 21, 1920, President Edsel B. Ford announced a reduction in the prices of the Ford products, that of the touring car being cut from $575 to $440, and other models being similarly reduced. The new prices meant a loss on the immediate orders of the Company, according to the announcement, because of the large volume of inventories purchased at the high prices previously prevailing; but the reductions were made to stimulate sales. A short spurt in the business of the Company followed the price cuts, but sales soon fell off again.

In view of the period of liquidation in general business which was then setting in throughout the country, the vulnerable financial position of the Ford Motor Company at this time may be seen from a survey of its balance sheet of December 31, 1920: [1]

ASSETS		LIABILITIES	
Real estate	$ 50,861,001	Capital stock	$ 17,264,500
Other tangible goods	124,350,295	Liability on unsecured	
Cash	13,557,245	indebtedness	143,025,301
Good-will	21,262,833	Surplus	124,265,141
Credits	54,438,634		
U.S. Bonds			
Stock in subsidiaries			
Prepaid expenses	20,084,934		
Investments in other companies			
	$284,554,942		$284,554,942

1 Annual report to the Michigan Secretary of State.

FROM Lawrence H. Seltzer, A *Financial History of the American Automobile Industry* (New York, 1928), pp. 114–18.

In spite of the new insertion of a good-will item of $21,262,833 in the list of assets, the net worth of the Company as exhibited by the balance sheet above showed a decrease of more than $60,000,000 as compared with the net worth on July 31, 1919. Liability on unsecured indebtedness had increased from $96,271,959 to $143,025,301; credits had decreased from $96,182,704 to $54,438,634; cash had decreased from $59,829,279 to $13,557,-245; and tangible goods other than real estate had increased from $88,506,-436 to $124,350,295.

In this situation, the Company took radical steps, open only to a concern of its size, to force down the prices of raw materials and of manufactured parts, and thus to permit it to stimulate its sales by further price reductions. Cognizant of the effect of its action on many firms of which it was the sole or chief customer, the Company suddenly ceased purchases of raw materials and parts; and, while maintaining its production at highest pitch, it made preparations for a sudden shut-down of the great Highland Park plant so soon as the accumulated inventories of materials had been turned into finished products. In justifying the action of his Company, Henry Ford is quoted as having said: [2]

I knew something drastic had to be done, and was determined to do it. When the war ended, the excuse for war prices ended, but those who sold us raw materials did not seem to know it.

Late in December, 1920, after its inventories had been made up into finished parts and shipped to its thirty-five branch assembling units throughout the country, the Company suspended operations at its Highland Park plant—first, for two weeks, and then, 'indefinitely.'

During January, all the assembled cars were shipped from the Company's branches to the more than 10,000 Ford dealers, draft bills of lading attached. About 125,000 cars were thus marketed, and much of the burden of emergency financing was thus shifted to the dealers, who were requested to take up the cars under their annual quota-arrangement with the Company. At the same time, foreign agents were called upon to remit $3,000,000 on outstanding accounts; $3,700,000 was realized from the sale of by-products of the Ford operations; and $7,900,000 from the sale of Liberty bonds.[3] After six weeks of shutdown, the Highland Park plant was reopened for operation.

Striking economies were now effected in the productive operations. The office force was cut in half; all order blanks and statistical forms that did not aid directly in production were abolished; sixty per cent of the telephone extensions were removed; the number of foremen was cut to one-fourth of the previous number (one foreman being now employed for every twenty men instead of one for every five men); the number of employees per car per day was reduced from fifteen to nine.[4] 'We cut the overhead charge from $146

2 [Allan L.] Benson, *The New Henry Ford*, p. 184.

3 Henry Ford, *My Life and Work*, p. 173 ff.; see also, Dow, Jones & Co., quoted in the *Literary Digest*, September 30, 1922; Benson, *op. cit.*, p. 187 ff.

4 *Ibid.*

to $93 a car, and when you realize what this means on more than four thousand cars a day you will have an idea how . . . it is possible to make an impossible price,' wrote Mr. Henry Ford, in discussing these changes, in his autobiography.[5] Continuing, he declared:

Most important of all, we found out how to use less money in our business by speeding up the turnover. And in increasing the turnover rate, one of the most important factors was the Detroit, Toledo, & Ironton Railroad—which we purchased. . . . We discovered . . . that freight service could be improved sufficiently to reduce the cycle of manufacture from twenty-two to fourteen days. That is, raw material could be bought, manufactured and the finished product put into the hands of the distributor in (roughly) 33 per cent less time than before. We had been carrying an inventory of around $60,000,000 to insure uninterrupted production. Cutting down the time one-third released $20,000,000. . . . Counting the finished inventory, we saved approximately $8,000,000 more—that is, we were able to release $28,000,000 in capital. . . . On January 1 (1921), we had $20,000,000. On April 1, we had $87,300,000, or $27,300,000 more than we needed to wipe out all our indebtedness.

The success of the Ford Motor Company in extricating itself from financial embarrassment without the customary expedients of long- or short-term borrowing provoked widespread comment. While operating economies played a large role in this success, an equally important one was that involved in the shifting of the burden of credit to the Company's sales dealers and suppliers. When other firms were facing acute embarrassment by reason of the sudden cancellation of orders by their customers, the Ford Motor Company prevailed upon its dealers to accept shipments (sight drafts attached) in advance of orders; and, at the same time, persuaded its suppliers of parts and materials to extend credit. The power of the Company to employ such expedients in a period of acute distress in general business can be explained only by the extraordinary profitableness to its dealers and suppliers of their relations with the Ford enterprise.

Recovery and Integration

THE Ford Motor Company emerged from its embarrassment with a greatly improved manufacturing organization and in a liquid financial condition. In the six months between December 31, 1920, and June 30, 1921, its cash and bank balances rose from $13,557,245 to $54,844,538; its current liabilities (including reserves and accruals) declined from $143,025,301 to $89,417,027. The fruits of its new manufacturing economies were strikingly displayed in the years immediately following. The price of the Ford touring car was reduced from $440 to $355 in 1921; the Company's net profits in this year of depression totaled $75,890,836. In 1922, the Company's net worth increased by more than $133,000,000; and in 1923, with the price of its touring car reduced to $295, the Company's output and sales exceeded 2,000,000 vehicles—the largest volume it has yet achieved. The operations of the Company for the years 1919–23, inclusive, in so far as they are re-

5 Page 173.

flected by figures of output, receipts, profits, and net worth, are summarized below.

TABLE 1. OUTPUT, RECEIPTS, PROFITS, AND NET WORTH OF FORD MOTOR COMPANY, 1919–23, INCLUSIVE

YEAR	OUTPUT [a]	RECEIPTS [b]	PROFITS [c]	NET WORTH [d]
1919	537,452	$305,637,115	$ 69,924,411	$202,135,296 (July 31)
	401,982			
1920	1,074,336	429,866,663	53,448,480	141,529,641 (Dec. 31)
		483,896,483		
1921	1,013,958	546,049,450	75,890,836	173,951,173 (June 30)
1922	1,351,333	608,341,082	133,248,623	307,199,796 (June 30)
				359,962,693 (Dec. 31)
1923	2,090,959	858,863,758	99,342,888	459,305,581 (Dec. 31)

[a] From *The Ford Industries*, p. 11, published by the Ford Motor Company. Upper figure for 1919 represents output for the 12 months ended July 31, 1919; lower figure, for the five months ended December 31, 1919; remaining figures are for calendar years.

[b] Figure for 1919 is for the fiscal year ended July 31, 1919; upper figure for 1920 is for the nine months ended April 30, 1920, and lower figure, for the eight months ended December 31, 1920; the remaining figures are for calendar years. Figures for the years 1919, 1920, and 1921 were taken from Benson, *loc. cit.*, who obtained them from the books of the Company; those for 1922 and 1923 were obtained from *Moody's Industrials*, 1926, p. 2499, and do not include interest on bank balances or bond investments, rents on buildings, etc.

[c] Figures are for the calendar years; those for 1919, 1920, and 1921 were obtained from Benson, *loc. cit.*; those for 1922 and 1923 represent the differences in the Company's surplus account as shown in its annual reports to the Michigan Secretary of State and the Massachusetts Commissioner of Corporations, and, therefore, do not reflect profits distributed in dividends. They may, on the other hand, reflect changes in valuation practices.

[d] From the annual reports of the Company to the Michigan Secretary of State and the Massachusetts Commissioner of Corporations.

Looking forward to the future with undiminished confidence, the Company made great strides in its policy of industrial integration and in further expanding its productive capacity.

.   .   .   .

5] Business Commentators Describe Ford's Strong Position at the End of the Crisis

THE CLOSING of the Ford plant on September 16, because of the high price of coal, apparently found the Ford Motor Company at its record peak of cash, working capital, surplus and earning power. Production, says *The Michigan Manufacturer and Financial Record* (Detroit), "has been running at the rate of 5,000 to 5,400 cars a day, making possible a production of 1,300,000 vehicles for the current year and a gross business of $700,000,000. Net profits on this gross business are expected to reach $75,000,000 for 1922." These estimates, of course, may be too high if the Ford shut-down lasts any considerable time. The Ford Company, which started a score of years ago with invested capital of $28,000, now has assets amounting to $409,820,132.97, according to a statement filed with the Michigan Secretary

FROM "Ford Prosperity," *Literary Digest*, Vol. 74 (September 30, 1922), p. 50.

of State. When the present strong financial status of the Ford Company was revealed in reports filed in Massachusetts, Dow, Jones and Company commented on Ford's recovery from his embarrassment of two years ago as follows:

Ford's financial crisis came in the winter of 1920. He mastered his difficulties by shipping out nearly 125,000 cars, with bills of lading attached, forcing his 17,000 agents to accept them at cash. At the same time he compelled suppliers to extend credit. He established coordination with his railroad, the Detroit, Toledo & Ironton, releasing, through improved transport, $28,000,000 previously tied up in inventories. He inaugurated a ruthless house-cleaning and scaling down of expenses, extending even to the point of removing 60% of the factory telephone connections, and reducing from fifteen to nine the number of employees necessary to produce a Ford car a day. Fortune's smile has never been clouded since early 1921. Tho blest with a record-breaking business of 5,200 cars a day, Mr. Ford has displayed a degree of financial astuteness totally unexpected, and resented by many agents and suppliers because of its relentlessness; yet marvelous in its results.

The Michigan Manufacturer points out that between December 1, 1920, and June 30 of this year, Henry Ford's total assets were almost doubled, and his cash on hand grew from $13,557,244 "to the present staggering figure of $145,985,669.31." The balance sheet of June 30, 1922, is as follows:

ASSETS	JUNE 30, 1922	LIABILITIES	JUNE 30, 1922
Cash on hand	$145,985,669.31	Accounts payable	$ 37,967,056.14
Accounts receivable	46,647,597.37	Pay rolls, salaries	4,340,514.40
Notes receivable	79,572.81	Employees' investment	11,903,499.59
Interest receivable	608,027.93	Accrued expenses	1,276,802.76
U.S. and municipal bonds	8,334,119.84	Reserved for income tax	44,848,892.81
Merchandise and supplies	56,045,121.30	Reserved for other taxes	2,283,570.87
Stocks, bonds of subsidiaries	9,548,375.02	Capital stock	17,264,500.00
Miscellaneous investments	500,814.85	Surplus	289,935,296.40
Prep. expenses	395,754.35		
Plant, land, buildings	81,626,015.03	TOTAL	$409,820,132.97
Machinery, tools	39,531,079.34		
Good-will	20,517,985.82		
TOTAL	$409,820,132.97		

The Detroit weekly goes on to call attention to the great variety of the Ford interests as follows:

The total Ford interests' investments in land, plants and inventories now are in excess of $400,000,000, while the various plants and industries employ 73,000 men in this country and abroad. The properties include the Highland Park plant of 305 acres, producing cars and employing 42,000; River Rouge plant, 665 acres, making tractors, sedan and touring bodies, coke, gas, benzol, sulphate, tar, oil, and employing 9,000; Ford City, Ont., 56 acres, producing cars and employing 2,400; Manchester, Eng., cars and tractors, 2,000 employees; Iron Mountain, Mich., sedan and touring bodies; Cork, Ireland, tractors, 713 employees; Dearborn, Mich., experimental, 280 men; Northville, Mich., auto and tractor valves, 245 men; Hamilton, Ohio, transmission assembly, 283 men; Lincoln Motor, Lincoln cars, 3,000 men;

assembling branches in 27 American cities employing 30 to 2,000 men each; eight service branches in the United States and foreign assembly branches in Buenos Aires, Cadiz, Copenhagen, London, Ont., Manchester, Eng., Montreal, São Paulo, Brazil, Bordeaux, Toronto, Winnipeg, and foreign service branches in Calgary, Regina, St. Johns, Vancouver, Windsor, London, Eng., and Montevideo, Uruguay.

There [are] also the Banner Fork coal mines at Wallins Creek, Kentucky; Nuttall-burg coal mine, in West Virginia; Imperial iron mine, Michigamme, Mich.; timber lands in Baraga, Marquette, Houghton, Iron and Dickinson counties, Michigan, and the Detroit, Toledo & Ironton Railroad, operating 614 miles of line, 2,200 cars and locomotives and employing 1,700 men.

PART II

The Strategy of Competition

The Coming of Modern Management and Marketing

INTRODUCTION

THE CRISIS of 1920–21 was brief. By the late spring of 1921 demand returned. But by 1924 the market began to level off at a high plateau of about 3.5 million car sales a year. This leveling-off, or saturation of the market, had a profound effect on the industry. Recall the statistics. In 1920 just under 2 million new passenger cars had been sold. The drop in demand during the following year reduced the annual total to 1.5 million. Recovery in the following spring and summer brought the 1922 output to 2.3 million. In 1923 it jumped to 3.6 million. And there it remained. Except for 1929, when Ford forced the market with his new Model A, passenger-car sales did not rise above the 4-million mark in any one year until the great growth of the economy and the national income in the years after World War II. By 1924 most Americans who could afford a car had purchased their first one. From then on the important customer was no longer the man buying his first car but the man who already owned one.

This change in the market called for a radical change in the automobile makers' business strategies. Marketing and management now became tasks as critical as production and finance had been in the years before 1920. The saturated market increased competition. Expansion of output by one company could come only at the expense of another. Such competition for a larger share of a market of relatively fixed size put a premium on the use of product differentiation, mass advertising, consumer financing, and other instruments of modern marketing. Price was no longer the major competitive weapon in selling new cars. As important as the price tag to the buyer who had already purchased his first car were comfort, style, ease of performance, and the trade-in deal on the old car. (Such a trading business, of course, enhanced the role of the dealer.) For those to whom price was still the primary consideration, a good used car could usually be had more cheaply than a new one.

As the battle for customers intensified, efficient management became almost as vital a need as imaginative marketing. No longer could expanding output assure continuing profit margins by lowering unit costs. If profit margins were to be maintained, detailed attention had to be given to the flow of goods through the enterprise. Supplies had to be carefully purchased. Inventories had to be kept as low as possible. Cars had to be distributed so that dealers had enough, but not too many, to meet current demand. Mean-

ingful information on costs had to be developed if the exact amount of current profits was to be known. Since costs were closely related to volume, their determination—as well as that of the quantities of supplies purchased, the size of the labor force needed, and the anticipated business for the dealers —depended greatly upon accurate forecasts of the future market. Efficient management came to require a continuous flow of detailed data on future, as well as current and past, performance. It also called for a more clearly defined allocation of duties if over-all coordination, appraisal, and long-term planning were to be effectively achieved; if long-term and short-term changes in the market were to be acted upon quickly; if the best use was to be made of technological innovations; and if competitors' actions were to be successfully countered.

It should be remembered that the history of the automobile paralleled the experience of nearly all American consumer-goods industries as well as many industries making producer goods. In their initial drive for the American mass market, the makers of a new product had to concentrate on production and finance; then the saturation of that mass market turned them to improving marketing and management methods. The automobile was (and still remains) one of the most costly and technologically intricate of the consumer durables. Therefore it raised more complex problems of buying, manufacturing, and distribution than did other consumer durables. Of the two leaders of the industry during the 1920's, Ford, despite (or maybe because of) his brilliant response to the challenges of expansion, failed to meet the challenges of competition. General Motors, on the other hand, pioneered in many of the ways of modern management and marketing.

Ford Sticks to Tested Strategies

❬ WITH the passing of the economic tempest of 1920–21, Ford's future looked bright indeed. He had captured over 55 per cent of the market, while his closest rival held only 12 per cent. In 1922 General Motors was concentrating on internal reforms. As yet it had no car comparable with the Model T in price. As prosperity returned and the demand for cars rose rapidly, Ford saw every reason to move forward with the policies that had proved so successful in the past.

In 1922 Ford therefore decided to continue to concentrate on producing his well-engineered, cheap utility car as efficiently and swiftly as possible. He would continue to expand output, thus cutting unit costs—a strategy which would in turn permit him to reduce prices and thus increase his market still further. Ford's policy demanded the enlarging of his plants and production facilities and called for an expanded pool of reliable sources of supplies and raw materials. Even before the end of World War I, Ford had begun to expand the size and number of his assembly plants and to build a huge

central production works on the River Rouge near Detroit. After 1921 he moved quickly to complete the mammoth industrial complex on the Rouge. With its own glass works, its $35-million steel mill, its foundries, its assembly lines, and its shipping facilities, it became the magnificent manifestation of Ford's fundamental policies of mass production and vertical integration.

To Henry Ford, production continued to be the basic challenge. All his plans were based on the assumption of an ever expanding market. But after 1923 this assumption was no longer tenable. As the market leveled off, most automobile makers began to realize that marketing was becoming a more serious challenge than production. Nearly everyone in the industry—competitors, suppliers, dealers, and business and industrial analysts—watched eagerly to see how Ford would respond to the changing situation. Would he continue to produce a cheap utility car for the man buying his first automobile when the number of first buyers had become so small? Would he still consider price the basic competitive weapon when good used cars could be had at much lower prices than that of a new Model T and when prosperous Americans who were turning their first car in on a new one wanted more than mere utility?

The drop in demand for the Model T struck at the basic assumptions underlying Ford's policies. If volume production declined, then the cost of each unit produced rose. Price cuts could only slice more deeply into profits, unless they encouraged sizable further buying. Yet the Rouge plant was built to produce the T. A change to a new line or even a new model would be enormously expensive. Many argued, however, that Ford still might meet the changing market by improving his relations with his dealers, by providing ways in which a customer could buy a Ford on an installment plan, by increasing his advertising, and by improving his distribution methods.

Many people within and without his company warned Ford of the need to overhaul or at least temper his basic policies. He would not listen. Those within the company who urged new policies were fired. Ford justifiably believed he knew the automobile business better than any other man in the country. Who then had the right to tell him how to run his company? In fact, competition from outside and discontent from within only encouraged Ford to gather more and more control into his own hands. By the mid-1920's nearly all of his more able executives had resigned or had been fired. Ford was perfectly confident that he and one or two trusted lieutenants could easily administer the enormous industrial empire. He had only scorn for those who suggested that a business as immense as his needed to be more systematically organized.

In 1927 and 1928 management and marketing weaknesses finally laid the Ford Motor Company low. In May 1927 Ford decided to abandon the Model T. The Rouge and his thirty-four assembly plants in the United States and fourteen overseas factories were completely closed down for a retooling for at least six months and did not return to full-scale production for more than a year. Ford never fully recovered from this long model changeover. It reduced his profits, caused his suppliers and dealers suffering, and brought unemployment to much of Detroit. Still more serious for Ford, it permitted General Motors to get a firm grasp on the market—a grasp never again lost. Even though the new Model A was an excellently designed car, it failed to achieve the dominating place of the T. And although Ford began to modernize his marketing methods by setting up a finance company and by improving relations with his dealers, he continued throughout the period to lose his share of the market. Not until the years following World War II and Henry Ford's death was the Ford administrative pattern reshaped along lines similar to those of General Motors. And only then did the Ford Motor Company become an effective competitor once again.

The first selection in this section describes Ford's policies, and the second one questions their validity. In the first, an excerpt from *My Life and Work*, Ford outlines clearly his policies as he saw them in 1922. The selection indicates as clearly the assumptions on which they were based. The second selection was written in the spring of 1926 by an industrial analyst, James Dalton. It remains one of the most concise and perceptive presentations of Ford's marketing problems written to date.

Critical questions are raised by these readings. Why was Ford so slow to recognize the changing market situation? What alternatives were open to him when he did become aware of it? Why was he so reluctant to change even then? Why should the persistent pioneer and innovator of the years before 1920 become so set in his ways? Related to these questions are those concerning his basic assumptions about industrial production. What were the sources of Ford's assumptions and why were they clearly valid for one period in an industry's history but not in another? It is important, too, to keep in mind how the history of the American automobile industry would have differed if Ford had heeded the warnings he received from both within and without his company and had turned his attention to marketing and management in the mid-1920's.

THE "T" AND THE ROUGE

1] Ford Outlines His Basic Policies of Production and Integration

OUR POLICY is to reduce the price, extend the operations, and improve the article. You will notice that the reduction of price comes first. We have never considered any costs as fixed. Therefore we first reduce the price to a point where we believe more sales will result. Then we go ahead and try to make the price. We do not bother about the costs. The new price forces the costs down. The more usual way is to take the costs and then determine the price, and although that method may be scientific in the narrow sense, it is not scientific in the broad sense, because what earthly use is it to know the cost if it tells you you cannot manufacture at a price at which the article can be sold? But more to the point is the fact that, although one may calculate what a cost is, and of course all of our costs are carefully calculated, no one knows what a cost ought to be. One of the ways of discovering what a cost ought to be is to name a price so low as to force everybody in the place to the highest point of efficiency. The low price makes everybody dig for profits. We make more discoveries concerning manufacturing and selling under this forced method than by any method of leisurely investigation.

The payment of high wages fortunately contributes to the low costs because the men become steadily more efficient on account of being relieved of outside worries. The payment of five dollars a day for an eight-hour day was one of the finest cost-cutting moves we ever made, and the six-dollar day wage is cheaper than the five. How far this will go, we do not know.

We have always made a profit at the prices we have fixed and, just as

FROM Henry Ford in collaboration with Samuel Crowther, *My Life and Work* (New York, 1922), pp. 146–55.

we have no idea how high wages will go, we also have no idea how low prices will go, but there is no particular use in bothering on that point. The tractor, for instance, was first sold for $750, then at $850, then at $625, and the other day we cut it 37 per cent to $395.

The tractor is not made in connection with the automobiles. No plant is large enough to make two articles. A shop has to be devoted to exactly one product in order to get the real economies.

For most purposes a man with a machine is better than a man without a machine. By the ordering of design of product and of manufacturing process we are able to provide that kind of a machine which most multiplies the power of the hand, and therefore we give to that man a larger rôle of service, which means that he is entitled to a larger share of comfort.

Keeping that principle in mind we can attack waste with a definite objective. We will not put into our establishment anything that is useless. We will not put up elaborate buildings as monuments to our success. The interest on the investment and the cost of their upkeep only serve to add uselessly to the cost of what is produced—so these monuments of success are apt to end as tombs. A great administration building may be necessary. In me it arouses a suspicion that perhaps there is too much administration. We have never found a need for elaborate administration and would prefer to be advertised by our product than by where we make our product.

The standardization that effects large economies for the consumer results in profits of such gross magnitude to the producer that he can scarcely know what to do with his money. But his effort must be sincere, painstaking, and fearless. Cutting out a half-a-dozen models is not standardizing. It may be, and usually is, only the limiting of business, for if one is selling on the ordinary basis of profit—that is, on the basis of taking as much money away from the consumer as he will give up—then surely the consumer ought to have a wide range of choice.

Standardization, then, is the final stage of the process. We start with [the] consumer, work back through the design, and finally arrive at manufacturing. The manufacturing becomes a means to the end of service.

It is important to bear this order in mind. As yet, the order is not thoroughly understood. The price relation is not understood. The notion persists that prices ought to be kept up. On the contrary, good business—large consumption—depends on their going down.

And here is another point. The service must be the best you can give. It is considered good manufacturing practice, and not bad ethics, occasionally to change designs so that old models will become obsolete and new ones will have to be bought either because repair parts for the old cannot be had, or because the new model offers a new sales argument which can be used to persuade a consumer to scrap what he has and buy something new. We have been told that this is good business, that it is clever business, that the object of business ought to be to get people to buy frequently and that it is bad business to try to make anything that will last forever, because when once a man is sold he will not buy again.

Our principle of business is precisely to the contrary. We cannot conceive how to serve the consumer unless we make for him something that, as far as we can provide, will last forever. We want to construct some kind of a machine that will last forever. It does not please us to have a buyer's car wear out or become obsolete. We want the man who buys one of our products never to have to buy another. We never make an improvement that renders any previous model obsolete. The parts of a specific model are not only interchangeable with all other cars of that model, but they are interchangeable with similar parts on all the cars that we have turned out. You can take a car of ten years ago and, buying to-day's parts, make it with very little expense into a car of to-day. Having these objectives the costs always come down under pressure. And since we have the firm policy of steady price reduction, there is always pressure. Sometimes it is just harder!

Take a few more instances of saving. The sweepings net six hundred thousand dollars a year. Experiments are constantly going on in the utilization of scrap. In one of the stamping operations six-inch circles of sheet metal are cut out. These formerly went into scrap. The waste worried the men. They worked to find uses for the discs. They found that the plates were just the right size and shape to stamp into radiator caps but the metal was not thick enough. They tried a double thickness of plates, with the result that they made a cap which tests proved to be stronger than one made out of a single sheet of metal. We get 150,000 of those discs a day. We have now found a use for about 20,000 a day and expect to find further uses for the remainder. We saved about ten dollars each by making transmissions instead of buying them. We experimented with bolts and produced a special bolt made on what is called an "upsetting machine" with a rolled thread that was stronger than any bolt we could buy, although in its making was used only about one third of the material that the outside manufacturers used. The saving on one style of bolt alone amounted to half a million dollars a year. We used to assemble our cars at Detroit, and although by special packing we managed to get five or six into a freight car, we needed many hundreds of freight cars a day. Trains were moving in and out all the time. Once a thousand freight cars were packed in a single day. A certain amount of congestion was inevitable. It is very expensive to knock down machines and crate them so that they cannot be injured in transit—to say nothing of the transportation charges. Now, we assemble only three or four hundred cars a day at Detroit—just enough for local needs. We now ship the parts to our assembling stations all over the United States and in fact pretty much all over the world, and the machines are put together there. Wherever it is possible for a branch to make a part more cheaply than we can make it in Detroit and ship it to them, then the branch makes the part.

The plant at Manchester, England, is making nearly an entire car. The tractor plant at Cork, Ireland, is making almost a complete tractor. This is an enormous saving of expense and is only an indication of what may be done throughout industry generally, when each part of a composite article is made at the exact point where it may be made most economically. We are constantly experimenting with every material that enters into the car. We cut most of our own lumber from our own forests. We are experimenting in the manufacture of artificial leather because we use about forty thousand yards of artificial leather a day. A penny here and a penny there runs into large amounts in the course of a year.

The greatest development of all, however, is the River Rouge plant, which, when it is running to its full capacity, will cut deeply and in many directions into the price of everything we make. The whole tractor plant is now there. This plant is located on the river on the outskirts of Detroit and the property covers six hundred and sixty-five acres—enough for future development. It has a large slip and a turning basin capable of accommodating any lake steamship; a short-cut canal and some dredging will give a direct lake connection by way of the Detroit River. We use a great deal of coal. This coal comes directly from our mines over the Detroit, Toledo and Ironton Railway, which we control, to the Highland Park plant and the River Rouge plant. Part of it goes for steam purposes. Another part goes to the by-product coke ovens which we have established at the River Rouge plant. Coke moves on from the ovens by mechanical transmission to the blast furnaces. The low volatile gases from the blast furnaces are piped to the power plant boilers where they are joined by the sawdust and the shavings from the body plant—the making of all our bodies has been shifted to this plant—and in addition the coke "breeze" (the dust in the making of coke) is now also being utilized for stoking. The steam power plant is thus fired almost exclusively from what would otherwise be waste products. Immense steam turbines directly coupled with dynamos transform this power into electricity, and all of the machinery in the tractor and the body plants is run by individual motors from this electricity. In the course of time it is expected that there will be sufficient electricity to run practically the whole Highland Park plant, and we shall then have cut out our coal bill.

Among the by-products of the coke ovens is a gas. It is piped both to the Rouge and Highland Park plants where it is used for heat-treat purposes, for the enameling ovens, for the car ovens, and the like. We formerly had to buy this gas. The ammonium sulphate is used for fertilizer. The benzol is a motor fuel. The small sizes of coke, not suitable for the blast furnaces, are sold to the employees—delivered free into their homes at much less than the ordinary market price. The large-sized coke goes to the blast furnaces. There is no manual handling. We run the melted iron directly from the blast furnaces into great ladles. These ladles travel into the shops and the iron is poured directly into the moulds without another heating. We thus not only get a uniform quality of iron according to our own specifications and directly under our control, but we save a melting of pig iron and in fact cut out a whole process in manufacturing as well as making available all our own scrap.

What all this will amount to in point of savings we do not know—that is, we do not know how great will be the saving, because the plant has not been running long enough to give more than an indication of what is ahead, and we save in so many directions—in transportation, in the generation of our power, in the generation of gas, in the expense in casting, and then over and above that is the revenue from the by-products and from the smaller sizes of coke. The investment to accomplish these objects to date amounts to something over forty million dollars.

. . . .

Now as to saturation. We are continually asked:

"When will you get to the point of overproduction? When will there be more cars than people to use them?"

We believe it is possible some day to reach the point where all goods are produced so cheaply and in such quantities that overproduction will be a reality. But as far as we are concerned, we do not look forward to that condition with fear—we look forward to it with great satisfaction. Nothing could be more splendid than a world in which everybody has all that he wants. Our fear is that this condition will be too long postponed. As to our own products, that condition is very far away. We do not know how many motor cars a family will desire to use of the particular kind that we make. We know that, as the price has come down, the farmer, who at first used one car (and it must be remembered that it is not so very long ago that the farm market for motor cars was absolutely unknown—the limit of sales was at that time fixed by all the wise statistical sharps at somewhere near the number of millionaires in the country) now often uses two, and also he buys a truck. Perhaps, instead of sending workmen out to scattered jobs in a single car, it will be cheaper to send each worker out in a car of his own. That is happening with salesmen. The public finds its own consumptive needs with unerring accuracy, and since we no longer make motor cars or tractors, but merely the parts which when assembled become motor cars and tractors, the facilities as now provided would hardly be sufficient to provide replacements for ten million cars. And it would be quite the same with any business. We do not have to bother about overproduction for some years to come, provided the prices are right. It is the refusal of people to buy on account of price that really stimulates real business. Then if we want to do business we have to get the prices down without hurting the quality. Thus price reduction forces us to learn improved and less wasteful methods of production. One big part of the discovery of what is "normal" in industry depends on managerial genius discovering better ways of doing things. If a man reduces his selling price to a point where he is making no profit or incurring a loss, then he simply is forced to discover how to make as good an article by a better method—making his new method produce the profit, and not producing a profit out of reduced wages or increased prices to the public.

. . . .

THE OLD WAYS FALTER

2] An Industrial Writer Analyzes the Impact of the New Market and New Competition on Ford

FOR SEVENTEEN years the Ford Motor Co. forged steadily onward and upward under the impetus of a virtual price monopoly. There was little in the way of competition and there seemed a limitless reservoir of buyers for its products to whom price was the major appeal.

Then something happened. Real competition on both a price and quality basis came into the field. The country became extraordinarily prosperous. Its people were well supplied with money and more of them became dissatisfied with the cheapest form of individual transportation.

Ford sales were checked. New body models failed to stimulate them and a moderate price reduction had little more effect. His percentage of total production fell 10 per cent last year as compared with 1925 and his portion of the total for the first two months this year averaged only 34 per cent.

The whole industry is speculating avidly on what Ford will do to bring his business back and regain his ascendency. Can he do it and if so, how? Whatever he does it is likely to produce a form of competition in automobiles far keener than anything yet known.

The first question Ford must answer conclusively is whether or not means can be devised to move the present line in satisfactory volume. If it can't be done, the only other alternative is to design another line—a step which he will be reluctant to take because of the tremendous production difficulties involved.

Two moves already have been made to overcome sales resistance. Body lines were materially changed early last fall but the improvements failed to expand sales enough to offset the losses attendant upon delays in getting into quantity production. The next attempted sales stimulus was a price cut ranging from $20 on the coupe to $60 on the two-door sedan and $95 on the four-door sedan. These concessions also failed to increase demand materially.

Ford's possible remedies are not yet exhausted, however. He might make a price slash of such substantial proportions that competitors could not approach it. Such a reduction, however, would cut deeply into profits and might wipe them out entirely on present volume, for Ford body costs are

FROM James Dalton, "What Will Ford Do Next?" *Motor* (May 1926), pp. 30–31, 84, 102 ff. Reproduced from *Motor* magazine. Copyright 1926 The Hearst Corporation.

considered higher, in proportion, than those of his rivals because of chassis peculiarities.

The next most important move might be a sincere attempt to allay dealer discontent which has been gaining headway steadily for the past two or three years among all classes, from the biggest to the littlest. It has been just as difficult for Ford retailers to make satisfactory profits as it has been for the rank and file handling other lines. This has been due partly to the slicing of territories, partly to competition of several other very popular lines and partly to increased used car difficulties resulting largely from increased demand for closed models. Until recently the Ford had been preeminently an open car but now nearly 75 per cent of all he makes are closed.

It is not probable that Ford will reduce the number of his retail outlets, but it is quite possible that he may be compelled to increase the average dealer discount, bringing it into line with that given by most of his competitors.

One reason why Ford has not held his own in sales is that he has lost a large number of experienced dealers, both in large and small towns. Many of these men have taken on rival lines in similar price classes. They have entered into bitter competition with the new Ford representatives and in numerous cases have been able to carry with them a considerable percentage of their former Ford customers.

Another logical step, in conjunction with substantial price cuts and dealer reforms, would be better time sale facilities for Ford dealers to aid them in financing both new and used cars. This business up to now has not been on an entirely satisfactory basis and a good many of his retailers have had real reason to complain of the facilities available to them.

With his enormous resources it would be comparatively simple for Ford to organize a subsidiary finance and insurance company, thus employing a part of his $620,000,000 surplus. If this plan did not appeal to him he could enter into a contractual arrangement with two or three of the present finance companies. No one of them has available the resources to handle all the business, so that it probably would be necessary to operate on something like a zone basis.

Only when these remedies, or something similar to them, had been given a fair trial could it be determined accurately whether it would be possible to maintain production at recent levels with the present line which has undergone no material mechanical change since 1908.

If these potential stimulants failed to increase sales substantially it would be perfectly patent that Ford would have to bring out an entirely new line or be content with a steadily diminishing volume of production.

Ford sales might be helped by a general business recession or even by hard times. As long as the country remains as prosperous as it has been most of the time for more than three years, the trend will be toward larger sales of motor cars costing more than $750. In this connection *Motor* said in December:

After three years of widespread prosperity the people of the country are more plentifully supplied with money than at any time in their history, except during the war inflation, and more of them will find it possible to go into higher price brackets in their car buying.

There is now a plentiful supply of high-class closed cars which can be bought for as little as new cars in the under $750 price class.

Dangerously liberal time sales terms will make it possible for almost every one who could really afford a car costing less than $750 to buy one costing more than that.

When these facts are understood it is easy to see why many companies have been able to increase their output so sharply this year and why they may be able to show another gain in 1926, although not all of them will be able to make as much progress as they profess to expect.

Gains of manufacturers making cars selling for more than $750 have been made largely at the expense of some of those making cars selling for less than $750, and the gains promise to be more marked in 1926 than they have been this year.

As a matter of fact, production of cars selling for $750 or less constituted 69.3 per cent of the total last year as compared with 73.8 per cent in 1925, a decline of 4.5 per cent. The discrepancy is accentuated by the fact that the total production gain last year was 555,000 over the preceding year, while cars selling for less than $750 gained only 253,000. The percentage loss of Ford alone was nearly 10 per cent, which means that his competitors took about half the business he lost. Much of it went to Chevrolet, Overland and Essex.

The Ford market always has been primarily for first car buyers. In the beginning this promised an inexhaustible reservoir, for no one dreamed that a quarter century would see 18,000,000 automobiles in use in this country. But facts far outstripped imagination.

From the time the Ford Motor Co. was organized in June, 1903, until late in 1908, it was experimenting continually to determine upon a satisfactory standard model. Only about 25,000 cars of different models had been made prior to the fall of 1908 when the now universally known Model T was introduced to the public. The first car of this type was turned out on October 1, 1908, but it was not until December 10, 1915, that the 1,000,000th left the assembly line. The first million was the hardest. After that they went faster and faster. Two million were made between January 12, 1923, and December 26 of the same year. The following table and an accompanying chart [see facing page] show the dates on which the million marks from one to twelve were reached:

CAR NUMBER	DATE	CAR NUMBER	DATE
1	Oct. 1, 1908	7,000,000	Jan. 12, 1923
1,000,000	Dec. 10, 1915	8,000,000	July 11, 1923
2,000,000	June 14, 1917	9,000,000	Dec. 26, 1923
3,000,000	April 2, 1919	10,000,000	June 4, 1924
4,000,000	May 11, 1920	11,000,000	Jan. 3, 1925
5,000,000	May 28, 1921	12,000,000	June 15, 1925
6,000,000	May 18, 1922		

Ford ate up his primary market with amazing rapidity, but it was not until last year that he reached the "point of diminishing returns." In the

FIGURE 1

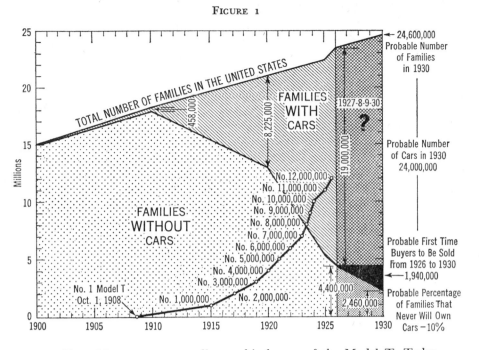

Families without any car at all were big buyers of the Model T. Today
few families have no car at all and the business is largely one of replacement. The "No. 2,000,000" locates the date when the 2,000,000th Model T
was built, etc.

biggest year the industry as a whole ever had, his domestic sales actually
fell off slightly and so far this year they have fallen off still more.

The trend towards higher priced cars has been even more marked thus
far this year, but Ford has been the principal loser. It is no secret that his
organization was much disappointed at the reception given the new models
last fall. After the orders which had accumulated while plants were virtually
out of production had been cleaned up it was found that the average
monthly sales volume had not increased appreciably. It might have been
considerably smaller, however, if the model changes had not been made.

Results, or lack of results, from the most recent price reduction were
equally disappointing. It was the first time in the history of the company
that price recessions, no matter how small, had failed to give a sharp impetus to demand.

If another and sharper revision of prices were made it would remain
to be seen what effect it would have. If the cut were large enough there
undoubtedly would be an upward swing in sales which might or might
not continue for some time. It would depend to a considerable extent upon
general business conditions and the prosperity of the people.

The consensus of opinion among the keen observers of the industry, how-

ever, is that Ford has passed the peak with his present model and that price
will have little permanent effect upon his sales curve. The price monopoly
he enjoyed so long is no longer his.

In 1921, five years ago, there were—omitting roadsters and coupes and
counting only four and five passenger open and enclosed cars—only three
models selling for less than $1,000 and only one for less than $750. Two
of the three were Fords and the spread between the Ford open car and the
nearest competing car of any kind was $455. The Model T cost only $440.
At the beginning of 1926 there were 27 four and five passenger open and
enclosed models under $1,000; 11 for less than $750 and 3 for less than $500.
Sixteen of the 27 were enclosed and 11 open. If the roadsters and coupes
are counted there are under $1,000 today 41 models. This shows how the
Ford competition has grown in half a decade.

With less than 4,500,000 families in the United States without motor cars,
it is perfectly obvious that the country is approaching the saturation point
for Fords inasmuch as the number of families which buys one Ford after
another is relatively small as compared with repeat orders for a good many
other lines of cars.

This does not mean, nevertheless, that any other producer will outstrip
Ford in the measurably near future, even if he were content to proceed as
he is now, cultivating his remaining market as intensively as possible. It is
probable another decade would pass before he would sell less than 1,000,000
a year or any other maker would be on even terms with him in point of
output.

But can he afford to go ahead on any such basis?

The whole Ford policy has been based on a tremendous annual output
which shall be increased from year to year without regard to competition.
As production declines costs rise. And if Ford is giving the public the best
prices possible on his closed models, which now constitute the major part of
his output, his production economies as compared with other lines are more
theoretical than real. The changes in four years in this respect, on the sedan
model, are rather striking as the following table shows:

	1922	1926	REDUCTION
Ford	$ 645	$565	$ 80
Overland Four	895	595	300
Chevrolet	875	735	140
Dodge	1,785	895	890
Chrysler (Maxwell)	1,485	995	490

· · · · · · · · · · · ·

Reasons for the decline in the relative popularity of the Ford car are
perfectly obvious to those familiar with the trade. Mechanically it is virtually
the same as it was seventeen years ago. There is little criticism of its quality
or its value. But other automobiles which have more nearly kept pace with
changing mechanical trends are not much higher in price. Furthermore,
there is an unlimited supply of good used cars which sold originally for

FIGURE 2 — THE "UNDER $1,000" MARKET

Left axis: **Price Spread to Nearest Competitor $455 or 103.4% Over Price of Ford's Popular Model** — **$551**

Diagonal line: *AVERAGE PER CAPITA EARNINGS*

	1921	1922	1923	1924	1925	1926
~$900+	Harroun Dort-Dodge CHEVROLET Chevrolet Buick Overland	Jewett-Oakland-Cleveland Dort Columbia Oldsmobile Studebaker Gardner Nash	Studebaker Gardner Elcar Columbia Buick Oakland	Gardner Elcar Dodge CHEVROLET Essex ESSEX		AJAX CLEVELAND JEWETT Dodge OLDSMOBILE
~$820–870		OVERLAND Durant Maxwell	DURANT Buick-Maxwell Dodge OVERLAND Dort CHEVROLET	Rollin Durant Dodge Essex GRAY	Maxwell-GRAY Dodge Oldsmobile OVERLAND Durant STAR	OVERLAND Chrysler Cleveland STAR Dodge Oldsmobile Ajax PONTIAC
~$800	FORD			Maxwell CHEVROLET OVERLAND STAR Oldsmobile	CHEVROLET Overland	CHEVROLET STAR ESSEX
~$680–730	FORD	--FORD	FORD	FORD	FORD Chevrolet Gray	OVERLAND CHEVROLET STAR FORD $610
~$600	Overland	--STAR: FORD	FORD	FORD	Star Overland Chevrolet	OVERLAND FORD { Chevrolet / Star }
~$540	Chevrolet	Overland Chevrolet	Overland Chevrolet	{ Overland / Chevrolet }	{ Overland / Chevrolet / Star }	Overland
~$500		Gray	Gray	Star		
~$480		Star				
~$420	Ford	Ford	Ford	Ford	Ford	Ford
~$360	Ford	Ford		Ford	Ford	Ford
~$300					Ford	Ford
text		The Start of the Era of Cheaper Cars	Time Payments Become Big Factor in Sales of Cheap Cars			The Start of the Era of Cheaper Enclosed Cars
choices	**3** CHOICES **2** TOURING / **1** SEDAN	**13** CHOICES **10** TOURING / **3** SEDAN	**24** CHOICES **19** TOURING / **5** SEDAN	**23** CHOICES **17** TOURING / **6** SEDAN	**24** CHOICES **16** TOURING / **8** SEDAN	**27** CHOICES **11** TOURING / **16** SEDAN

Closed Cars Shown in CAPITALS (GRAY)   Touring Cars Shown in Small Letters (Ford)

The chart at the left shows how competition has grown "under $1,000." In 1920 the Model T touring car practically had a monopoly. Today there are 27 choices. Figures each year are as of January. Only 4- and 5-passenger cars are listed. Names in capitals are enclosed cars; small type, open cars.

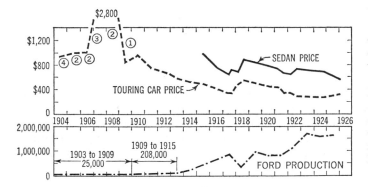

FIGURE 3

The Ford price has been coming down and production going up for nearly twenty years. (1) Model T begun. (2) Engine changed. (3) Only two-seaters in 1907. (4) Model A, tonneau.

much more than the Ford but which now can be bought for no more and often for less than the price of a new Ford.

An added factor has been the extraordinarily liberal time sales terms which have made it possible for almost everyone with a steady income to buy a higher priced car than a Ford.

The Ford has been for years the butt of countless printed or spoken jests. There was a time when these gibes were held to be good advertising but their cumulative effect has not been favorable to the Ford business. They have driven a very large number of prospects to other cars.

Standardization of product and production methods, together with control of raw materials and other advantages, have made Henry Ford a modern Croesus—a veritable billionaire. But it is becoming evident the time has come when he must make genuine concessions to public demand and also to his dealers.

The Fords have built up the most powerful industrial organization in the world and their resources are almost limitless. They can experiment until the cows come home without making serious inroads on their gigantic "profit and loss" surplus. They have demonstrated time and again that they are resourceful, sagacious and courageous. The mere fact that they seem to have run up against an economic condition which they cannot change does not mean that they will not be successful once they have found a means of meeting this condition.

It may be that they can again dominate the motor car market as completely as they have in the past, but it is quite possible that before such domination can be regained they may have to go through another period of experimentation as they did in the first years of the company's history. In the original experimental period there was a market for any kind of a motor vehicle which would run, because the nation was hungry for individual transportation and the market was untouched.

The Fords are not prone to discuss their plans for the future. Many of those who profess to be somewhat familiar with them contend that within a year they will make drastic mechanical changes in their car or bring out an entirely new line. Their decision in this respect, if they should conclude to bring out a line powered with a six cylinder engine would seal the fate of the four-cylinder motor so far as automobiles are concerned. Then, too, there might be possibilities in a really low priced eight.

Even a comparatively unimportant mechanical change in the Ford is costly. But to install a conventional transmission and remove the gasoline tank to the rear, for example, would cost a huge sum. Furthermore, the effect of changes, no matter how radical, on the present line would be entirely problematical. They might or might not materially stimulate demand. If they didn't it would necessitate further expensive experiments.

It might be cheaper, therefore, to bring out an entirely new line. If that were done it would necessitate the most careful engineering. Although it has been asserted repeatedly for years that Ford has had new lines ready for the market to meet any emergency which might arise it is to be doubted that entire reliance is to be placed in these reports, although he and his engineers must have given more or less consideration to such a contingency.

In any event there can be no junking of present Ford production and sales methods. His entire organization has been built around the quantity idea and he will have to continue on that basis. Price, therefore, must be the main consideration, just as it always has been.

Great as is the country's prosperity, merchandising on a price basis is just as successful as it ever was. The only trouble with the present Ford line is that so many of his cars have been sold that he is reaching the saturation point. By turning out something entirely new he can create a great new market.

If, for example, he were to bring out a six cylinder car which embodied all the most modern ideas in design, with comfortable bodies, attractive lines and colors, at prices materially lower than those offered by any of the present makers, there would be opened to him immediately an enormous market. He would have as prospects all the present Ford owners as well as a very large percentage of those who are prospects for other makers of low priced lines. To accomplish such a result, however, it would be necessary for him to produce something different, distinctive and attractive, as well as to offer superior values.

All the logic of the situation points to some such step as the ultimate solution of his present difficulties in the passenger car field.

General Motors' Innovations in Management

❲ AT GENERAL MOTORS the years immediately after 1921 were ones of retrenchment and reform. The top executives concentrated on bringing order out of the administrative chaos left by Durant and on thus transforming an agglomeration of many varied business units into a single coordinated enterprise. They also worked hard at planning and carrying out new business strategies to cut their costs and expand their sales. Besides Pierre du Pont, the men most responsible for these changes were Alfred P. Sloan, Jr., who became operating vice-president in 1921 and president in 1923, and Du Pont-trained F. Donaldson Brown and John Lee Pratt.

These four represented a new breed of businessmen. In their personalities, education, and business training they all differed greatly from Durant and Ford. All four had received formal engineering training. Du Pont and

Sloan had graduated from the Massachusetts Institute of Technology, Brown and Pratt from the engineering school of the University of Virginia. They had little of Billy Durant's optimistic outgoing charm. Few men, for example, ever called Du Pont or Sloan by their first names. Of these highly rational, somewhat reserved professional executives, Sloan was mainly responsible for creating the modern decentralized administrative structure at General Motors, Pratt and Brown for developing the detailed statistical information necessary for the operation of a complex modern organization.

Both the creation of the new structure and the development of the new type of data came out of administrative needs so startlingly revealed by the crisis of 1920. Because Sloan had long been troubled by the lack of control over the divisions, he had drawn up a proposal for administrative reorganization even before the crisis. By this plan division managers were to retain their autonomy, but their activities were to be coordinated and controlled by a sizable general office consisting of general executives and advisory staff officers. The general executives would include the president, operating and financial vice-presidents, and group executives who had major jurisdiction over separate groups of divisions. Besides meeting their individual responsibilities, the men acted collectively in the Executive Committee to appraise, plan, and make policy for the corporation as a whole. The staff officers in the general office could only give advice. They could not give orders to division managers or other personnel. They were to provide expert information and advice to both the divisional officers and the general executives. Durant found Sloan's plan interesting, but he never acted on it. Pierre du Pont moved quickly, however, after

the events of the fall of 1920 dramatically emphasized the need for effective administrative control. Adopted December 30, 1920, Sloan's plan has remained the basic "constitution" under which General Motors has been governed ever since.

The development of statistical data grew even more directly out of the crisis of 1920. In order to regain control of divisional spending, Durant set up an Inventory Committee in October 1920, which Du Pont strengthened when he took office. This committee had full power over purchasing, payrolls, and the disposal of existing inventories of all General Motors divisions. It also allocated the funds needed to pay suppliers and wages. As the committee began to achieve control, its chairman, John Lee Pratt, asked each division to report its inventories monthly, along with its estimated production for each of the next three months. The committee's approval of the estimate then became the authorization for the division manager to make the purchases necessary to complete the estimated production schedule. By April 1921 procedures had become systematized enough to disband the Inventory Committee and have the new general Financial Staff and Executive Committee supervise these controls.

It took four years of effort and experimentation to transform Sloan's plan and Pratt's procedures into an efficient, smoothly running administrative organization. The duties of the staff and the general officers had to be defined and redefined. New channels of communication had to be fashioned, particularly to bring together the general executives, staff advisers, and divisional officers. The creation of the Interdivisional Committees for major functions—such as sales, research and development, production, purchasing, and advertising—

achieved this last purpose. In these years, too, forecasting became more sophisticated and covered longer periods of time. The vice-president in charge of the Financial Staff, Donaldson Brown, and his assistants worked out "standards" or "estimated normal average conditions" for volume, production costs, commercial expenses, pricing, and investment. These standards provided criteria to test existing performance in all of these areas. They also became tools for evaluating the increasingly complex data flowing in from dealers and factories. The Financial Staff further worked out methods of adjusting the forecasted schedule of production, purchasing, employment, and distribution to the actual sale of cars to customers, based on reports made every ten days by the dealers. Through such techniques Brown tried to make the flow of materials through the enterprise from the original supplier to the final consumer as smooth and, therefore, as inexpensive as possible. Finally the Financial Staff developed comparable rational methods for planning and carrying out the long-term allocation of resources through budgets and carefully defined capital-appropriations procedures. By 1925 General Motors had created the structure and techniques of the new decentralized type of organization that many other American industrial firms later copied.

If other companies followed General Motors' organizational example, the Ford Motor Company did not. Ford did more than ignore these innovations. He expressed a positive contempt for the formal definitions of executive or supervisory duties, for explicit channels of communication and authority, and for the development of detailed and accurate information to flow through these channels. As a result, Ford's management became still more personal, far less rational, and, in the terms of return on investment, far less efficient than General Motors.

The readings presented here on General Motors suggest the evolution of its administrative structure and techniques between 1920 and 1925. The first reading comes from Sloan's initial proposal for reorganization, which Durant ignored and Du Pont quickly put into effect. The next reading is from a description of the corporation's administrative structure written by Charles S. Mott, a vice-president and member of the Executive Committee, in the spring of 1924 just as the reorganization was being completed. In the final selection on General Motors, Albert Bradley, Brown's able assistant, who became chairman of the Corporation's Board of Directors after World War II, explains the forecasting system developed by 1926 and indicates its uses.

In the selection from his *My Life and Work*, Ford makes crystal clear his views on the value of administrative structures and control. If he found formal administration worse than unnecessary, he also was convinced that his type of informal, personal organization assured his men and managers of getting "the exact recognition they deserve." Readers interested in the fate of the Ford executives under this personal rule should certainly look at Keith Sward's chapter on "The Ford Alumni Association" in *The Legend of Henry Ford* (New York, 1948). Sward dramatically describes in absorbing detail the departure of one able executive after another. As these men resigned or were fired, the control of the vast industrial empire fell into the hands of a very few aggressive, forceful, indeed ruthless, men. At first Charles E. Sorensen and Ernest Liebold were the favored crown princes. But in time they gave way to Harry Bennett, a prize fighter with long and close associations with Detroit's underworld.

In studying these selections the reader should keep in mind the training, business experience, and personalities of the innovators at General Motors. Would they have created as rational and systematic a structure if they had not had the formal technical education an engineering school provides? Or would they have done so if the crisis of 1920 had not occurred? Were they out to build a more "democratic" and less autocratic type of business organization? What were the advantages of the decentralized form over those of the standard centralized, functionally departmentalized operating structures of the day or over those of the loosely held financial holding companies? And what were its disadvantages? What did Brown and Bradley hope to achieve by defining "standards" for volume, costs, prices, and investment? Why has the use of "standards" in forward planning brought the charge of "administered" prices? Why did Bradley feel that accuracy in determining the flow of materials through the organization and the ability to even out the flow in the face of short-term fluctuations of demand was of value to suppliers, employees, and distributors, as well as to the corporation itself?

The selections on Ford raise the question of why he refused to see the need for systematic or rational management. What was the connection between these attitudes and the mass exodus of the more able Ford executives? Would the average American of the 1920's or even of the 1960's have agreed with Ford or with Sloan on the need for extensive business structures? Keep in mind the popularity of C. Northcote Parkinson's satirical polemics on modern administration—for example, *Parkinson's Law* (Boston, 1957).

THE CREATION OF A DECENTRALIZED STRUCTURE

1] Alfred P. Sloan, Jr., Plans Administrative Reorganization

General Motors Corporation
Study of Organization

THE OBJECT of this study is to suggest an organization for the General Motors Corporation which will definitely place the line of authority throughout its extensive operations as well as to co-ordinate each branch of its service, at the same time destroying none of the effectiveness with which its work has heretofore been conducted.

FROM "Organization Study," 1920. Du Pont-General Motors Anti-trust Case, Defendants' Trial Exhibit, GM 1.

The basis upon which this study has been made is founded upon two principles, which are stated as follows:—

1. The responsibility attached to the chief executive of each operation shall in no way be limited. Each such organization headed by its chief executive shall be complete in every necessary function and able to exercise its full initiative and logical development.

2. Certain central organization functions are absolutely essential to the logical development and proper control of the Corporation's activities.

Having established the above principles as fundamental, and it is believed that all interests within the Corporation agree as to such principles, the definite objects which it is hoped to attain by this study, are enumerated as follows:—

1. To definitely determine the functioning of the various divisions constituting the Corporation's activities, not only in relation to one another, but in relation to the central organization.

2. To determine the status of the central organization and to co-ordinate the operation of that central organization with the Corporation as a whole to the end that it will perform its necessary and logical place.

3. To centralize the control of all the executive functions of the Corporation in the President as its chief executive officer.

4. To limit as far as practical the number of executives reporting directly to the President, the object being to enable the President to better guide the broad policies of the Corporation without coming in contact with problems that may safely be entrusted to executives of less importance.

5. To provide means within each executive branch whereby all other executive branches are represented in an advisory way to the end that the development of each branch will be along lines constructive to the Corporation as a whole.

[Sloan then spelled out in detail his proposal for the reorganization of the corporation. His plans are summarized by the chart on the following pages, which he appended to the report.]

2] A General Executive Describes the Nearly Completed Structure in 1924

I N SPEAKING of the principles of organization as applied to a large corporation I must naturally speak of General Motors as one of the largest of our industrial activities and one with the administration of which I have been connected for several years.

General Motors is made up of 62 divisions and subsidiary and affiliated

FROM C. S. Mott, "Organizing a Great Industrial," *Management and Administration* (May 1924), pp. 523–27.

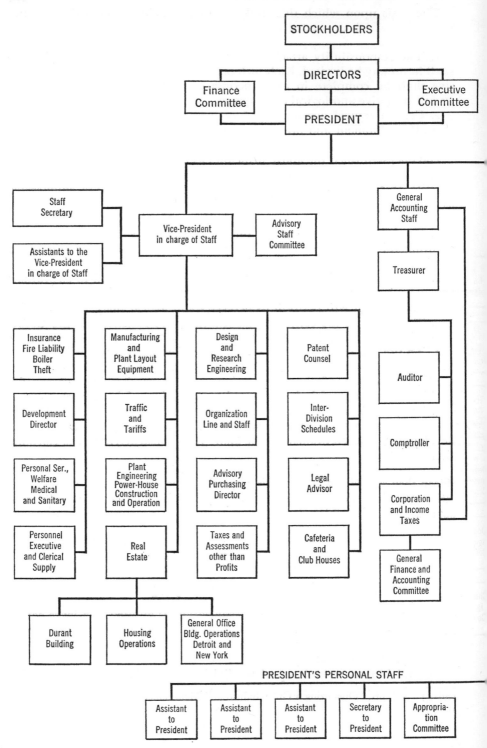

FIGURE 1. SLOAN'S INITIAL PLAN OF REORGANIZATION
FOR GENERAL MOTORS, 1920

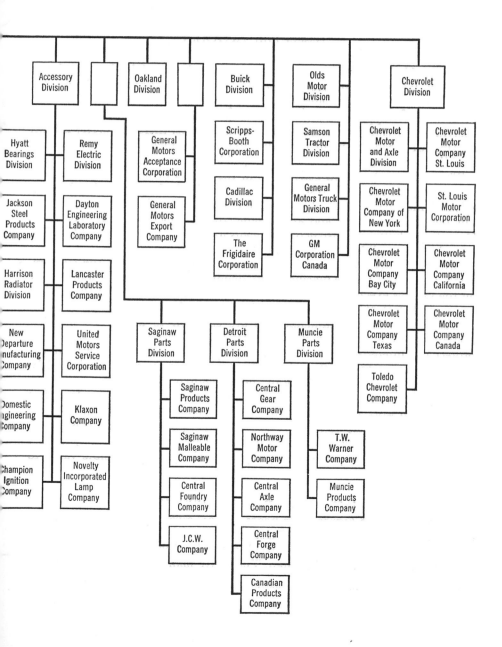

companies.[1] The public is perhaps most familiar with the names and the products of the six vehicle divisions—Buick, Cadillac, Chevrolet, Oakland, Oldsmobile and General Motors Truck—but besides these the General Motors family includes many parts and accessories factories, assembly plants, and other industrial activities. These are located in 12 states and the Dominion of Canada in the western hemisphere, and in the British Isles in the eastern hemisphere. Closely allied with this are the activities of our export company with its 18 distributing centers. From these strategic points, the sales and service of General Motors are extended to 144 countries.

Assets and Activities

THE assets of General Motors are in excess of $565,000,000. It has more than 70,000 stockholders and more than 135,000 employees. Added to the latter are many times this number of other workers, who depend upon the managing and operating efficiency of the corporation. It would be difficult to make even an approximate estimate of the total number of families and individuals directly associated with General Motors; there is scarcely a town in America in which one or more divisions of the organization have not an establishment engaged in serving the public.

The enormously varied activities and the armies of men and women for which General Motors is responsible have established a tremendously complicated industrial fabric. The fundamental problem is, of course, to run this business at a profit and at the same time to operate it constructively. Operating a business constructively means to increase not only its intangible assets but its tangible assets as well.

Briefly, all this is accomplished by the proper organizing of the corporation's man-power and by placing a very definite and individual responsibility on the various executives. There has always been, and doubtless always will be, a good deal of discussion as to the best methods of organization and operation, but certain fundamentals are common to all business undertakings. Any plan adopted should crystallize policies in such a way as to protect the interests of stockholder, employee, and customer, while at the same time, in operating, there is the least possible restriction on the initiative and the constructive ability of the individual.

It is generally recognized that men are more important than plans, but the best men work best by following the best plans. It is a General Motors policy to decentralize control, at the same time taking advantage of the strength, resources, and experience of the organization as a whole, so that every General Motors product may represent the greatest possible value to the customer.

General Plan of Organization

THE chart shown in Figure 1 [on pages 120–21] gives a graphic presentation of the operating organization of General Motors.

In detail, General Motors is governed by the stockholders, through the board of directors and its chairman. The active management of the corpora-

1 [Over half of these carried on manufacturing activities.]

tion is in the hands of the president, who is subject to the control of the Executive and the Finance Committees. In the formulation of the corporation's financial policy, the vice-president who is chairman of the Finance Committee governs. The financial staff, necessarily a large and well-organized body, includes in its activities the company's relations with banks, the department of the treasurer and of the comptroller, the insurance department, the tax department, and so on. An important activity of the financial organization within General Motors is the establishment of certain fundamental services, such as those of the General Motors Acceptance Corporation, which assists General Motors dealers and General Motors customers in financing purchases under the deferred payment plan, and the General Exchange Corporation, handling insurance of General Motors products.

Our president is chairman of the Executive Committee and the active head of all our operations. Under his jurisdiction come the financial department, already mentioned, the production and sales activities, gathered together under the head of the operations staff, and the advisory staff.

Organization of Operations Staff

THE operations staff is divided into several major groups, each under the charge of a vice-president of General Motors, who acts as a group chief. These groups comprise the Affiliated Companies Group, the Car Group, the Accessories Group and the Export Group, which in turn comprises General Motors Export Company and General Motors, Ltd., our British company. The Affiliated Companies Group has for its group chief the president of the General Motors Corporation. The companies in this group are those in which General Motors has a majority stock ownership.

As stated, a vice-president of General Motors is in charge of the Car Group. The activities of this group include the operation of the car and the truck divisions already enumerated and a number of companies manufacturing accessories and other products of general use. It may be mentioned here that the products of General Motors in a number of cases are not utilized solely in General Motors vehicles, but form important component parts of other trustworthy cars. We have, besides, a number of subsidiaries whose products go to the public at large. Important manufacturing and distributing divisions of the corporation are General Motors of Canada, Ltd., Delco, Remy, New Departure, Hyatt, Delco-Light, Klaxon, Jaxon, Fisher Body Corporation, Harrison Radiator, Brown-Lipe-Chapin, Doehler Die Casting, and Lancaster Steel Products. United Motors Service, Inc., on this continent is in charge of servicing the products of several of the accessories divisions, through more than 6,000 authorized representatives.

As stated, each of the principal groups or divisions is in charge of a manager, who is a vice-president of the parent corporation. Generally speaking, each division is in charge of a general manager, who has the entire responsibility for the success or failure of his operation, subject only to the clearly formulated policies of the corporation as a whole.

Each division operates as an independent unit, the head of which is practically as independent as if he were the president of a separate company, but at the same time his work is co-ordinated by the functioning of certain

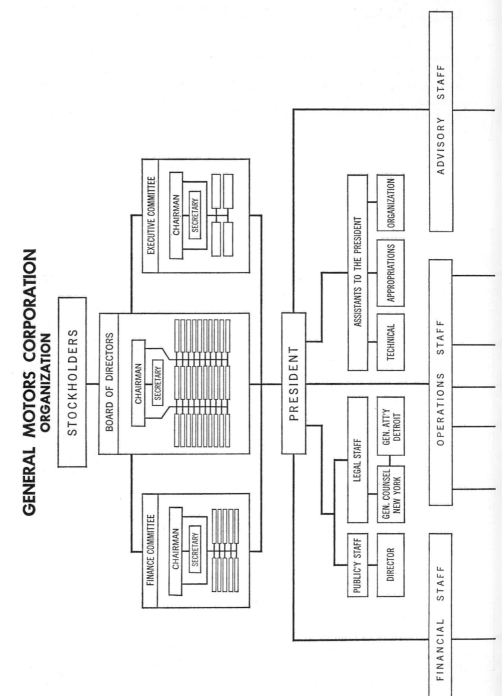

GENERAL MOTORS CORPORATION
ORGANIZATION

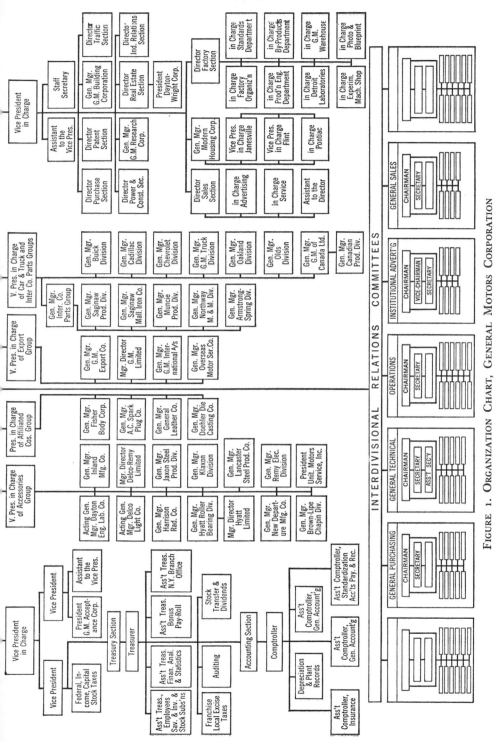

FIGURE 1. ORGANIZATION CHART, GENERAL MOTORS CORPORATION

committees and the advisory staff described below. Under this arrangement, each division enjoys advantages that would be beyond the reach of individual organizations. Among these may be mentioned research facilities, which furnish what amounts to an engineering audit on design; forecast and control of budget expenditures; forward commitments, with the solid advantages of quantity buying; and a consolidated cash plan, which has worked out to the advantage of everyone connected with General Motors, from stockholder to consumer.

Organization of Advisory Staff

THE advisory staff is in charge of a vice-president and is composed of several sections headed by members of the staff. These staff members act in an advisory capacity only; their services are available when they are sought by the divisions and the associate companies.

The chief of the advisory staff heads the directors of the following important sections:

Patent Department.   All patent matters pertaining to the interests of the corporation are referred to the head of the patent department, who acts very largely on his own authority as an expert. He has complete charge of, and responsibility in, the divisions of his department located at Detroit, Michigan, at Dayton, Ohio, and at Bristol, Connecticut. These divisions handle all matters dealing with patents, trade-marks, copyright, and related subjects. The work is assigned at the discretion of the department head. All divisions refer all patent matters to him direct and he is responsible for the decisions made. Every month a comprehensive report of the patent department's activities dealing with matters of infringements, inventions, and litigation is forwarded to the Executive Committee.

Real Estate Section.   The real estate section, also under its own responsible head, handles the purchase, sale, or lease of all real property which has been turned over to it by the corporation or any of its divisions. The section acts in the capacity of consultant in all real estate matters. A monthly report is made by its head to the Executive Committee; this report gives the status of all individual parcels of land owned by the corporation. Valuations on these parcels, if a change in valuation from the figure at which they are carried on the books is proper, are made as the result of consultation by the real estate section with other experts familiar with the individual piece of property involved. Offers for property are also referred for consideration to individual experts.

Office Building Section.   The General Motors Building Corporation, of which the vice-president in charge at Detroit is the president, is a separate corporation. It has charge of the general office building at Detroit through a general manager and assistants; the general manager reports to the president of the General Motors Building Corporation. The corporation office building at New York is also managed by the same general manager and his assistants. Periodical reports covering the building corporation's operations are made by its general manager to the Executive Committee of General Motors.

Housing Section. Housing activities are operated through another individual corporation, of which a vice-president of General Motors is the president. Active management is under the charge of a vice-president and general manager of the Modern Housing Corporation, the subsidiary; he has entire responsibility for the activities at Flint, Pontiac, and elsewhere. Periodical reports to the Executive Committee are made by the vice-president and general manager of the Modern Housing Corporation.

[*Research Section.*] A very important activity of the corporation's advisory staff is that of the General Motors Research Corporation, which operates at Dayton, the industry's largest experimental and testing laboratories, under the charge of a vice-president of General Motors. The work of the laboratories at Dayton and that of the factory section's laboratories at Detroit, of which mention will be made later, represent a portion of the General Motors' contribution to the advance of the automotive industry. The information and data gathered by the laboratories at Dayton and Detroit are at the service of any division of the corporation for development, experimental, and testing work.

Sales, Advertising, and Service Section. This section is headed by a director assisted by a corps of experts in the several lines that have to do with sales effort, advertisements of various kinds—display and direct, periodical, and outdoor—and service matters. The director and the experts act as consultants on all matters of sales and service, and recommendations in accordance with their investigations are made by the director to the vice-president at the head of the advisory staff. Proposals for appropriations for advertising are reported on by this section, which also deals with retail sales plans, branch operation, showrooms, service stations, and so on. The final approval of the vice-president in charge is based on the investigations and reports of this section.

Purchase Section. This is similar in its organization to the sales, advertising, and service section. A director and a corps of experts collect and digest data on the requirements of the corporation's divisions for purchases in large quantity. Arrangements are perfected by which each division and plant in General Motors has available the advantages of participating in purchasing its materials on corporation requisition.

Another important activity of the corporation is that of its Purchase Committee, closely allied, by the nature of its work, to the Purchase Section. This committee's regular membership consists of the president, two vice-presidents, the head of the purchase section, the purchasing agents of the vehicle divisions and of an accessory division, and a committee secretary. From time to time representatives from the divisions which are not represented on the permanent committee are asked to attend the committee meetings. Examinations of conditions and markets are conducted, and recommendations, of advantage to the corporation and the divisions alike, are made as the result of the committee's work.

Power and Construction Section. At the head of this section of the advisory staff is a director who reports to the staff's chief. He is a consulting engineer whose services are at the disposal of the divisions in matters relating to power and construction. His work includes investigation of rates charged for power, a study of fuel supply and markets, and building construction costs. It includes also the collection of data on the efficiency of boilers and ovens, heat-treating plants and allied equipment. He also has charge of negotiations with public utility corporations in matters relating to power supply.

Factory Section. This section is also headed by a director reporting to the advisory staff's head. His section handles a number of important matters, and makes available to all divisions information dealing with production, cost analysis, lubrication, waste prevention, salvage, metallurgical data, standards, factory layout and tool design. Connected with this section are the laboratories at Detroit, previously mentioned. These laboratories are well equipped for making physical and chemical tests and their activities form an important basis for accurate information on production, which is available to all the divisions and subsidiaries.

The same section has charge of General Motors Warehouse, a depository for the corporation's surplus tools and equipment. Sales are made from the stock kept on hand in this warehouse, which acts as a sort of equipment clearing-house among the divisions. All appropriations requests, having to do with matters in which the section is interested, are referred to the section for report before final approval. Special requirements are listed by the divisions and checked by the factory section; wherever possible, machinery on hand is utilized in filling divisional requirements. The director makes a formal monthly report to the staff chief.

Traffic Section. The director of this important section is a vice-president of General Motors, who heads the traffic experts of the corporation and makes available their knowledge and experience for the corporation's individual traffic departments.

Industrial Relations Section. This section operates under a director who works in conjunction with one man in each division to correlate and standardize, so far as possible, matters pertaining to industrial relations. Under his direction also is an expert who works at the central office at Detroit, gathering data on the important matter of industrial safety, and making them available on request.

Committee Organization

IN ADDITION to the activities of the operating staff and the advisory staff there are several important committees functioning in [the] General Motors organization. These have been formed for the purpose of pooling experience and co-ordinating information so that each division is given the advantage of as much common knowledge as possible.

Operations Committee. This is made up of the general managers of the car divisions and is headed by the president of General Motors with the principal executives. At the meetings of the committee there are discussed the corporation policies as regards manufacture and distribution.

General Purchasing Committee, General Sales Committee. These committees are similarly constituted, with divisional heads as their members. They function for the same purpose as the other committees of executive heads in divisions—to act as a clearing house of information and to lay out plans of campaign that will have a general application throughout the organization.

General Technical Committee. Emphasis should be laid on the importance of this committee. It is headed by the corporation president, with several of the vice-presidents, the president's technical advisor, the chief engineers of the principal divisions, members of the advisory staff whose work deals with technical matters, the head of the patent section and the vice-president in charge of the accessories group of plants. Other members of the organization are from time to time invited to assist in the deliberations of this committee; the plan is to avoid reaching a definite membership, but because of the importance of the matters discussed, many are invited to be present at particular sessions. Technical matters affecting the corporation and the divisions are discussed and recommendations made.

Institutional Advertising Committee. The corporation's institutional advertising is handled by a committee of which a vice-president of General Motors is the chairman. On the committee are the sales managers of some of the divisions, the presidents of the advertising agencies handling General Motors advertising, the director of the sales, advertising, and service section of the advisory staff and several of his aids, also the president and several vice-presidents of the corporation. Appropriations for institutional advertising are discussed and approved by this committee before recommendation of a budget is made to the Finance Committee.

Operating Details—Forecasting

IT WILL be seen that in General Motors the policies of the corporation are developed as the result of the functioning of these various committees, side by side with the development of financial policies by those in charge of finance.

The operating staff, the advisory staff, and the various committees deal with matters as they arise. In addition to these there is of course necessary the establishment of certain standard methods of handling matters affecting all divisions of the corporation alike.

In the matter of appropriations, a general manager has the authority to make capital expenditures up to a certain amount. If it is a case, for ex-

ample, of the manufacture of certain parts instead of their purchase from
outside sources, he develops a complete estimate of buildings, equipment,
and material, shows the amount of working capital required and so on. He
lists the estimated savings to be effected by the plan and shows the reasons
for individual manufacture. These plans and expenditures must be approved by an executive or a committee, according to the amount of expenditure involved and also according to the scope of the plan. For amounts in
excess of those which may be made on the authority of a division general
manager, the authority rests with the general manager in conjunction with
the group chief and the president; larger amounts are authorized by the
Executive Committee; and still larger amounts call for authorization by the
Finance Committee. An Appropriation Committee is responsible for requi-
sitions coming through in proper form and with proper signature.

Inventory, production, and sales forecasts are presented every 30 days, on
a blank which covers a period of 90 days. In the case of a report made on
October 25, 1923, for example, the blank shows actual inventory at October
1, with estimates for November 1, December 1, and January 1, which of
course include commitments already made or to be made, within the period.
Production and sales forecasts are given in the same manner and all of the
information given as of October 25 is compared with similar information
given as of the twenty-fifth of one, two, and three months previous. Thus
actual results are compared automatically with previous forecasts; and this
tends to secure accuracy in forecasting.

These data are given for the vehicle divisions and for the intercompany
parts group as well. On another portion of the blank are set down actual
production for October 1923, and estimated sales and production by months
for November and December 1923, and January and February 1924. Data
are also furnished, showing the total estimated for four months, in all
vehicle and parts plants, both in the United States and in Canada. Each
month, therefore, opportunity is given to the executives to observe the
closeness of relation between forecast and actual results. The figures as they
stand are reported [to] the president [as chairman] of the Executive Committee. The report in the form outlined brings clearly forward the conditions
of the individual plant, inventories, and so on.

Up to a certain amount, the general managers of divisions make forward
commitments for three months to cover material and other productive
requirements of their manufacturing schedules. Beyond that, the approval
of the group chief and the president is required. Practically, the forward
commitment request is sent to the group chief and the president and unless
the division is notified of disapproval within a week commitment is made
by the division. The forward commitments are forwarded to the Executive
and the Finance Committees for approval and for combining these commitments with the future liabilities of the corporation.

A most important development along financial lines, as a fundamental
policy of General Motors, has been the establishment of Consolidated Cash.
A plan has been worked out by which the income from the several manufacturing divisions and the other income-producing sources of the corporation is sent to the treasurer, who releases funds on requisition from the

divisions as they are required. This financial plan, which operates very much along the lines of the federal reserve system, provides almost automatically for funds where they are needed at the time and makes the liquid assets of the corporation available to the best advantage.

No system of administration can, of course, be entirely free from faults; but in General Motors a judicious combination of the advantages of the decentralized system, with its incentive to individual initiative, and those of a closely knit central organization, has operated to the obvious benefit of the corporation. A consistent effort is made all along the line by General Motors to individualize the divisions and the departments in such a way as to develop their initiative to the fullest extent. At the same time, the organization's composite knowlege and experience are pooled in such a way as to make them available and of value to everyone concerned.

3] A Financial Staff Officer Explains the General Motors Forecasting System

ACCORDING to no less an authority than Webster, to forecast is only "to plan before execution" or "to consider or calculate beforehand." Apparently no knowledge of astrology is required or even implied. It is also comforting to find a budget defined as "a statement of probable revenue and expenditure and of financial proposals for the ensuing year as presented or passed on by a legislative body." The forecasting program of General Motors Corporation is nothing more than systematic planning applied to the conduct of its business, from the point of view of fundamental financial policies and of current operating control.

A Forecasting Program Must Give Consideration to Four Major Factors. Systematic planning for the future, then, is the subject of this paper, with particular reference to the financial and economic aspects of the business. For each industry taken as a whole, the three major economic factors which must be appraised and dealt with are:

1. Growth, which is primarily dependent upon the increase of the country in population and wealth, after a condition of stabilization in the particular industry has been reached.

2. Seasonal Variation, i.e. differences in activity which may be attributed to the change in seasons, as distinct from other factors.

3. Operation of those forces which are generated within the general business situation itself, and which make for the alternating periods of depression, revival, prosperity, and crisis, usually referred to as the business cycle.

Each representative member of an industry is affected not only by the three factors just enumerated, but also by competition from other members of the same industry.

FROM Albert Bradley, "Setting Up a Forecasting Program," *Annual Convention Series,* American Management Association, No. 41 (March 1926), pp. 3–18.

The four factors, then, (1) Growth, (2) Seasonal Variation, (3) Condition of General Business, and (4) Competition, must all be given thorough consideration in setting up a forecasting program.

A forecasting program should serve two separate and quite distinct general purposes. In its broadest aspects, the forecast affords a means of gauging an operating program in terms of the fundamental policy of the Corporation regarding the rate of return on capital investment, as related to the pricing of the product, and the conditions under which additional capital will be provided for expansion. The second, and the more frequent, use of a forecast is as a tool for the control of current operations.

Whether a business be large or small, there is need of a policy in regard to the relation of capital investment to price of product, and the condition under which additional capital is to be used to expand the business (either through retention of earnings instead of paying dividends, or from sale of capital securities). The governing considerations are rate of return on investment and the relationship of capacity to average and peak demands. In a small business where ownership and management are identical, the fundamental policy may never be formally expressed, but it will nevertheless be taken into account by the owner-manager in making up his mind whether or not to make any additions to his plant. In the typical large industry, however, where capital is supplied by a large number of stockholders, many of whom are not active in the management, and particularly where the operations are diversified and scattered, it is essential that machinery be established by which the fundamental considerations of pricing of product and expansion programs can be related to the established policies.

The forecasting program now employed by General Motors Corporation is a product both of past experience and present needs. It serves certain specific purposes related to the activities of a large and growing business; and also is the preventive medicine or anti-toxin to ward off certain ills which have afflicted the Corporation in the not very distant past. The present forecasting procedure is in theory essentially simple, and rests upon certain broad general principles which are applicable to most other lines of manufacturing enterprise.

·   ·   ·   ·   ·   ·   ·   ·   ·   ·   ·   ·   ·

Forecasting Program in Relation to Fundamental Policies

DEALING with the forecasting program in relation to fundamental policies, it may be said that return on investment is the basis of the policy in regard to the pricing of product, but it must be understood that the fundamental consideration is the average return over a protracted period of time, not the specific rate of return over any particular year or short period of time. This long-time rate of return on investment represents the official viewpoint as to the highest average rate of return which can be expected consistent with a healthy growth of the business and may be referred to as the *economic return attainable*.

Pricing Policy Must Consider Normal Average Rate of Plant Operation (Standard Volume). The fundamental policy in regard to pricing of product and expansion of the business necessitates also an official viewpoint as to the normal average rate of plant operation.

Rate of plant operation is affected by such factors as: general business conditions; the extent of seasonal fluctuation in sales likely within years of large volume; policy with respect to seasonal accumulation of finished cars or their components (semi-finished product) for the purpose of leveling the production curve; the necessity or desirability of maintaining excess plant capacity for emergency use, and many other factors. The percentage accepted by the Corporation as its policy in regard to the relationship between assumed normal rate of plant operation and practical annual capacity, is referred to as *standard volume,* and represents, so far as practicable, the economic situation of the industry, rather than any abnormal situation pertaining to a particular plant.

The Corporation's Price Policy Is Completely Expressed in the Conception of Standard Volume and Economic Return Attainable. The Corporation's fundamental price policy, once formulated, is completely expressed in the conception of standard volume and expected long-time average rate of return on investment. The price of any product which will satisfy these conditions is its Standard Price. It is expected that in actual practice prevailing price will be above standard price at certain times, and below at other times, and it may never exactly coincide with the standard price; but the determination of standard prices is desirable for two reasons:

1. It affords a standard with which the actual prices or contemplated prices can be compared, so that variances can be given necessary consideration, thus guarding against the possibility of unintentionally pricing either an entire line or certain models in a manner inconsistent with the fundamental price policy in the matter of return on investment.

2. The policy itself is thereby submitted to the test of experience, so that if over a long period of time standard price cannot be realized, then the fundamental policy as to return on capital attainable in the business requires modification.

The forecast covering a year's operations affords an opportunity to consider a proposed program from the standpoint of the fundamental policies, since the matter of price must be dealt with, and this requires consideration of rate of return on investment and rate of operation in relation to capacity. The forecast must, of course, be predicated upon an estimate of the volume of business to be done, and the price at which the product is to be sold. Given the two basic estimates as to quantity and price, an estimate of the year's earnings, the capital required to handle the business, and the per cent earned on the investment, can be prepared.

The practice of General Motors Corporation is for each car division, some time prior to the beginning of the sales year, to submit to the Executive Committee a so-called "Price Study," which embodies the Division's estimates of sales in units and in dollars, costs, profits, capital requirements, and return on investment, both at Standard Volume and at the forecast rate of operations for the new sales year, all on the basis of proposed price. This Price Study in addition to serving as an annual forecast, also develops the standard price of each product; that is, the price which, with the plant operating at standard volume, would produce the adjudged normal average rate of return on capital which has been referred to as the economic return attainable. Proposed prices can therefore be directly compared with the standard prices which express the Corporation's fundamental policy, and a means is thereby provided for the measurement of departures from the policy which are necessitated by competitive conditions and other practical considerations.

This method of analysis necessitates the establishment of standards of capital requirement and expense factors, representative of the normal average operating condition, in terms of their respective ratio to annual sales or annual factory cost of production according to whichever is the more direct relationship. (Attention is called to the fact that the word "standard" as used in this connection represents the estimated normal average condition, not the goal of efficiency towards which operations are directed.)

A brief description of the development of these standards follows:

Standards of Capital Requirement. The rate of capital turnover is an important factor in a consideration of price to be established on product, since the margin of profit, multiplied by the annual capital turnover, determines the rate of return upon capital.

The standard fixed investment ratio is readily obtained, once standard volume and standard cost have been determined. The amount tied up in working capital items should be directly proportionate to the volume of business. For example, raw materials on hand should be in direct proportion to the manufacturing requirements, so many days' supply of this material, so many days' supply of that material, and so on, depending upon the condition and location of sources of supply, transportation conditions, etc. Work in process should be in direct proportion to the requirements of finished production, since it is dependent upon the length of time required for the material to pass from the raw to the finished state, and the amount of labor and other charges to be absorbed in the process. Finished product should be in direct proportion to sales requirements. Accounts receivable should be in direct proportion to sales, being dependent upon terms of payment and efficiency of collections.

Manufacturing Expense Standards. Costs of production and distribution per unit of product vary with fluctuation in volume, because of the fixed or non-variable nature of some of the expense items. The three elements of factory cost, i.e. manufacturing cost, are: (1) productive labor (labor expended directly on the product), (2) productive materials (materials which enter into the composition of the final product), and (3) manufacturing expense or burden, consisting of so-called indirect labor (foremen, inspectors, material handling) and indirect material, taxes, plant maintenance, light, heat and power, etc., etc. The first two items, productive materials and productive labor, representing perhaps 80 per cent of the total factory cost, may be referred to as 100 per cent variable, since the aggregate varies directly with volume within reasonable limits, and the cost therefore remains uniform per unit of product.

Among the items which are classified as manufacturing expense or burden, there exist varying degrees of fluctuation with volume, owing to their greater or lesser degree of variability. Among the absolutely fixed items are such expenses as depreciation, taxes, etc., which may be referred to as 100 per cent fixed, since within the limits of plant capacity the aggregate will not change, but the amount per unit of product would vary in inverse ratio to the output.

There is another group of items which may be classified as 100 per cent variable, such as inspection, material handling, etc., the amount of which per unit of product is unaffected by volume. Between the classes of 100 per cent fixed and 100 per cent variable is a large group of items, partially variable (light, heat, power, salaries, etc.). Lacking an exact means of determining the degrees of variation, a practicable method is to approximate the condition by applying a variability factor calculated on the basis of past experience.

Having determined the degree of variability of manufacturing expense, the estimated total expense at standard volume can be established. A standard burden rate is then developed which represents the proper absorption of burden in costs at standard volume. In periods of low volume, the unabsorbed manufacturing expense is charged directly against profits as "unabsorbed burden," while in periods of high volume, the over-absorbed manufacturing expense is credited to profits, as "over-absorbed burden." By this generally accepted method, there is avoided the distortion of costs and inventory values which would result from spreading a fixed overhead over a fluctuating volume.

Commercial Expense Standards. The usual practice of charging off commercial expenses from month to month eliminates the problem of over and under-absorption of expense made necessary in the case of manufacturing expense to avoid the distortion to asset values in consequence of fluctuating volume. In the consideration of price to be established on the product, and in the preparation of estimated profits at various volumes, it is nevertheless important to analyze as to the variable and non-variable character of the expense. An analysis of commercial expenses along the lines suggested for manufacturing expenses can be made. Non-variable expense includes the principal administrative salaries, rents, etc. Expenses 100 per cent variable are commissions, loading and shipping, etc. Between these extremes comes the third class, expenses partially variable and partially non-variable, the amount of which increases or decreases with changes in volume, but not in direct proportion to those changes. This class includes such items as salesmen's and other salaries, traveling expenses, etc., and the degree of variability can be determined for all practical purposes on the basis of past experience.

The analysis as to the degree of variability of manufacturing and commercial expenses with increases or decreases in volume of output, and the establishment of standards for the various investment items, makes it possible not only to develop "standard prices," but also to forecast, with much greater accuracy than otherwise would be possible, the capital requirements, profits, and return on capital at the different rates of operation which may result from seasonal conditions or to changes in the general business situation. Moreover, whenever it is necessary to calculate in advance the final effect on net profits of proposed increases or decreases in price, with their resulting changes in volume of output, consideration of the real economics of the situation is facilitated by the availability of reliable basic data.

The fundamental policy therefore provides standards of measurement for normal average return on investment and long-run average rate of operation in relation to capacity. Based on these, it is possible to establish standard cost and capital factors which in turn permit the expression of the fundamental policy in terms of price of product, i.e., Standard Price. Proposed and actual prices, profits, and return on capital can therefore be gauged in terms of the fundamental policy, and a means is afforded of judging the extent of necessary departures due to competition and other practical considerations. Similarly, cost and capital requirements' estimates taken into account in the original consideration of prices of product can be currently compared with actual results, and important variances from the forecast given necessary consideration.

Forecasting in Relation to Current Operating Control

TURNING now to the use of a forecast scheme as a means of current operating control, the same "Four Horsemen"—Growth, Seasonal Variation, Trend of General Business, and Competition, must again be dealt with. It cannot yet be said that Napoleon's first rule of warfare "Divide the enemy and conquer them in detail" has been successfully carried out, since the opposing forces must be dealt with collectively, as well as individually.

Growth. The limits of this paper do not permit a discussion of the growth factor beyond the statement, that, while the industry has been subject to an unusually rapid rate of expansion in the past, the volume has now reached such large proportions that it seems altogether unlikely that tremendous annual increases will continue. The expectation is rather for a healthy growth, in line with the increase in population and wealth of the country, and the development of the export market.

The condition of general business and the trend of competition are, of course, important factors affecting current demand for the Company's product. These factors, however, must be dealt with throughout the year simultaneously with the Growth and Seasonal Variation factors.

In regard to the seasonal character of the business, it may be said that the spring months always have been and still are the months of heaviest retail purchases of motor cars by the public. Although by far the larger proportion of automobiles are in service the year round, the buying urge still appears to be strongest in the spring, when everyone wishes to buy a new car, and, if he has enough resources remaining, to invest in a new suit of clothes. Even the trend towards closed cars, the proportion of which for General

Motors Corporation has more than doubled during the past three years, and now amounts to over 70 per cent of the total, does not appear to have materially altered the seasonal trend.

Seasonal variation, therefore, makes it necessary to have a greater number of cars available to retail purchasers at certain times of the year than at others. An analysis based primarily on our own experience for the past three years indicates a distribution by months as follows (See Figure 1):

STANDARD TREND OF DOMESTIC DELIVERIES TO CUSTOMERS
MONTHLY PERCENTAGE DISTRIBUTION OF YEARLY VOLUME

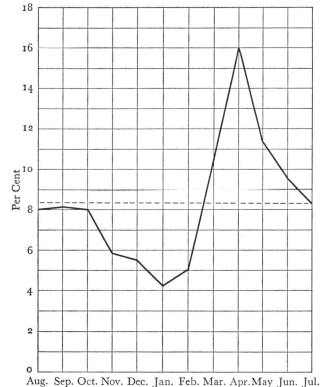

FIGURE 1. ANALYSIS OF DISTRIBUTION BY MONTHS

	PER CENT		PER CENT
January	4.2	July	8.3
February	5.0	August	8.0
March	10.2	September	8.1
April	16.0	October	8.0
May	11.3	November	5.9
June	9.5	December	5.5

There must, therefore, be available for delivery in the peak month of April almost four times as many cars as during December or January, and about

twice as many as during each of the months July, August, September and
October. The peak three months' period, March, April and May, represents
37.5 per cent of the year, or half as great again as the rate based on distributing the year's business evenly throughout the twelve months.

From the retail dealer's standpoint the ideal way of meeting the seasonal
situation would, at first glance, appear to be for the factory to vary its output
in order to conform to the seasonal consumer demand. There are several
good fundamental reasons why this cannot be done:

In the first place, factory capacity, in order to permit the manufacture in
one month of April requirements, 16 per cent of the year's volume, must
be almost twice as great as would be required to operate on an absolutely
level production basis, which would require but 8.3 per cent of the year's
volume each month. The result would be that the capital investment in
plant must be excessive, fixed charges for depreciation, taxes, etc., would
be increased, so that larger earnings would be necessary to provide an
equivalent return on the increased capital and to absorb the additional burden of plant maintenance, etc. This would require higher list prices for the
finished product, which, however, would create sales resistance and thereby
decrease the market. Such a plan of increasing capacity to take care of the
peak month's requirements is, therefore, fundamentally unsound from the
economic standpoint.

In the second place, even though the factory capacity were available, the
plan of adjusting monthly production to monthly consumer demand would
be fundamentally unsound from a standpoint even more important than
that of cost. I refer to the labor situation. Workmen are entitled to steady
employment, or as nearly steady employment as can be provided. Moreover, it is unlikely that the necessary amount of labor would be available
when needed; and it is absolutely certain that no factory operating on such
a varying manufacturing program would be able to keep its skilled employees, with the result that the quality of the product would suffer.

Operating on a Level Production Schedule. It is a fundamental principle,
therefore, that in order to operate economically, and thereby offer the
greatest value to the public, factories should operate on as level a line of
production as can reasonably be attained; and that radical changes in
production schedules should be eliminated as far as possible. Operating on
a level production schedule means, of course, that during months of low
retail demand the surplus of cars produced over and above those purchased
by the public must be stocked by the dealers, distributors, and the manufacturers, to be liquidated in the months of peak retail demand.

From the standpoint of economical distribution, of course, it is desired
to keep finished stocks down to the minimum, since the storing of this product not only requires additional capital, with its interest charge, but also
expenses for insurance, and other storage costs. There is also the danger,
if sales do not come up to expectations, not only that the cost of carrying
stocks of finished product may be unduly increased through prolonging the
period of storage, but also that losses may result from the necessity of forced
selling, i.e., distress merchandising, of the excess stock at the end of the

regular selling season. This phase of the problem is of vital consideration when plans are under way for the factory to manufacture a new line of products, since the new program may be seriously delayed, with resulting loss to the manufacturer, the dealers and distributors. In short, at first glance, economical manufacture requiring level production, and economical distribution, involving minimum stocks of finished product, appear to be diametrically opposed.

The operating program of General Motors Corporation is a compromise between the two plans just described. Factories vary their production schedules within the three limits established by (1) plant capacity, (2) the accumulation of stocks of finished product which are not excessive when viewed in their relationship to current retail demand and the necessities of seasonal requirements, and (3) the maintenance of reasonably steady rates of operation with resulting benefits to employees through continuous employment and the avoidance of the economic loss which results from violent fluctuations in the rate of manufacturing operations.

The original estimate of the year's domestic sales volume is based upon an estimate of the number of cars which are likely to be sold to the public by the entire automotive industry, segregated into (1) Low Price Group (2) Medium Price Group and (3) High Price Group. The estimate for the industry is based primarily upon actual experience for the last three sales years, after giving careful consideration to the probable number of automobiles needed to replace those which will be worn out or otherwise destroyed during the coming year, and an appraisal of the general business situation for the coming year.

The expectation of each car division is determined after giving consideration to the expected total amount of business available for its respective price group and the competitive situation of the division. It must be borne in mind that these estimates concern a future period and must of necessity reflect an appraisal not only of the general business situation, but also of the effect of new models, price reductions, and other factors, not only by ourselves, but also by competitors, all of which must be weighed beforehand. The estimate for each division, on approval by the Executive Committee, is referred to as the original Divisional Index.

So far the procedure is not radically unlike that followed for the past six years. There is undoubtedly a better background for the estimates for the industry, and the distribution of the total among the three major price groups; also more experience for gauging the performance of the several Divisions. The step forward which General Motors Corporation has taken, however, consists not so much in more accurately forecasting the year's business, as in developing a method which insures a change in its production schedules the moment actual experience indicates a change in the trend of retail deliveries to the public.

The first and controlling principle in the establishment of General Motors production schedules is that they shall be based absolutely upon the ability of its distributors and dealers to sell cars to the public. Each car division now receives from its dealers every ten days the actual number of cars delivered to consumers, the number of new orders taken, the total orders on hand, and the number of new and used cars on hand. Each ten-day period the actual results are compared with the month's forecast, and each month, as these figures are received, the entire situation is carefully analyzed to see whether the original estimate was too high or too low. If it is decided that the estimate was too high, the production schedule is immediately reduced. If, on the other hand, it is found that the retail demand is greater than had been estimated, the production program is increased, provided the plant capacity permits. In this way the production program is compared month by month, in fact, ten-day period by ten-day period, and the necessary adjustments in the production schedule and in the estimate of the year's volume (i.e., Divisional Index) are made. In other words, instead of attempting to lay down a hard and fast production program a year ahead and to stick to it regardless of the retail demand, the Corporation now follows the policy of keeping production at all times under control and in correct alignment with the indicated annual retail demand, and with the minimum accumulation of finished product in the hands of dealers for seasonal requirements, which the flexibility of production schedules permits.

Coordination of Inventories and Purchasing Commitments. Under the Corporation's system of inventory and purchase control, installed as a result of the liquidation losses of 1920–21, inventories and purchase commitments cannot get seriously out of line if the production schedule itself is properly controlled. Each operating division submits monthly a definite forecast of operations of the current month and the three succeeding months, covering sales and production each month, and indicating the amount of investment at the end of each month in inventories and other items of working capital, and also outstanding inventory commitments. These forecasts, if accepted (and each Division's forecast is considered as accepted unless the President takes exception thereto and contacts with the Division affected), constitute the authority for each Division to proceed upon the indicated manufacturing schedule and to make forward commitments up to the requirements of the forecast. Special authority is required from the central office to cover any commitments beyond the requirements of these authenticated forecasts, and is requested only in exceptional circumstances.

The usual practice is to release immediately upon adoption of the schedules the materials required for the following month, and to make definite commitments beyond that time, that is, one month, only for those items which require a longer period for their manufacture and delivery to the plant. The major items, constituting say 95 per cent of material purchases for the entire car, are item by item released on the basis of analysis as to number of days which must elapse between date of placing order and date of arrival of materials in the plant; in other words, the overall period which takes into account the time required for manufacture by the supplier, which, of course, varies widely as between different items, and also distance of supplier from plant, transportation conditions, etc. A reasonable working stock and flow of the large number of small items which constitute the other 5 per cent is maintained. The necessary bank of materials to be held at the plant is also given consideration, this bank being changed with more or less permanent changes in the rate of operation, in transportation conditions, ability of suppliers to adjust their schedules, etc. Commitments finally are made only for the minimum quantity of materials necessary to insure the requirements of the schedule, taking into account all circumstances affecting the situation.

The result of this plan of operation is the minimum total of materials on order and/or in the plant, which is necessary to insure the flow of materials necessary to proceed with the production schedule for one month. From a current operation standpoint, a balanced inventory condition does not represent a quantity of materials which could be made up into a certain number of automobiles, with nothing left over as is the case from the standpoint of liquidation. It represents the quantity of the different items which must be either on hand or on order for shipment within a given period, in order to permit manufacture at a given rate of output. For example, assume a schedule of 10,000 cars for the current month, March, and for each of the next three months, April, May and June. Towards the end of March, there will have been released all of the balance of the materials not already ordered or available and which are necessary for April production, perhaps one-half of the materials for May, and less than one-fourth of June's requirements, and, except in unusual instances, nothing beyond June. A month later a similar procedure will be followed, this time the balance of materials being released to complete the May schedule (say one-half), an additional one-fourth of June's requirements, and the first quarter of July's requirements. During the intervening month there will likely have been some change in the total schedule. It is quite certain there will have been considerable change in the distribution by model types. Such a plan makes it possible to reflect with minimum delay any changes in requirements, since manufacturing operations are proceeding upon the basis of minimum inventories and minimum commitments. In other words, to the extent that commitments have not been made and/or inventories accumulated beyond immediate requirements, there exists a slack to take up subsequent changes in the schedule without the necessity of either piling up inventories beyond the Corporation's own requirements, or of deferring delivery of materials committed for, but still held by suppliers.

This plan not only protects the Corporation, but it safeguards the supplier as well, through insuring him more continuous operation. Assume, for example, the Corporation's own inventories were larger, and commitments also were greater. It would follow that a reduction in the schedule would mean to the supplier either smaller orders or no orders at all for a considerable time. It is self-evident that the ultimate total material requirement for the schedule for the entire period of manufacture of the product in question is the same whether the Corporation carries large or small inventories, and/or makes large or small forward commitments. It follows, therefore, that the smaller the inventories and commitments at any time, the larger must be the balance of materials to be ordered from suppliers within the manufacturing period; so that suppliers are less likely to be cut off without further business, or their operations seriously curtailed, if the manufacturer has not accumulated materials or made commitments beyond immediate requirements.

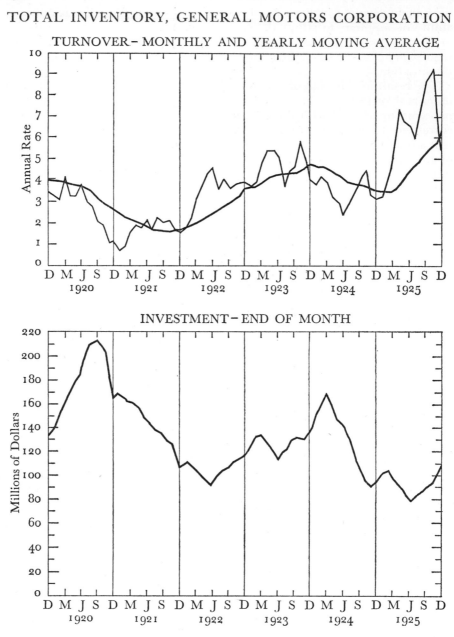

FIGURE 2. COMPARISON OF TURNOVER OF TOTAL INVENTORIES, 1920–1925.

Results of Forecasting Program

THE results of this forecasting procedure of General Motors Corporation may be considered from the standpoint of their relationship to the fundamental policies and to current operating control.

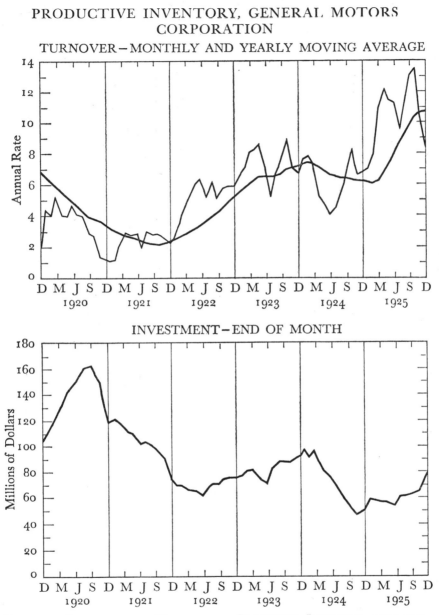

PRODUCTIVE INVENTORY, GENERAL MOTORS
CORPORATION

TURNOVER–MONTHLY AND YEARLY MOVING AVERAGE

INVESTMENT–END OF MONTH

FIGURE 3. COMPARISON OF TURNOVER OF PRODUCTIVE INVENTORY, 1920–1925.

The establishment of cost, expense and investment standards has not only made possible the development of standard prices, by means of which actual or proposed prices can be gauged in terms of the fundamental policies as to return on investment and relationship of normal average rate of plant operation to capacity, but it has also subjected the fundamental policies themselves to the test of actual experience, and has made these policies better understood throughout the organization. There has also resulted a marked improvement in accuracy of the basic estimates themselves. Accuracy in estimating and a clear understanding of fundamental policies facilitate systematic planning for the future in even the simplest type of organization; but they have an even greater value, in fact, are absolutely essential, in a large, complex and decentralized organization like General Motors Corporation, consisting of thirty-five different and distinct manufacturing divisions.

Dealing with the matter of current operating control it may be said that increases or decreases in production schedules have been less violent than heretofore. Operations at a more level rate and the closer scheduling of materials have made it possible to manufacture a larger quantity of cars with a smaller amount of capital tied up in inventories. For example (See Figure 2), the turnover of total inventories of the Corporation for the entire year 1925—6.3 times represented an improvement of 33 per cent over the best previous year, 1923. An even greater improvement was shown in the turnover of productive inventory (total inventory less finished product—see Figure 3) which reached 10.6 for the year 1925—an increase of 50 per cent over the best previous year, 1923.

Moreover, as a result of the more even rate of operations of the car divisions, it seems safe to assume that the inventory turnover of suppliers was favorably affected, since we know that such a favorable influence was enjoyed on the part of our own Accessory and Parts Divisions.

Steadier employment for the workmen is shown by the fact that in 1925, the maximum number of employees was 93,284, the average 83,278, the minimum 68,085. Thus the maximum varied only 11 per cent, and the minimum only 18 per cent from the average, by far the best performance in the Corporation's history.

Moreover, with the improvement in capital turnover, it has been possible to pass on to the public not only savings in cost, but also to considerably reduce the profit margin per car, without impairing return on investment. In other words, with no increase in capital the Corporation has been able to conduct a larger volume of business at a smaller net profit per unit, and to make a very satisfactory return on its capital; and to pass along to the public the savings resulting from increased volume and increases in efficiency.

The closer alignment of current production schedules with the movement of the final product into the hands of consumers has resulted in improving the economic position of the 15,000 dealers in General Motors' products through the more rapid rate of turnover of stocks of cars carried by dealers. For example, for the entire United States, the turnover of General Motors dealers' new car stocks for the entire year 1925 was 12 times, or approximately 25 per cent greater than any previous year.

The automobile business, in common with other businesses, undoubtedly will continue to have its good and poor years. The business is also to a considerable extent seasonal in character, which means that finished goods must be stocked beforehand in order to meet the demand of peak months. There is the growth factor, possibly less significant for the future than for the past. It is not possible accurately to forecast very far ahead the trend of general business, since it depends so largely on concurrent developments within the entire business situation during the intervening period. The Corporation has, however, taken a real step forward in obtaining by ten-day periods from its 15,000 dealers actual data regarding movement of the finished product into the hands of consumers. By this method a change in trend can be detected much more quickly and with much greater certainty than has been possible heretofore, so that necessary adjustment of manufacturing programs can be made more promptly.

It is an economic principle, if not yet an economic law, that the closer one gets to the consumer, the less fluctuation there is in the purchase and consumption of goods; and the view is generally accepted that the wide variations in business activity result to a very large degree from production having proceeded at a rate in excess of current demand or consumption at certain times, which must be followed by periods of subnormal activity, during which stocks of goods must be liquidated before business can proceed on an even keel with current production in line with current consumption. It is to avoid the economic loss resulting not only to itself from uneven schedules and excessive inventories, but to its dealers through excessive carrying charges, and its employees through less regular employment, that General Motors Corporation has taken this constructive step forward in adjusting its current operations to ultimate consumer demand. To the extent that it can accomplish this purpose, it will contribute something towards stabilizing its own business, a result which, if it can be made widespread, will contribute much toward the elimination of waste resulting from dislocation or ill-adjustment of industry, and thereby increase the economic well-being of the country as a whole.

FORD REJECTS MODERN MANAGEMENT METHODS

4] Ford Derides Systematic Organization

THAT which one has to fight hardest against in bringing together a large number of people to do work is excess organization and consequent red tape. To my mind there is no bent of mind more dangerous than that which is sometimes described as the "genius for organization." This usually results in the birth of a great big chart showing, after the fashion of a family tree, how authority ramifies. The tree is heavy with nice round berries,

FROM Henry Ford in collaboration with Samuel Crowther, *My Life and Work* (New York, 1922), pp. 91–96.

each of which bears the name of a man or of an office. Every man has a title and certain duties which are strictly limited by the circumference of his berry.

If a straw boss wants to say something to the general superintendent, his message has to go through the sub-foreman, the foreman, the department head, and all the assistant superintendents, before, in the course of time, it reaches the general superintendent. Probably by that time what he wanted to talk about is already history. It takes about six weeks for the message of a man living in a berry on the lower left-hand corner of the chart to reach the president or chairman of the board, and if it ever does reach one of these august officials, it has by that time gathered to itself about a pound of criticisms, suggestions, and comments. Very few things are ever taken under "official consideration" until long after the time when they actually ought to have been done. The buck is passed to and fro and all responsibility is dodged by individuals—following the lazy notion that two heads are better than one.

Now a business, in my way of thinking, is not a machine. It is a collection of people who are brought together to do work and not to write letters to one another. It is not necessary for any one department to know what any other department is doing. If a man is doing his work he will not have time to take up any other work. It is the business of those who plan the entire work to see that all of the departments are working properly toward the same end. It is not necessary to have meetings to establish good feeling between individuals or departments. It is not necessary for people to love each other in order to work together. Too much good fellowship may indeed be a very bad thing, for it may lead to one man trying to cover up the faults of another. That is bad for both men.

When we are at work we ought to be at work. When we are at play we ought to be at play. There is no use trying to mix the two. The sole object ought to be to get the work done and to get paid for it. When the work is done, then the play can come, but not before. And so the Ford factories and enterprises have no organization, no specific duties attaching to any position, no line of succession or of authority, very few titles, and no conferences. We have only the clerical help that is absolutely required; we have no elaborate records of any kind, and consequently no red tape.

We make the individual responsibility complete. The workman is absolutely responsible for his work. The straw boss is responsible for the workmen under him. The foreman is responsible for his group. The department head is responsible for the department. The general superintendent is responsible for the whole factory. Every man has to know what is going on in his sphere. I say "general superintendent." There is no such formal title. One man is in charge of the factory and has been for years. He has two men with him, who, without in any way having their duties defined, have taken particular sections of the work to themselves. With them are about half a dozen other men in the nature of assistants, but without specific duties. They have all made jobs for themselves—but there are no limits to their jobs. They just work in where they best fit. One man chases stock and shortages. Another has grabbed inspection, and so on.

This may seem haphazard, but it is not. A group of men, wholly intent upon getting work done, have no difficulty in seeing that the work is done. They do not get into trouble about the limits of authority, because they are not thinking of titles. If they had offices and all that, they would shortly be giving up their time to office work and to wondering why did they not have a better office than some other fellow.

Because there are no titles and no limits of authority, there is no question of red tape or going over a man's head. Any workman can go to anybody, and so established has become this custom, that a foreman does not get sore if a workman goes over him and directly to the head of the factory. The workman rarely ever does so, because a foreman knows as well as he knows his own name that if he has been unjust it will be very quickly found out, and he shall no longer be a foreman. One of the things that we will not tolerate is injustice of any kind. The moment a man starts to swell with authority he is discovered, and he goes out, or goes back to a machine. A large amount of labour unrest comes from the unjust exercise of authority by those in subordinate positions, and I am afraid that in far too many manufacturing institutions it is really not possible for a workman to get a square deal.

The work and the work alone controls us. That is one of the reasons why we have no titles. Most men can swing a job, but they are floored by a title. The effect of a title is very peculiar. It has been used too much as a sign of emancipation from work. It is almost equivalent to a badge bearing the legend:

"This man has nothing to do but regard himself as important and all others as inferior."

Not only is a title often injurious to the wearer, but it has its effect on others as well. There is perhaps no greater single source of personal dissatisfaction among men than the fact that the title-bearers are not always the real leaders. Everybody acknowledges a real leader—a man who is fit to plan and command. And when you find a real leader who bears a title, you will have to inquire of someone else what his title is. He doesn't boast about it.

Titles in business have been greatly overdone and business has suffered. One of the bad features is the division of responsibility according to titles, which goes so far as to amount to a removal altogether of responsibility. Where responsibility is broken up into many small bits and divided among many departments, each department under its own titular head, who in turn is surrounded by a group bearing their nice sub-titles, it is difficult to find any one who really feels responsible. Everyone knows what "passing the buck" means. The game must have originated in industrial organizations where the departments simply shove responsibility along. The health of every organization depends on every member—whatever his place—feeling that everything that happens to come to his notice relating to the welfare of the business is his own job. Railroads have gone to the devil under the eyes of departments that say:

"Oh, that doesn't come under our department. Department X, 100 miles away, has that in charge."

There used to be a lot of advice given to officials not to hide behind their titles. The very necessity for the advice showed a condition that needed more than advice to correct it. And the correction is just this—abolish the titles. A few may be legally necessary; a few may be useful in directing the public how to do business with the concern, but for the rest the best rule is simple: "Get rid of them."

As a matter of fact, the record of business in general just now is such as to detract very much from the value of titles. No one would boast of being president of a bankrupt bank. Business on the whole has not been so skill-fully steered as to leave much margin for pride in the steersmen. The men who bear titles now and are worth anything are forgetting their titles and are down in the foundation of business looking for the weak spots. They are back again in the places from which they rose—trying to reconstruct from the bottom up. And when a man is really at work, he needs no title. His work honours him.

. . . .

Of course, there are certain factors in the desire for recognition which must be reckoned with. The whole modern industrial system has warped the desire so out of shape that it is now almost an obsession. There was a time when a man's personal advancement depended entirely and immediately upon his work, and not upon any one's favour; but nowadays it often de-pends far too much upon the individual's good fortune in catching some influential eye. That is what we have successfully fought against. Men will work with the idea of catching somebody's eye; they will work with the idea that if they fail to get credit for what they have done, they might as well have done it badly or not have done it at all. Thus the work sometimes be-comes a secondary consideration. The job in hand—the article in hand, the special kind of service in hand—turns out to be not the principal job. The main work becomes personal advancement—a platform from which to catch somebody's eye. This habit of making the work secondary and the recogni-tion primary is unfair to the work. It makes recognition and credit the real job. And this also has an unfortunate effect on the worker. It encourages a peculiar kind of ambition which is neither lovely nor productive. It pro-duces the kind of man who imagines that by "standing in with the boss" he will get ahead. Every shop knows this kind of man. And the worst of it is there are some things in the present industrial system which make it appear that the game really pays.

. . . .

General Motors' Innovations in Marketing

⟨ As soon as it took office late in 1920 the new General Motors management began to define basic marketing, as well as administrative, policies. The completion of the administrative organization in 1925 permitted these executives to concentrate even more intensely on developing ways and means to increase the sales of General Motors' products. Of the initial marketing decisions the most critical were those that shaped the corporation's product line. Durant's concern had always been for the expansion of facilities rather than the formation of a rationally defined product line. In 1920 Buick, Olds, Oakland, and even Chevrolet competed directly with one another in the middle-price market. Only Buick and the high-priced Cadillac had a national reputation as reliable vehicles. In 1921, for example, Chevrolet sold only 75,667 passenger cars, less than Buick did, to obtain all of 4 per cent of the market, while Olds and Oakland each held less than 1 per cent of the market. The first step then was to bring the products of these other three divisions up to the standards and market acceptance of those of Buick and Cadillac.

The second step was to arrange the offerings of each of the divisions so that together, they covered all price ranges and met the tastes of different customers. This new policy of a full line—or in the corporation's phrase, of "a car for every purse and purpose"—was not fully worked out until 1925. The primary reason for the delay was technological. The corporation's research director, Charles F. Kettering, had planned to improve the offerings of the weaker divisions by developing a lighter, more efficient, and cheaper air-cooled engine for them. Only after the experiment failed in 1923 did the corporation concentrate on rounding out its line with cars using conventional water-cooled engines. In 1925, with the development of the six-cylinder Pontiac to meet the high-volume demand in the market just above the low-priced four-cylinder Chevrolet, the full line neared completion. The Pontiac put a General Motors car in practically every price class. Cadillac was a leader among the most expensive cars. Then came Buick, Olds, and Pontiac. At the bottom of the price ladder Chevrolet now began to challenge Ford.

General Motors' fashioning of a full line of products was only a start toward conquering the market. After 1921 the divisions were under constant pressure from the general office to improve the performance and appearance of their products. General Motors, for example, moved into the six-cylinder engine more rapidly than other companies. It adopted the closed body more quickly than Ford. The divisions and Kettering's Research Staff worked on producing better products by improving tires, brakes, gears, and so on. In 1926 the corporation brought in Harley Earl, a designer from Hollywood, to head a new "Styling Section" of the Advisory Staff. Finally General Motors began to rationalize the introduction of technical improvements and style changes by incorporating them annually into new models. Each year the new model was introduced with all the fanfare of a massive sales campaign employing nearly every modern advertising technique.

After its formation in 1924 the General Sales Committee came to handle the details of setting up and supervising the execution of marketing policies for the corporation as a whole. Besides working out strategies for the introduction of new models and for impressive advertising campaigns, it concerned itself with defining the relations of the corporation's many divisions with their dealers. Through 1925 the problem was still one of creating a dealer organization. But after General Motors had fashioned the largest dealer network of any corporation in the country, the committee had to see that it operated efficiently. This task became arduous because as the market stabilized and competition increased, dealers found it more and more difficult to make large profits. As Dalton's comments suggest, they grew restive and more deeply concerned about their relations with the manufacturer.

Unlike the Ford executives, the General Motors General Sales Committee moved quickly to meet the new situa-

tion. It asked the Sales Section of the General Office Staff to make studies of the potential for cars in every area of the country. On the basis of this rational study it defined the territories of its different dealers. It also developed schemes to prevent dealers from encroaching on one another's territories and devised policies for trade-ins and used cars. To give the dealers more scope for trading, the committee raised their markup from 17 per cent to 24 per cent. The committee did not insist, as did Ford, that they show a sizable profit on the sale of used cars. Moreover, since General Motors paid much more attention than Ford to coordinating the flow of material through the enterprise from the suppliers to the actual market, the General Sales Committee was more able than Ford to prevent effectively the overstocking of dealers. The General Sales Committee and the Sales Section also worked hard to indoctrinate their retailers in the advantages of modern accounting methods.

Through this rational approach to marketing and by aggressive and thoroughly systematic sales methods, Chevrolet's brilliant sales manager, Richard C. Grant, quickly took a deep slice out of Ford's markets and profits. Only after the Fords had abandoned the Model T did Henry and his son Edsel begin to follow the patterns set by General Motors. In 1928 they finally organized a finance company to make it easier for customers to buy Fords on the installment plan. Until then their one concession to the customers' desire to buy on time had been to set up a type of "Christmas Club" plan. According to this scheme a potential customer put aside a weekly deposit in a local savings bank until he had enough to pay most of the initial cost of his Ford. Only in 1930, after the depression had already begun to crack the market, did Ford raise his dealers' margins from 17½ per cent to 22 per cent, still 2 per cent less than General Motors'. Two years later his company began its initial drive to improve dealer accounting. Even by the end of the 1930's, the Ford Motor Company had not yet developed systematic methods for allocating sales territories or setting quotas. Nevertheless, during this decade the Fords did much more to improve their marketing than they did to develop more efficient management structure and methods.

If the dealers had problems as the market leveled off, such difficulties were nothing compared to the ones they experienced after the 1929 stock-market crash. Annual automobile sales fell from 4.5 million in 1929 to 1.1 million in 1932, rising slowly to 3.3 million in 1935 and 3.7 million in 1936. Manufacturers' practices or even errors of judgment that the dealers might have accepted earlier were no longer tolerable. A dealer could hardly remain solvent if the company flooded him with nonsalable products or permitted other dealers to invade his territory. Again General Motors took the lead in bettering dealer relations. The Distribution Policy Group, which had replaced the General Sales Committee as the determiner of marketing policy for the corporation as a whole, improved the dealer's contract and set up a Dealer Council. It also formed a Dealer Relations Board to hear complaints and to review contract cancellations. Ford and Chrysler followed suit, but not before a Congressional committee and the Federal Trade Commission had begun to investigate the relations between dealers and the large automobile companies.

The readings in this section cover marketing during the period of the leveling-off of demand in the 1920's followed by its sharp decline in the difficult years of the depression. The first set covers the creation of the General Motors product line and includes excerpts from Alfred Sloan's testimony in the Du Pont–General Motors Antitrust case and from the corporation's annual reports for 1923 and 1925; the last selection gives a listing of the completed line in 1926 from *Motor Age* magazine. The second set consists of a short passage from a *Fortune* article on Chevrolet plus nearly all of another *Fortune* article entitled "How to Sell Automobiles." The latter is the most complete short summary available of the development and carrying out of General Motors' marketing policies. The final selection, taken from the Federal Trade Commission's *Report on the Motor Vehicle Industry*, was chosen to emphasize how differently General Motors and its major competitor handled one critically significant selling problem— that of the used car and the trade-in.

In studying these selections, the reader needs to keep in mind that the creators of General Motors' marketing organization and policies were not men with backgrounds in the selling of automobiles. Just as Brown and Pratt brought with them from Du Pont concern for rational and systematic administration, so Richard C. Grant applied the "principles" of modern marketing he had learned at the National Cash Register Company to the more complex marketing tasks of General Motors. An important question is then, what exactly was brought from the outside in the development of General Motors' marketing as well as management policies? How were the importations modified to meet the needs of the automobile industry in general and of General Motors in particular?

Other questions raised by these selections deal with the costs and methods of modern marketing. Its costs were then and still are challenged as being wasteful. Why should so much time, energy, and money be spent in advertising, in changing models, and in carrying out high-pressure sales campaigns? What might be other ways of maintaining or increasing one's share of the market? Is it necessary to maintain or increase one's share of the market? If so, is competition then inherently wasteful? What were the points at issue between the dealer and the manufacturer? Was this an inherent conflict? Why was so little said on these issues before the mid-1920's and so much after that time? How might the dealers' lot have been improved, particularly during the depression years? One solution would have been to have had the companies take over their dealers and carry out their retailing activities with salaried employees. Why was this alternative not tried or even suggested? In other words why did the automobile companies, who did their own wholesaling from the very start, never attempt to do their own retailing? Were there other reasons besides Ford's personality or his personal views that helped prevent the Ford Motor Company from pioneering in the ways of modern management? Conversely, what elements in General Motors' situation in 1921 put a premium on innovation? And, finally, how might Ford have made an effective comeback in the 1930's?

CREATION OF A PRODUCT LINE

1] Sloan Describes the Beginning of a New Marketing Strategy

[Mr. Sloan described the qualities of General Motors' two acceptable lines—those of Cadillac and Buick. He then added:]

THE OTHER cars were very bad. Chevrolet was a mess, Oakland and Olds were about the same category.

In fact, one of the first questions that was raised after Mr. Pierre du Pont became president in November or December 1920, was to change the name of the Chevrolet and the Oakland, and I protested against it on the basis that a change of name did not improve the quality, if we improved the quality we would not have to change the name. And that was accepted, and we carried the name through.

.   .   .   .

FROM Direct testimony in deposition of Alfred P. Sloan, Jr., in the Du Pont-General Motors Anti-trust Case, April 28, 1952, pp. 18–19, 30–31.

Q. To what extent, under Mr. Durant's administration, was there an attempt made to produce different kinds of cars for different needs, if you understand what I mean? A. There was practically no coordination or planning of the products in relation to the then-existing market. The cars were brought into existence sometimes, it seemed to me, in a very haphazard way; there was no proper engineering coordination between the various parts of the car. It was something like a man wanting to get a new change of clothes, and he goes and buys a coat in one place and a pair of trousers in another and a vest in another and all different fits, and you don't get a complete ensemble, especially at less cost, and that is something like we were approaching at that time in the development of our car products.

. . . .

We improved the engineering departments. Under Mr. Durant's regime, for instance, there was only one dynamometer in the General Motors. A dynamometer is an instrument by which you measure the performance characteristics of an engine, and any engineer that wanted to have a new engine tested, or anything, had to send it to Detroit. Now I presume in our engineering departments we have fifty dynamometers in each engineering department. It is a very essential thing.

There was no concept at all in our engineering departments as to the market and what should be done to make a quality product. There was no accredited means of testing our products. A new car would come out, there was no yardstick set-up for determining the various performance characteristics of either our cars or cars [with] which we were in competition. Nothing of the kind [existed] in General Motors at all. Mr. Durant did not think in terms of those kind of things.

. . . .

Q. Were any steps taken with respect to the problem of lining your products with the various categories of customer demand? A. Well, there was a policy adopted that might be expressed as a car for every person and purpose; that is, instead of having a miscellaneous lot of cars that were priced in competition with one another, developed the way I previously stated, it was a comprehensive plan whereby the organization would go into the market with a properly developed car in each price position, something like a commanding general would have to have an army in every point of the front line, so that he could not be attacked. That was the thought behind the thing, and through evolution over the years we reached that point.

. . . .

2] The Annual Reports Indicate the Evolution of This Strategy

a] THE 1923 ANNUAL REPORT

IN 1921 a definite policy was adopted. The Corporation should establish a complete line of motor cars from the lowest to the highest price that would justify quantity production. Its endeavors at all times should be to develop the best value in each price class which large volume, effective manufacturing methods, aggressive engineering and efficient means of distribution, all supported by large resources, make possible.

Limitations already dealt with in previous reports necessarily added to the time when this policy could be made effective. During the year substantial progress has been made. The products of the Corporation have been re-aligned and adjusted and competition which heretofore existed within the car manufacturing Divisions has been largely eliminated. Such a policy makes possible co-ordination, not otherwise practical, in engineering, manufacturing and particularly in distribution.

The absolute necessity of realigning the products, all of which was effected during the second half of the year 1923, manifestly resulted in a considerable loss in profits. The development and bringing into production on a quantity basis of an entire line of new models by each of the Motor Car Divisions, with the exception of Chevrolet, was an important undertaking. A considerable interval of time exists between the introduction of a new article into manufacture before a competitive cost can be obtained. This is particularly true with a complicated and highly technical product such as the modern motor car. Moreover, in changing models, production must largely cease for a considerable interval which in turn means reduced sales. It is the policy of the Corporation to maintain the present alignment of products, refining and improving in detail. With the possible exception, however, and then only in degree, of the lower price models, recognition of new technical developments affecting performance, cost of manufacture and improvement in appearance, must be given proper weight and be recognized from time to time by changes of more or less major character. On the other hand, it is not believed that it will be essential in any one year to make as complete a realignment of products as was required during the year 1923.

FROM *Annual Report of General Motors Corporation for 1923* (March 24, 1924), pp. 6–7; *Annual Report of General Motors Corporation for 1925* (February 24, 1926), p. 7.

b] THE 1925 ANNUAL REPORT

AN OPERATING review of the year would not be complete without specific reference to the following:

The Pontiac Six

THE Corporation has established the fundamental policy of building a car for every purse and purpose and in line with that policy added during the year to its car line, a new six-cylinder car—the Pontiac Six. It is built and marketed by the Oakland organization as a companion car to the Oakland Six and has a distinct field of its own—quite different from the place now so well occupied by the Oakland Six. The Corporation was convinced that there is an enormous potential market for a car of quality at a price between that of the Chevrolet and the Oldsmobile. There are many who require more than the four-cylinder Chevrolet affords yet do not need what the Oldsmobile six-cylinder offers. All the Corporation's accumulated experience was built into this new product and it is believed that such a car at this price will add greatly to the position of the Corporation and its dealer organization and will enable the Corporation to materially increase its volume.

3] The Competing Lines, 1926

a] THE GENERAL MOTORS LINE

SHIP WT.	PASS.	BODY STYLE	PRICE	SHIP WT.	PASS.	BODY STYLE	PRICE
CHEVROLET				2460	5-p	Coach	950
				2660	5-p	De Luxe Coach	1,040
		"Superior" (Series K)		2535	5-p	Sedan	1,025
				2735	5-p	De Luxe Sedan	1,115
1730	3-p	Roadster	$ 525				
1875	5-p	Touring	525	**OAKLAND**			
2030	2-p	Utility Coupe	675				
2130	5-p	Coach	695			"6"	
2215	5-p	Sedan	775	2425	2-p	Roadster	$ 975
				–	4-p	Roadster	–
PONTIAC				2500	5-p	Touring	1,025
				2640	5-p	Coach	1,095
		(110 in. W. B.)		2615	3-p	Landau Coupe	1,125
–	2-p	Coupe	$ 825	2765	5-p	Sedan	1,195
–	5-p	Coach	825	2885	5-p	Landau Sedan	1,295
				BUICK			
OLDSMOBILE						"Standard"	
		"30"		2845	2-p	Roadster	$1,125
2235	5-p	Touring	$ 875	2955	5-p	Touring	1,150
2445	5-p	Sp. Touring	930	3020	2-p	Coupe	1,195

COMPILED FROM *Motor Age* (January 7, 1926), pp. 90–91.

SHIP WT.	PASS.	BODY STYLE	PRICE
		BUICK [*Cont.*]	
3150	5-p	2 d. Sedan	1,195
3110	4-p	Coupe	1,275
3230	5-p	4 d. Sedan	1,295

"Master"
(120 in. W. B.)

SHIP WT.	PASS.	BODY STYLE	PRICE
3350	2-p	Roadster	$1,250
3515	5-p	Touring	1,295
3765	5-p	2 d. Sedan	1,395
3670	5-p	Sedan	1,495

(128 in. W. B.)

SHIP WT.	PASS.	BODY STYLE	PRICE
3570	3-p	Sp. Roadster	$1,495
3635	5-p	Sp. Touring	1,525
3855	3-p	Country Club	1,765
3805	4-p	Coupe	1,795
3940	5-p	Brough. Sedan	1,925
4025	7-p	Sedan	1,995

CADILLAC

"314" Standard Line
(132 in. W. B.)

SHIP WT.	PASS.	BODY STYLE	PRICE
4075	5-p	Brougham	$2,995
4040	2-p	Coupe	3,045

SHIP WT.	PASS.	BODY STYLE	PRICE
4155	5-p	Sedan	3,195
4240	7-p	Sedan	3,295
4115	4-p	Victoria	3,095
4360	7-p	Imperial	3,435

Custom Built
(132 in.)

SHIP WT.	PASS.	BODY STYLE	PRICE
3920	–	Roadster	$3,250

(138 in. W. B.)

SHIP WT.	PASS.	BODY STYLE	PRICE
4300	7-p	Touring	$3,250
3960	–	Phaeton	3,250
4190	5-p	Coupe	4,000
4190	5-p	Sedan	4,150
4250	7-p	Suburban	4,285
4355	7-p	Imperial	4,485

[Since the Oakland models overlapped those of other divisions in price, that division soon concentrated wholly on the new Pontiac, phasing out its other models. In addition, the Cadillac Division began building the LaSalle to fill the price gap between its lowest-priced car and the highest offered by Buick.]

b] THE FORD LINE

SHIP WT.	PASS.	BODY STYLE	PRICE
		FORD	

WITHOUT STARTER AND DEM. RIMS

SHIP WT.	PASS.	BODY STYLE	PRICE
1526	2-p	Runabout	$ 260
1557		*With Balloon Tires*	305
1607	5-p	Touring	290
1640		*With Balloon Tires*	335

WITH STARTER AND DEM. RIMS

SHIP WT.	PASS.	BODY STYLE	PRICE
1645	2-p	Runabout	$ 345
1655		*With Balloon Tires*	370
1728	5-p	Touring	375
1738		*With Balloon Tires*	400
1851	2-p	Coupe	520
1860		*With Balloon Tires*	545

SHIP WT.	PASS.	BODY STYLE	PRICE
1961	5-p	Sedan, Tudor	580
1972		*With Balloon Tires*	605
1994	5-p	Sedan, Fordor	660
2004		*With Balloon Tires*	685

LINCOLN

SHIP WT.	PASS.	BODY STYLE	PRICE
4460	2-p	Roadster	$4,000
4580	7-p	Touring	4,000
4565	4-p	Phaeton	4,000
4740	5-p	Sport Touring	4,900
4750	4-p	Coupe	4,600
4885	4-p	Sedan	4,800
4760	5-p	Sedan	4,900
4890	7-p	Sedan	5,100
4945	7-p	Limousine	5,300

SELLING THE PRODUCT

4] A Leading Business Journal Analyzes General Motors' Marketing Innovations

a] CHEVROLET

THE ECONOMIC philosophers are still arguing over the question of whether Ford made a boner or General Motors pulled a fast one. Model T was a wonderful car, but it certainly did not flatter your pride of ownership. And neither its wheel base (100 inches) nor its horsepower (22½) nor its outward appearance changed appreciably from one year to the next. Actually the Chevrolet, with its spare, stretched cowl and the blue cross on its radiator, didn't change radically in the middle twenties either. To be sure, its horsepower crept up, and its clutch changed from a cone to a single-dry-plate type. But most of all it was the three inch longer wheel base, the standard transmission, and the annual new styling that made the Chevrolet, priced near Model T, seem like more money. For General Motors had become aware of the Used Car, and of the fact that the automobile market was becoming a replacement market. It therefore took the lead in the habit-forming campaign that has made the annual model a practical necessity. But to breed dissatisfaction with all old models was *ipso facto* to breed dissatisfaction with all Model T's. Hence Mr. Knudsen's [1] sales kept climbing and reached 732,-000 in 1926, while Mr. Ford's production, which reached a peak of 2,091,000 in 1923, fell thereafter for three successive years. Model T, despite a brief effort to restyle it, was doomed. And when Ford shut down for six months in 1927 to tool up for Model A, Chevrolet swarmed into the breach and passed both Ford and the million mark for the first time.

Since then, of course, the race has been more intense than ever. By the time Ford had regained his stride with the four cylinder Model A, Mr. Knudsen, in what was then the fastest change-over on record, had turned the Chevrolet from a four to a six. To which Ford's answer was the V-8 of 1932, which soon superseded the A entirely. Plymouth's entry meanwhile had raised the low-priced-field ante with hydraulic brakes, forcing Chevrolet (and

---

1 [William S. Knudsen became production manager and then general manager of Chevrolet after he resigned from a top production job at Ford in 1921. In 1937 he accepted the presidency of General Motors when Sloan became chairman of the board.]

FROM "Chevrolet," *Fortune* (January 1939), pp. 39–40, 46, 103–04.

this year Ford) to follow suit, Plymouth itself being forced by the competition to change from four to six cylinders in 1933.

·   ·   ·   ·   ·   ·   ·   ·   ·   ·   ·   ·   ·

Styling

A CHEVROLET is made up of thirty-odd thousand separate parts, and was never conceived as a whole in any one man's mind. But a logical starting point is with the corporation's administration committee, chairmaned by Mr. Sloan, which lays down the rule that the Chevrolet must be low priced and must sell big. This dictum, together with the pace already set in that field, gives Jim Crawford and his engineering staff their first points of reference, and they go to work. But no sooner have they fixed upon the basic chassis measurements and body size than the corporation reënters the picture, with its styling section.

This is an autonomous fount of designing ideas that G.M. set up twelve years ago to create the lines of all its cars. Housed (along with the Fisher Body engineers) in a special building across the street from Chevrolet, it consists of about a hundred mechanics, a hundred designers, and an immensely tall man of natty dress named Harley Earl. Mr. Earl is a former car-body designer of Hollywood who came east to head the styling section when it was founded. He is a designer *pur sang,* employs no engineers, and avoids engineering influence so far as he can, fearing his designs might suffer if he knew too much about the workings of the car beneath. This approach is, of course, anathema to those industrial designers who believe that all form should be dictated by function. But such criticism would sound as out of place in Mr. Earl's *moderne* workrooms as would a reproach to Darryl Zanuck for not eschewing happy endings. Mr. Earl quarrels proudly with the divisional engineers. They argue (or veto) him out of his extremisms, but there is a residue of pure, unfunctional style in the grille, hood, fenders, ornamentation, and lines of every G.M. car that is Mr. Earl's own contribution and is unquestionably a primary factor in how well it sells.

Some time in early summer you might find Mr. Coyle,[2] Mr. Crawford, and Ed Fisher [3] in Mr. Earl's draped office discussing the car that will be presented to the public one year from the ensuing fall. First, will it be a really new model or a modification of the preceding model? For thorough body changes, owing to the high cost of dies, are made only every other year, such as 1937 and 1939. Will Chevrolet give up the optional big trunk and conceal the spare on all body styles? If Mr. Coyle will sacrifice the accessory revenue, Mr. Earl can draw a cleaner rear end. What about the headlights? Other cars are sinking them in the fenders, but G.M.'s Customer Research . . . says that buyers really like them the old way. And so on, through a hundred and thirty or forty details. Mr. Earl is left alone to explain the problem to his artists, who then go off and think.

The thinking is done in a locked workroom sacred to Chevrolet. There

2 [M. E. Coyle, general manager of the Chevrolet Division.]
3 [E. F. Fisher, head of the Fisher Body Division.]

are four other similar workrooms sacred to the other divisions, and little osmosis of designing ideas between them. It happens that the artists who inhabit the Chevrolet cell, though not engineers, know more about engineering than any of Mr. Earl's other employees. The special problems of Chevrolet force practicality upon them. No plant in the country could die-cast enough grilles for Chevrolet; they must be designed for stamping. Because of the huge warehouse stocks of parts, front fenders must be designed with their stacking characteristics in mind. And nothing must be costly: Chevrolet once turned them down on an arty bumper because it cost three cents per car extra to make. For all Styling's precautions, there is usually a battle with Mr. Crawford somewhere along the line. In the 1938 model Styling took so long to suit him that he finally had the front end designed in his own department. But normally Mr. Earl's men proceed through a series of compromises from a blackboard sketch to a quarter-sized clay model to a full-sized clay model, to a complete wood car. And if Mr. Coyle likes the wood model, the final show is arranged. In Mr. Earl's auditorium, under a single 50,000-watt bulb, the model is hushedly uncurtained before Messrs. Sloan, Knudsen, and the other Brass Hats. Mr. Knudsen has usually seen it before, and nine times in ten there is nothing but praise. It is now January. The approved wood model, shrouded in canvas, is trundled over to Chevrolet, and it is now up to Fisher and Mr. Crawford.

Engineering

MR. CRAWFORD'S staff of 500 engineers, draftsmen, and clerks has been working steadily right along. Some of his men work on experimental cars; they have had rear-engine Chevrolets, $300 Chevrolets, and eight-cylinder Chevrolets on and off their boards for years. Others make production drawings of actual Chevrolets. But none of them has ever designed a whole Chevrolet. Mr. Crawford, though an able engineer (he was responsible for the old Auburn), does not do that either. He is rather an executive coördinator of specialists. His staff, both design and production, is a congeries of expert groups: carburetor experts, clutch experts, transmission, brake, engine, gear, spring, and other experts.

Twice in the last eleven years, however, this staff has quickened its even pace into a memorable group charette. The first time, when Chevrolet became a six with the 1929 model, was by far the easier of the two, although the actual change-over, accomplished in a record two months, was the occasion of a complimentary dinner tendered by the corporation to Mr. Knudsen. The second time was in preparing the 1937 model, when the Chevrolet got not only a whole new engine but a new body, frame, transmission, and rear axle as well. A greater change over the previous year than any model in Chevrolet's history, it was starting production scarcely one month after the last 1936's had been assembled.

After the 1929 change, and especially during the period of interchangeability with Pontiac, the Chevrolet had begun taking on a lot of weight from year to year without a comparable increase in performance. Ford had gone to an eight, Plymouth to a six, and the need for a wholly new Chevro-

let was apparent a long way off. Mr. Crawford accordingly was given the
objective of reducing the weight 200 pounds and increasing performance by
15 per cent without sacrifice of body space. How did he do it?

Certain things (apart from cost) were given. Chevrolet has had a valve-in-
head engine since 1911. It got it originally because a group of ex-Buick
engineers formed the Mason Motor Co. at Flint and sold their first valve-in-
head engines to Mr. Durant. It has never been changed to an L-head because
a valve-in-head usually gives more power per cubic inch of piston displacement and because Chevrolet, like Buick, has a lot of advertising money invested in it.

Not given, but determined by circumstance, was the frame. Knee action,
introduced on the Chevrolet in 1934, had forced it to brace its frame with a
K-Y cross-member, which proved both heavy and expensive. Accordingly Mr.
Crawford began work the same year on a box-section frame, which was put
on the standard (no knee action) model in 1936, using no X-member at all.
But Fisher came along in 1935 with the turret top, which gave the car
enough rigidity so that Mr. Crawford was able to extend the box frame to
all models in 1937.

The main points of attack in the 1937 change were thus the rear axle,
transmission, and engine. The hypoid rear axle, which permits a lower floor,
had already been around some time in the Packard and other cars, and Mr.
Crawford began designing his early in 1935. Work on a more compact transmission was also begun well ahead of time; Chevrolet had introduced syn-
chromesh in 1932 and the improved version was performing well on the
dynamometer by November, 1934. As for the engine, the valve-in-head arrangement does not determine its length; so the crankshaft, which had been
resting on only three main bearings and was abnormally big, became the center of attention. Between April, 1934, and October, 1935, three different
series of engines and crankshafts were designed, built, and tested at the G.M.
proving grounds. One of the third series, a 216-cubic-inch job on a lighter
crankshaft, was finally approved. But at this point the manufacturing department, which had been in close touch all along, looked a little more closely at
the new crankshaft and said that if a few changes were made, they would be
able to line-bore the bearings more efficiently. So a new series was built, incorporating these changes, and tested all over again. It didn't work. Instead
of reverting to the previous design, however, Mr. Crawford then instituted a
series of further changes that meant a heavier crankshaft, a different crank-
case, and even a longer wheel base. By the time this new design had been
made to work it was April, 1936, just seven months before the first complete
car was due.

How narrow a margin this was can be understood only by appreciating the
manufacturing problems involved, which will be discussed shortly. In brief,
it could not have been done at all were not Mr. Crawford's department
closely coördinated with manufacturing at every step. Much of the experimental work, in fact, was done in the laboratories of the manufacturing
plants, with the day's production humming through the wall. Chevrolet's experimental models are not put together in a tool shop. Their parts are forged,
cast, and machined on the regular production lines in slack periods. By the

time Mr. Crawford's final engine was approved for production, therefore, the manufacturing department already knew how to make it. This is not the cheap way to make experiments. But when you are monkeying with a million cars, it is ultimately cheaper not to take chances.

Low-cost manufacturing requirements are indeed the chief limitation on Mr. Crawford's freedom of design. That is the reason why he has the reputation of being a hardboiled engineer. ("We don't want a sissy," says Marvin Coyle.) He has no trouble resisting the temptation to counter Ford's eight cylinders and Plymouth's aluminum-alloy pistons with something flashy of his own. Yet the Chevrolet is not merely a manufacturer's car. Its frame, clutch, and lubrication system are all unique. It was first in the low-priced field with six cylinders and with an all-steel top. And when you look at its performance records you begin to realize how superbly designed it really is.

·   ·   ·   ·   ·   ·   ·   ·   ·   ·   ·   ·

b] How to Sell Automobiles

It is no secret that the distributing process is the most inefficient part of the whole American economy. In some lines, such as whiskey and milk, distribution cost is from four to ten times the cost of production. With automobiles, it is nearly half the manufacturing cost. In other words, nearly one-third of the price you pay for a new automobile goes to cover the cost of getting it from the factory to you. And that doesn't mean freight. It means such things as the dealer's overhead, his salesman's commission, and the whole routine of teletypes, market statistics, movies, speeches, contests, brochures, brief cases, and advertisements that constitutes distribution. In keeping its distribution costs to less than a third of the total price, the automotive industry has done not much better and not much worse than others. But since the purchase of automobiles, parts, and accessories takes about 10 per cent of the national income—at retail, something over $6,000,-000,000 in a year like 1937—the distributing third of that business is, to put it mildly, huge.

General Motors' 40 per cent share of this distributive process is likewise huge. Huge, complicated, cushy, cockeyed, and controversial. . . .

Of the 150,000-odd men in the marketing and servicing of G.M. cars, some 17,000 are dealers and about 125,000 are dealers' employees. They are thus not technically G.M. men at all, unless in spirit. But they take a big cut of the cost of your car, and they constitute the nub of the distributive problem. In his own home town, the automobile dealer is typically a man of substance. But on a national scale, he is first and last a Little Businessman. As such he stands in marked contrast with the Big Businessmen—Messrs. Ford, Chrysler, and Sloan—who depend on him to buy, strictly for cash, their entire annual domestic output. He has a double importance to Detroit. Not only is he the factory's customer for its cars, trucks, salesmen's manuals,

from "How to Sell Automobiles," *Fortune* (February 1939), pp. 71–78, 105–09.

and a good many parts and accessories. He is also the factory's only direct link with the ultimate consumer, the mass market that Detroit has taken such special pains to please, and that has so richly rewarded Detroit for that effort. The automobile dealer, however, has not been so richly rewarded. In fact the importance to Detroit of his welfare has only recently been recognized, and his struggle for recognition is not wholly over yet. G.M. has recognized him, as we shall see; it was due largely to the timely intercession of Mr. Sloan that his struggle for recognition has not entirely degenerated into a class war between Big and Little Business. That war, however, is perhaps still latent in the factory-dealer relationship. And if social controls are ever to limit competition in the automobile industry, they will probably start with the Little Businessman.

Charade

OF THAT more presently. A quick tour of G.M.'s selling activities does not suggest a battlefield so much as it suggests Hollywood, especially around announcement time. Ordinarily the G.M. dealer may go regularly to church, and the G.M. salesman be home at five-thirty; but when the new models are coming out, all parties to the selling process seem to concentrate a whole year's selling effort into one extravagant nationwide charade. . . . The New York show, run by the Automobile Manufacturers' Association instead of by the dealers, yields to the Chicago show in blatancy but not in expense or importance. G.M. alone sends several hundred executives and lieutenants, from Mr. Knudsen down to the hairless cubs of the Campbell-Ewald copy staff, to New York in a body for three or four days at showtime. G.M.'s "private preview" of the new cars inundates the Waldorf-Astoria with so many invited guests that it takes Messrs. Sloan, Knudsen, Kettering, and Grant most of the afternoon just to shake hands with them; takes Eddie Duchin and twelve men just to be heard above them; takes the entire ballroom floor and a mezzanine just to hold the exhibits for them; takes five bars just to refresh them. Mary Pickford, Gloria Swanson, and every accessible debutante are photographed with the new Buick or Cadillac. Supernumeraries swarm and batten, space salesmen give parties, well-dressed engineering executives entertain the technical press at lunch. Anyone who has attended the New York show does not need to be reminded of the atmosphere, as colorful as a streamlined Ducoed fender and as metallic, with which G.M. and its rivals inflate the already enormous fact that new cars are news to America.

The *brouhaha* is not confined to the metropolitan shows. At that season, every automobile factory is a stage. For example, in Flint, where General Manager Harlow Curtice entertains some 5,000 Buick fieldmen, dealers, and salesmen, the loud-speaker is blaring *Flat Foot Floogee* into the vast auditorium by 9:45 A.M., while Mr. Curtice conscientiously shakes hands with every arriving guest. At ten-fifteen, after a verbal build-up, a life-sized model airplane on the stage with "$200,000" (the Buick quota) lettered on each wing sets up a deafening roar and from a runway in its belly appears a bright new yellow car that brings the entire auditorium to its feet. The Spanish girl with Jimmie Henschel's orchestra sings discreetly broad songs throughout the tented barbecue lunch, and the dry seriousness of the marketing and merchandising presentations in the afternoon are relieved by an animated cartoon and by witty anecdotes from Adman Arthur Kudner as he shows them the forthcoming campaign. Even dealers who missed the banquet of funny hats, boneless giant squab, and "Ice Cream de Esprit Buick 1939" the night before, go back to Seattle and Atlanta feeling pretty hopped up.

Meanwhile in Detroit and other cities, Chevrolet is entertaining 1,800 members of the trade and general press with a banquet, a ninety-minute vaudeville show, and favors that are seldom less valuable than a watch or a traveling bag, and a raffle ticket on a Chevrolet car. From these factory headwaters, the selling cascade tumbles down into every city and zone office in the land, so that half the big hotels in the U.S. during late September and October are full of music, speeches, bunting, new cars, and several hundred dealers and salesmen each. G.M. has been the employer of over fifty orchestras at once, in as many cities. . . .

NOW all this lavishness, it must be noted, is not the main reason why your car costs you half again as much as it costs to make it. The direct cost to G.M. of advertising, selling, and generally touting a Chevrolet is probably less than $25 a car, . . . (It is more, of course, with the smaller-volume cars.) This cost is probably not excessive for the results it achieves. The leverage of a selling dollar in producing volume is of course tremendous. Chevrolet's sales manager, Bill Holler, in the course of one of his high-tension speaking tours near announcement time, once took time off to address a gathering of service mechanics in the same bebannered town where a zoneful of dealers were being entertained. Sensing the thrifty skepticism of these practical men, Holler in effect spoke as follows:

"No doubt you wonder at the banquet down the street, and the band, and all those banners. Of course it costs money, plenty. It costs money for me and my men to cover the country in Pullmans, and to some people it might seem a lark to spend three weeks away from home, as I have. But we don't spend the money that way just to get rid of it. If anybody could show me a cheaper way than this banquet to infect four hundred dealers at once with the conviction that this year's Chevrolet can be made to hang up a record, I would welcome it." Whether or not the ham-backed mechanics felt ashamed of their doubts, they had nevertheless been given a straight story. For high-pressure selling is as crucial a job as it is exhausting. As for the social good-or-bad, that depends largely on what you think of the annual-model habit. But as a business proposition the sales end of the automobile business has since the depression become more critical than engineering itself.

The reason for that is the afore-mentioned Little Businessman, who buys Detroit's cars. Not counting taxes, freight, and similar extras, on which he takes no markup, about 25 per cent of the price you pay for a G.M. car is the dealer's discount, and is supposed to cover his expenses. This seemingly generous margin he all too often proceeds to give away in the form of an overallowance on your trade-in. He doesn't do this because he is stupid; it is more complicated than that. It is so complicated that to understand the problems of the Little Businessman, and the logic of G.M.'s selling policies, it will be best to go back to the beginning.

RICHARD RALPH HALLAM GRANT has been a G.M. Vice President since 1929. He is one of the four or five most influential G.M. executives, being a member of six policy groups and chairman of the Distribution Group. Mr. Grant, who is also known as Dynamic Dick and the Little Giant, is one of the greatest salesmen this nation of salesmen has produced. Short but graceful, with small hands and feet and a resonant, even-paced voice, he has been known to reduce dealers' conventions to tears of enthusiasm, and he is certainly the nearest thing to a professional orator in the G.M. high command. He was born in Ipswich, Massachusetts, graduated from Harvard in 1901, and still speaks with a marked down-East twang, although he has lived in the Middle West for more than thirty years. As a youth he worked in a bookstore and for the telephone company. But it was in Dayton, Ohio, that he learned to sell.

John Henry Patterson, tyrant of Dayton and its National Cash Register Co. . . . , was a type of businessman not much in evidence today, perhaps fortunately so. His way of quashing labor trouble was to shut down Dayton's biggest industry for two months and go traveling, reopening only when the city government itself cried "uncle." But he was a pioneer of American sales methods—the direct-mail circular, the yearly quota, the annual convention, and the salesmen's contest. Dick Grant, by 1913, had replaced so many department-store pneumatics with Mr. Patterson's cash registers that he became his general sales manager. And from Patterson he absorbed certain fundamental principles of how to sell goods. The adaptation of these principles, says Dick Grant, has been responsible for all the successful selling he has done since. They are: 1. Have the right product. 2. Know the potential of each market area. 3. Constantly educate your salesmen on the product, making them listen to canned demonstrations and learn sales talks by heart. 4. Constantly stimulate your sales force, and foster competition among them with contests and comparisons. (Mr. Grant later developed this to include booby prizes, although Patterson had never given booby prizes "because," says Mr. Grant, "he believed that humor had no place in business.") 5. Cherish simplicity in all presentations. 6. Use all kinds of advertising (Patterson had 104). 7. Constantly check up on your salesmen, but be reasonable with them and make no promises you can't keep.

In Dayton, Dick Grant got to know C. F. Kettering and Colonel E. A. Deeds, co-founders of Dayton Engineering Laboratories, who in 1915 invited him to become General Manager of their Delco Light. Within five years he had pushed Delco Light to a $15,000,000 business in the nearly virgin field of farm light and power, the Delco unit really breaking the ground for the subsequent rustication of utility high lines. Mr. Grant opened this market with the help of some forty distributors, thirty-five of whom had worked under him at the Cash. The farm market was quite different from the saloon, grocery, and department-store market, but the same sales principles worked. And when General Motors, which had meanwhile acquired

Delco Light, moved the unlikely infant Frigidaire from Detroit to Dayton in 1921, Mr. Grant tucked it in a corner of the Delco organization and applied his high-powered techniques to that too. In 1924, 20,000 Frigidaires were sold, and a new industry was born. But that same year Dick Grant moved on to Chevrolet.

THE automobile business, in the early twenties, was different. It was hardly conscious of any sales problem at all. Ford and Dodge, and to some extent Buick and Packard, had developed big, well-capitalized dealer organizations. Dodge's, the envy of the industry, was the chief reason Walter Chrysler paid $170,000,000 for Dodge in 1928; and Ford's, tyrannized but strong, had made automotive history by helping to tide Mr. Ford over his famous cash shortage of 1921. But with most factories the problem had hitherto been to make cars, not to sell them. There had developed a system of large distributors, who created dealerships as they pleased and made no trouble for the factory except to beg for bigger and faster deliveries. These big distributors, many of them, were the last vessels of the sporting blood that ran so freely through the industry in its youth. Inglis M. Uppercu (Cadillac, New York) used to race cars at the fairgrounds in Waverly, New Jersey; C. S. Howard (Buick, California) is the owner of Seabiscuit; Earl C. Anthony (Packard, California) was co-author with Johnny Noble of the song *Coral Isle*. With huge territories and a chronic seller's market, the distributors and indeed many of their dealers got rich without ever having to learn the fine points of competitive salesmanship at all.

When Dick Grant went to Chevrolet in 1924 the days of the big distributor were already numbered. Dodge and Packard had taken an interest in retail problems as early as 1920. In 1921 Mr. Sloan made a historic deal with R. L. Polk & Co. whereby, for about $50,000 a year, Polk gathered monthly registration figures by makes in thirty-one states, thus giving sales and production managers everywhere their first authentic measurement of the market on a national scale. And Chevrolet itself inaugurated a standard accounting system for all dealers in 1923. But Dick Grant carried all such "dealer operations" to a new pitch of intensity and invented many more. The Polk figures became the basis of the most minute checks on performance of every dealer in every county. The accounting system became compulsory and elaborate; it enabled the sales managers to set up bogeys in every department of the dealer's business—used-car, new-car, parts, service, etc.— and gave direction to their constant stream of canned demonstrations, convention shows, lantern-slide lessons, salesmen's and dealers' manuals, and other educational stimuli. There were other dimensions of the Chevrolet program. In 1925 the discount was increased from 21 to 24 per cent. This assisted Mr. Grant in getting new dealers, since Ford was then giving only 17 per cent; and from 6,700 dealers in 1925, the Chevrolet organization in 1929 had grown to 10,600 dealers in eight regions and fifty zones. Despite the rapid expansion, so well drilled was Mr. Grant's organization that Chevrolet also led the way in another technical revolution of the twenties: instead of Mr. Grant's adapting his sales programs to the number of cars Mr. Knudsen could make for him, Mr. Knudsen began to set his production schedules on the basis of advance sales estimates—one month firm and two months tentative, as is practiced throughout G.M. today. . . . With a good deal of help from Ford's obstinate devotion to Model T, Chevrolet sales jumped from 315,000 to over 1,000,000 in four years.

In 1929 Mr. Grant "moved upstairs," where the corporation executives dwell. As a G.M. Vice President, he had both a narrower executive authority and a wider range of influence than he had at Chevrolet. . . . Mr. Grant was able to instill most of Chevrolet's major selling methods in the other car divisions. Grant-trained Chevrolet salesmen turned up in charge of sales at Pontiac (C. P. Simpson, whose boss Harry Klingler is also a former Chevrolet man), at Oldsmobile (D. E. Ralston), even at Cadillac (the late J. C. Chick), and Buick's Bill Hufstader, an ex-Chrysler man, learned the lingo by working under Mr. Grant during BOP.[1] Thus most of the sales *techniques* practiced by all G.M. car divisions today can trace their lineage directly to Mr. Grant.

DISTRIBUTION *policies,* however, are another matter. And here we come squarely upon the problem of the Little Businessman. During the period when Detroit was teaching its dealers how to sell cars, two highly significant events took place. The first was the virtual saturation of the market for new cars at the lowest price (about $500) for which Detroit seems to be able to make them. This saturation was no secret; in 1927 Mr. Sloan pointed out publicly that "The industry . . . is practically stabilized. What has taken place is a shift of business from one manufacturer to another." And with this saturation came the problem of the used car, which began to back up on the new-car market like a clogged sewer. With a stabilized market the competition among the factories, already enlivened by the widespread adoption of Mr. Grant's sharp new selling weapons, became fiercer than ever. The brunt of this competition, however, was borne by the dealers, who were not only Detroit's customers but its front-line mercenaries, fighting Detroit's price battles with the public. Price cutting, in the form of overallowances on trade-ins, became so rampant that automobile dealers as a whole, in spite of somewhat more business, probably made less net profit in 1929 than in 1928.

Little Businessmen are inclined to trust Big Businessmen, and most dealers, perhaps, liked to think of themselves as the factories' partners. But to many of them it was growing clear that the risks and profits, under the new conditions, were no longer being equitably divided. The very terms of the franchise, hitherto academic, were called in question, and proved to give the dealer few rights except that of buying cars at a discount. Buick, Cadillac, and others had closed territories; but every franchise was cancelable with little or no notice and without cause. A "go-to-hell" contract, Mr. Sloan calls it today. This cancellation right gave the factory—and especially that familiar scapegoat, the "overzealous subordinate"—a lethal club for threatening the slow or cautious dealer. For even such a franchise, if not a bankable asset, was at least a necessity to the Little Businessman, and the threat of

1 [For a short time during the depth of the depression in 1932–33, the Buick, Oldsmobile, and Pontiac Divisions were temporarily combined as BOP.]

its summary removal could all too often make him overallow, and give away most of his profit, for the sake of appeasing some zone manager's thirst for new-car volume. It is small wonder that sales enthusiasm frequently turned into coercion. The line between them is shadowy at best. "If what you mean is salesmanship with a little pertinacity to it," said Dick Grant to a House committee a year ago, "some persons may call it coercion."

Of course the factories wanted the dealers to make money, provided they went on selling cars. But when the seller's market turned to a buyer's market, these objectives were no longer synonymous. When the depression deepened, the inconsistency was thrown into a garish light. Dealer capital was decimated. In 1932 G.M. dealers as a whole lost over $27,000,000. If fairness has a place in business, most factories were being unfair to their dealers and all of them were being tough. Wherefore in 1933 the whole problem was tackled, and tackled hard, by Mr. Sloan himself.

The Committee Meets

APART from the immediate emergency, Mr. Sloan already had a reason for getting interested in distribution. Having acknowledged to himself in the late twenties that engineering differences between one car and another were becoming less and less striking, he concluded that the only way for G.M. to go on outselling its competitors was by having better dealers. In 1931 some *Saturday Evening Post* space salesmen handed G.M. what Mr. Grant called "a real jolt." It was a survey that concluded that three-quarters of all car buyers *predetermine* what make they will buy before ever seeing a dealer. Later surveys by *Collier's* and others reached the same conclusion. These surveys were designed, of course, to confirm G.M. officials in their belief in the importance of advertising, and were successful to the extent that G.M. continues to be the biggest advertiser in the world, its budget (around $20,000,000 in a good year) even topping those of the tobacco companies. But Henry G. (Buck) Weaver, G.M.'s customer-research expert, had meanwhile been refining this statistic. His figures showed that while a third of the predetermination was due to advertising, the greater part was the direct result of the owner's past experience and that of his friends. This conclusion put a wholly new emphasis on the importance of adequate service, which in turn can be supplied only by a reliable, well-capitalized set of dealers. Furthermore, 25 per cent of sales could still be directly credited to the dealer's efforts, and in the words of Mr. Grant "it is out of this 25 per cent that we make our profit."

For all these reasons, Mr. Sloan's first move after BOP was to organize a Distribution Group, made up of G.M.'s brassiest hats—Messrs. Sloan, Knudsen, Grant, Brown, Bradley, L. P. Fisher,[2] and A. L. Deane.[3] It has met all day every other week since 1934. Although the divisional sales organizations have been kept relatively independent, there have come down to them since 1934 a series of resolutions and suggestions in which this group has formulated a new distribution policy for G.M.

2 [Lawrence P. Fisher was general manager of the Cadillac Division.]

3 [Albert L. Deane became president of the General Motors Holding Corporation in 1929.]

One of the group's first moves was to set up a Dealer Council. Mr. Sloan, Mr. Knudsen, Mr. Grant, and other G.M. executives have always spent a lot of time on field trips, talking to dealers and listening to their ideas. "We don't give any orders and we don't take any orders," in the words of Mr. Knudsen; "We just visit." The Dealer Council in effect formalizes, though it has not replaced, these visits. Three times a year, forty-eight big and little dealers from all parts of the country and from all sizes of towns come to New York, Chicago, or Detroit in groups of twelve to chew the rag with the Distribution Group. The dealer membership of the council rotates yearly. According to G.M. and also to dealers who have attended, the atmosphere of the meetings is candid, the corporation freely discusses its policies, and suggestions are cordially received. From the corporation's standpoint, these meetings eliminate a very real hazard in so huge an organization as G.M.— the hazard of misinterpretation of both G.M. policies and dealer beefs by the army of "overzealous subordinates," whose power to make trouble has been further limited by the creation of a Dealer Relations Board. To this board (it consists of Messrs. Sloan, Knudsen, Brown, and J. T. Smith [4]) any dealer may appeal any decision of the divisional sales managers, who have therefore become more scrupulous than before on such matters as cancellation.

In formulating actual dealer policies for the divisions to carry out, the Distribution Group first of all had to decide how many dealers there should be. "Experience has taught us," said Mr. Grant in 1936, "that packing dealers into a city in an effort to buoy up a falling price-class position is poor strategy and results in weakening dealers who heretofore have been strong." On the other hand, G.M. did not want its dealers to play golf all the time, and steering between too many and too few required a nice nautical judgment. What the Distribution Group did was to remove the question from the field of hunch and conjecture. Mr. Sloan's effort in all management questions is to apply "the scientific approach"; what that means is clearly illustrated in this case. To determine the number of dealers who will both sell all the G.M. cars the market will absorb and at the same time earn a good return on their capital over the business cycle, the corporation Sales Section (Mr. Grant's staff) has perfected an elaborate analytical technique. It begins with a determination of the market *potential* for each county and even each populous neighborhood in the U.S. It even decides where each dealership ought to be placed from the standpoint of traffic flow, and how much rent each ought to pay. For example, the national *planning potential* of Chevrolet, which is 40 per cent of its price class and is the basic criterion of the number of franchises Chevrolet will grant, is 800,000 cars and trucks a year and has been so since 1936. That is not the same thing as Chevrolet's sales *expectancy,* which may be more or less than the potential, depending on how good business looks; nor is expectancy the same thing as Chevrolet's *quota,* which is the expectancy plus a dash of optimism. Actual sales are still a fourth figure, and have twice exceeded the 800,000 potential without its being subsequently raised. The potential, broken down for each community, is by no means proportional to the population of each, and these local poten-

4 [J. T. Smith headed General Motors' legal staff.]

tials must be constantly raised and lowered with local conditions, as when a highway is diverted or an oil well dries up. But nationally an average sale of 800,000 Chevrolets is supposed to enable the present 9,000 dealers to make about 15 per cent on their capital over the business cycle. At any rate, neither Chevrolet nor any other G.M. division can now add or replace dealers in any metropolitan area unless Mr. Grant's statisticians, after applying their slide rules to a dozen considerations, say the potential will permit.

ALL this figuring, however, provided no answer to another dealer problem. The "fringe dealer," placed in the outskirts of a trading area with a small potential and a small overhead, was selling way over his quotas. He could invade the nearby downtown market and steal prospects from a big-overhead dealer by deliberate overallowance. In order to protect these dealers, many of whom had model service facilities and good reputations, G.M. had to discourage "cross selling"—in other words, to give the dealers territorial protection. Buick, Pontiac, and Oldsmobile installed new systems of protection soon after BOP. Chevrolet, after several years of experimenting, is beginning to install a system of its own. Protection takes the form of an infringement charge ($25 and up) paid by G.M. to one dealer and levied against the other. Each small-town dealer is protected within his home-town corporate limits, and all big-city dealers are protected against fringe dealers; but the dealers in multiple-dealer cities are not protected against each other, and the open country where there are no dealers is free for all.

Other G.M. reforms are reflected in the contract itself. Cancellation now usually requires a three-month notice, and the division shares the liquidation burden. At the end of each model year the factory will give the dealer a rebate on each car left on his hands in excess of 3 per cent of his current annual purchases; and there is an adjustment for price reductions during the year. Thus if the factory misjudges the market and the dealers take more cars than they can sell, the factory has to take part of the rap. With complete sales reports and inventory statements coming in from all dealers every ten days, and a hive of analysts constantly doping market conditions, the factories seldom make such mistakes any more, and the 3 per cent clause is seldom invoked.

The statistical information that G.M. extracts from its dealers is in fact a business in itself. In 1927 appeared a subsidiary called Motor Accounting Co., which set up a uniform accounting system for all G.M. dealers and made periodical audits for $15 a day. Even with this charge, G.M. was out of pocket some $6,000,000 for Motor Accounting between 1927 and 1933, when the dealers complained of the expense and it was dropped. Dealers' reports at once slipped back into a varied individualism, and three years ago Mr. Grant's staff set up an accounting section to make them uniform again. This costs G.M. some $300,000 a year, but it brings in detailed accounts from enough dealers so that Mr. Grant's staff, by simply projecting them, can estimate the financial and trading condition of the whole G.M. dealer organization at any time. Some dealers, however, keep books their own way, objecting that the G.M. accounting methods show the new-car profit in too favorable a light.

But whatever else they show, G.M.'s dealer accounts illustrate the effect of Mr. Sloan's new policies. According to Chevrolet figures, the 9,600 Chevrolet dealers made more money in 1936 than the 10,600 Chevrolet dealers made in either 1928 or 1929. Predepression figures for G.M. dealers as a whole are lacking, but they did make a profit of $51,000,000 in 1936 (by G.M. estimates) and have averaged over 12 per cent on their investment from 1932 to 1937 inclusive. This compares quite favorably with other retail lines, and with an average return of 14 per cent for G.M. Corp. itself. At any rate, dealers generally, as represented by organizations like the N.A.D.A., regard Mr. Sloan's policies with enthusiasm.

Mr. Sloan, who thinks of the dealer problem as the last big job of his career, has not finished it even yet. He is constantly working to iron out the remaining inequities in the factory-dealer relationship, and there is always the used-car problem to be solved. This work is not pure altruism on Mr. Sloan's part, since a strong dealer organization is the best guarantee of continuing sales. But there is this to be noted about Mr. Sloan's reforms. They were voluntary, and they indicate that one Big Business, at least, has been smart enough not to use all the power God gave it. Chrysler and Ford within the past year have followed G.M.'s lead with more liberal contracts and policies of their own. None of the three titans was any too soon. For the less patient dealers had begun to take matters into their own hands by the legislative route. As a result of their agitation, four states now have dealer-licensing laws, and there is a Federal Trade Commission investigation of the whole distribution question that is still going on. Nevertheless the agitation has largely abated, and a war between Big and Little Business has been averted, or at least postponed. That is, on the dealer front. But on another front, close by, the struggle is only beginning.

G.M.A.C.

ABOUT 60 per cent of all automobiles, new or used, are bought on time; and General Motors, as a sideline to its automotive business, owns and operates the largest sales financing company in the world. General Motors Acceptance Corp., set up in 1919 by John J. Raskob when he was chairman of the Finance Committee, became during the twenties the leading spur and beneficiary of the great American discovery that consumers' goods can be bought and sold without cash. A boom phenomenon over which financial graybeards shook their heads, installment selling acquired respectability during the depression, when good consumer paper proved far safer than many more seasoned forms of debt. G.M.A.C., whose volume first passed the billion-dollar mark in 1929, made a good profit all through the depression, and for the past four years it has steadily netted more than $12,000,000 a year. Though self-limited to cars sold by G.M. dealers, G.M.A.C. finances about one-fifth of all the time-bought automobiles in the U.S.

President of G.M.A.C. is John J. Schumann Jr., a tall, deep-voiced, well-dressed banker who came to G.M.A.C. from Harris Forbes after the War. He runs a corporation with some $400,000,000 in assets, 5,400 employees, and 150 branch offices. About half his business—$720,000,000 in 1937—is in wholesale paper; that is, when a G.M. dealer wants or has to "floor plan" his new cars, he pays as little as 10 per cent cash down and gives notes for the balance to G.M.A.C., which at once pays the car division the other 90 per cent cash and takes title to the car until the dealer sells it. The carrying charge to the dealer represents an interest rate of 4 to 5 per cent. This is safe business, but not so profitable as the dealer's retail paper; indeed the wholesale paper is taken with the tacit hope that the retail business will follow. Mr. Schumann bought $671,000,000 worth of retail paper in 1937 at an interest rate of slightly over 11 per cent on new cars and more than that on used. In good years repossessions run around 3 or 4 per cent on new cars and 10 or 12 per cent on used, going nearly twice as high in the 1932 depression. But G.M.A.C.'s actual losses on the dollar business have averaged less than one-tenth of 1 per cent over the past nineteen years. These losses Mr. Schumann keeps low in several ways.

One obvious way is to insure all the cars he finances. Virtually all this insurance is placed with another G.M. subsidiary, General Exchange Insurance Corp., which is therefore the biggest writer of automobile insurance in the world and earned $6,000,000 itself in 1937. G.E.I.C., whose Chairman is Mr. Schumann and whose President is blue-blooded Livingston Lyman Short, has 1,500 employees and $42,000,000 in assets, three-fourths of the latter being either cash or short-term government bonds. It has written 12,300,000 separate policies since 1925 and paid $99,000,000 in claims. Since a G.E.I.C. policy is tied to almost every G.M.A.C. installment purchase, G.E.I.C. has no acquisition costs and holds its rates about 25 per cent under conference standards.

Another way G.M.A.C. keeps down its losses is by fairly selective buying. Of G.M.'s 17,000 car dealers, not more than 15,000 meet G.M.A.C.'s credit standards; and of the 15,000, G.M.A.C. does business regularly with only 10,000, the others choosing to sell their paper elsewhere or carry it themselves. Still another way is by handing all repossessions back to the dealer. G.M.A.C. buys only what is called "recourse" paper. That means that the dealer endorses the car buyer's note, and if the car buyer doesn't pay out, the dealer is responsible to G.M.A.C. for the balance. In that case the dealer sells the repossessed car for what he can get, while G.M.A.C. gets paid in full. However, to help the dealer avoid a loss on his repossessions, G.M.A.C. puts about $9 of the finance charge on every car into a dealer's reserve, which ultimately reverts to the dealer whether the car is repossessed or not. This dealer's reserve is usually more than enough to compensate the average dealer for his repossession losses; and to dealers who check their risks carefully it often means a substantial profit.

Now G.M.A.C. is not alone in its field. There is Commercial Credit, which has been the favored company with Chrysler dealers; Universal Credit, specializing in Fords; and C.I.T., which bought Universal from Henry Ford six years ago. These (with G.M.A.C.) are the Big Four and they finance perhaps three-quarters of all the new and used cars sold on time in the U.S. But the Big Four have something like four hundred other competitors. Some of these "independents" are big companies too, but none of them has branches all over the country like the Big Four. And practically all the independents buy some non-recourse paper, taking their own repossessions and selling them for what they can get.

Because of their local nature, the rates of the independent finance companies vary widely from state to state. Automobile finance charges are too much for the average car buyer's arithmetic at best, and when divided among twelve or eighteen payments they look so much smaller than they really are that he doesn't feel like questioning them. This timidity leaves him wide open for a swindle. The unscrupulous dealer slips in an extra $50 or so—called the "pack"—and gets it back from the finance company to whom he sells the paper. Packing gives the dealer extra trading leeway; he can allow more for your trade-in. The generosity of the dealer's allowance helps blind you to the pack, and in fact it may cost you no more in the end than an honest deal. But the practice spreads like a price war through any community it starts in. At such times the nonpacking dealers and the finance companies who refuse packed paper lose business in great big chunks.

G.M.A.C., which always refuses to handle such packs, has been trying to establish a standard national finance rate. This is difficult for two reasons. One is that G.E.I.C.'s insurance rates vary with the insurance map. The other is that G.M.A.C. refuses to standardize its own terms, preferring to let each customer's ability to pay determine the number of payments. Nevertheless the actual finance rate of the Big Four is standard throughout the country, and is probably the lowest rate you can get anywhere except where the banks, taking selective risks and paying no dealer reserve to the dealer, have gone into the business, as have Mr. Giannini's banks in the West. Even there, its low insurance rates make G.M.A.C. competitive. But the nearest G.M.A.C. ever came to advertising its actual rates was late in 1935, with its now famous "6 per cent" plan. The Federal Trade Commission objected to this campaign because the 6 per cent finance charge, which is a flat percentage of the original unpaid balance on a twelve-month contract, sounded to the layman like an interest charge, the actual interest rate being (as we have seen) over 11 per cent. G.M.A.C. dropped the advertising, without prejudice to the merits of the case, which is still pending. But Mr. Sloan and Mr. Schumann are dashed and piqued by the FTC's position, for only by some such advertising can they educate the gullible as to the difference between one rate and another.

The 400 independent finance companies, however, feel that the Big Four have put their story over too well already. Not all swindlers by any means, the independents include many large and respected regional companies, and they have watched the inroads of the nationals on their business with mounting alarm. Indeed they have openly accused Ford, Chrysler, and General Motors of promoting their finance associates by discrimination and coercion —that is, by using the threat of cancellation to force dealers to sell their paper to Universal, Commercial Credit, and G.M.A.C. Last spring the Department of Justice, after one unsuccessful attempt in Milwaukee, secured an antitrust indictment against the Big Three and the Big Four in South Bend.

Thurman Arnold,[5] as is well known, likes to sign consent decrees, and after the South Bend indictment (a criminal suit) he signed a couple with Ford and Chrysler. These decrees outlaw such sharp practices as wage assignments and garnisheeing, and prohibit Ford and Chrysler from advertising any finance company by name unless (in the case of Chrysler) all companies offering the same service are advertised too. Ford had already sold Universal and Chrysler got rid of its Commercial Credit holdings a year ago, so that these decrees were not exactly signed in blood. Furthermore, they are not binding if the government loses its suit against G.M. and G.M.A.C. For G.M. and G.M.A.C., as soon as they learned that the government's idea of a consent decree was a complete divorce, walked out of the early meetings and did not come back, resolved to fight the suit to the end. Regarding the criminal-suit proceedings as a form of legal blackmail, Messrs. Sloan and Schumann are taking very high ground and refusing to talk to anybody but the judge. This suits Ford and Chrysler, who stand not to lose either way. As to whether G.M. and G.M.A.C. will win, that depends on whether the government can prove coercion. The indictment names the policy makers (Messrs. Sloan, Knudsen, Grant, Schumann, and fifteen others) instead of the "overzealous subordinates" on whose doorstep any overt cases of coercion should presumably be laid. Whether an overzealous subordinate can involve his boss in a crime is a question for the court. The government further claims that the dealer reserve itself is coercive and fraudulent, being more like a bonus than a reserve. Yet a liberal finance reserve is common practice, even with the nonrecourse companies at whose behest the government is suing; nor is it outlawed in the Ford and Chrysler decrees.

Perhaps little pity need be spent on so profitable a corporation, but G.M.A.C.'s dilemma is a neat one from the social point of view. If it were to use its full economic strength and either advertise or force its low and above-board rates down the consumer's throat, concededly saving him money, it might again run up against the FTC and the Department of Justice. An alternative would be to work for state rate legislation, which is decidedly backward in the small-loan field anyway. But legislation presents still graver problems. So closely linked are finance charges with the whole question of wild trading, the used car, and factory-dealer relationships, that a legislature that sets out to cure one evil is likely to end up fixing prices, as Pennsylvania attempted to do last year. And when it comes to striking a balance between too much competition and too much control, G.M., as we have already seen, prefers to assuage the hardships of the Little Businessman by timely concessions of its own free will.

The Grass Roots

SO MUCH for the distribution problem from the general policy point of view of Mr. Sloan, Mr. Grant, and Mr. Schumann. But a picture of G.M. sales is incomplete without a glimpse of a divisional sales department at work. The divisions, after all, are still pretty independent; they make most of their own decisions and they make G.M.'s actual sales. Moreover, in Bill

5 [In 1939 Thurman W. Arnold was Assistant U.S. Attorney General in charge of the department's antitrust division.]

Holler's sales department at Chevrolet we have the industry's prime object lesson in how a "Quality Dealer Program" works in practice, as well as in how to sell cars. Mr. Holler started his Quality Dealer Program soon after becoming sales manager of Chevrolet in 1933. The term has since been applied to the corporation's own program, but Mr. Holler originated it and many features of the corporation program were first worked out down in Chevrolet.

What, then, goes on in Mr. Holler's department? His setup has some parallels with the corporation's own. He has his own market analysts, his own dealer accounting staff, his own version of the Dealer Council. But some of his operations have no parallels in or out of G.M. He runs a school, for example, "the only school of its kind in American industry today," to teach dealers' sons how to become good dealers themselves and so lend continuity to the Chevrolet organization. The boys come to Detroit for an intensive eight-week curriculum under a faculty of G.M. executives.

For the dealers themselves, their sales managers, and salesmen, Mr. Holler has still other schooling, conducted by the zone men through lectures, movies, literature, and contests. For the general public he has a program called "Mass Selling," which consists of a steady output of 35-mm. educational movie shorts, newsreels, and cartoons; last year they cost him about $1,400,000 and were seen by some 32,000,000 people. For small boys he has the Soap-box Derby, which draws entrants from as far away as Panama, Hawaii, and South Africa, coasting past audiences of 3,500,000 Chevrolet prospects and costing about $150,000 a year. For dealers' used-car men he spends about $100,000 a year in lessons on reconditioning. For his own wholesale employees he has a secret society, Pi Alpha Pi Epsilon, complete with ritual, charm, and certificate. There is in fact something for everybody.

.   .   .   .

5] The Federal Trade Commission Describes Different Used-Car and Trade-In Policies at General Motors and Ford

Development of Used-Car Policies by Manufacturers

SO LONG as cars were few in number and most sales were to persons who had not previously owned cars, little attention was paid by manufacturers to the question of used-car merchandising. Dealers might take trade-ins if they wished, but that was a matter for the dealer to decide, and his decision was likely to be based upon whether he had, or thought he could readily find, a prospective purchaser for the used car at a price at least covering the amount paid for it. In general, this situation appears to have prevailed prior to and during the war period.

FROM Federal Trade Commission, *Report on the Motor Vehicle Industry* (Washington, D.C., U.S. Government Printing Office, 1939), pp. 213–17.

During the early 1920's, various manufacturers began to develop more or less definite policies which they recommended to their retailers respecting the handling of used-car business, and by 1925 the trade-in had become such an important factor in automobile distribution that manufacturers were forced to give increasing attention to it because of its vital relationship to the sale of new cars.

Early Ford Policy

DURING the period from 1920 to 1926, or even later, Ford Motor Co. took the position that the used-car business should be handled by Ford dealers on such a basis as to yield the dealer a commercial profit of about 20 per cent gross over cost of used cars to the dealers, and required reports from dealers covering their handling of used cars. Under Ford Motor Co.'s policy during this period, price cutting was a cause for dealer cancellation. Over-allowance on trade-ins was recognized as a method of price cutting and, upon occasion, was given as a reason for dealer cancellations. This policy was somewhat at variance with that of other manufacturers, apparently for the reason that during the time that Ford was producing model T cars Ford dealers did not face as severe a used-car problem as dealers handling gear-shift models made by other manufacturers. This was due to the fact that gear-shift cars were seldom traded in the purchase of model T cars. With the shift by Ford to the manufacture of the model A cars in 1928, however, Ford products came to be sold under conditions as to used-car merchandising quite comparable with those of other manufacturers, and Ford's used-car policy thereafter tended to develop along much the same lines as the policies of other manufacturers. The position that dealers should handle used cars on a basis to yield a profit was abandoned in favor of the position that used-car trading should be conducted on such a basis as to yield the maximum of new-car sales. To do this, recognition was given to the fact that dealers must often overallow on trade-ins in order to make sales. The percentage of dealer margins on new-car sales was increased by Ford Motor Co. from 17½ to 22 per cent in 1930 and later to approximately 25 per cent in recognition of the fact that dealers must give $50 or more overallowances on trade-ins to make new-car sales. In lieu of the position that both new cars and used cars should be merchandised at a profit, the position at present taken is that the total business done, including new cars, used cars, parts, and consumer service shall be conducted at a profit to the dealer. With this change in policy, Ford Motor Co. has shifted its attention to the development of a plan for used-car merchandising, and a field corps of retail business management specialists, including used-car managers working out of the company's various branches, has been developed by the company to bring about the widest possible use of the used-car plan and other plans and policies developed by the Ford Motor Co.

Early General Motors Policy

IN MAY 1925 the then-current Ford policy of insisting that dealers handle used cars at a profit was discussed by the general sales committee of General

Motors Corporation. Respecting this discussion, the minutes of this committee state:

This subject was discussed at some length, and it was brought out that in certain instances it might be better for a dealer to lose a small amount on a used car and move it than to insist that he make a profit on it. In general, we should not go out and get business by overbidding or overtrading, but in exceptional cases we might get into a situation where it would be good business to sell the used cars at not very much profit, or even at a loss. We are going to watch this new Ford policy and report on our findings from time to time.

Later in the year 1925, the general sales committee of General Motors Corporation discussed the subject of used cars in considerable detail and arrived at conclusions of fact and policy as shown in the committee's minutes under date of October 8, 1925, as follows:

USED CARS

1. Is it definitely established that the used car is the "dealer's own problem" and that it will be an increasingly important part of automobile retailing?
After considerable discussion, the following points were generally agreed upon:
The sale of new cars depends largely upon the used-car situation. This is especially true in the high-priced classes, where 80 per cent of the new-car sales involve trade-ins—in some instances it being necessary to sell two used cars in order to move one new car.
It was unanimously agreed that the future volume of sales on new cars would depend largely upon the efficient selling and servicing of used cars. It is, therefore, necessary for the manufacturer to take an interest in the sale of used cars.
As a step in this direction, Chevrolet are establishing quotas for used cars from a standpoint of the probable quantity of used cars it will be necessary to handle in order to realize the quota on new cars. This question, of course, involves the consideration of the dealer's capital, as well as his organization, both of which must be ample to cope with both the new- and the used-car situations.
It was agreed that the best way to approach the foregoing problems would be for each of the divisions to add to their respective organizations enough men specializing on the used-car problem to educate the dealers to cope with the situation to the best advantage.
2. Should used cars be regarded as transportation merchandise, just as are new cars, therefore, requiring sound merchandising practice in their handling; or should used cars be regarded merely as incident to new-car selling?
All agreed that the dealer should maintain the same contact with a customer to whom he has sold a used car as he does with a new customer. In due time, the customer will trade in his used car, and only by keeping such contact can the dealer expect to get 100-per cent replacement business on the used cars that he sells. In short, the dealer has a new-car client and a used-car client, and from a selling standpoint they should be treated exactly alike in every respect.
3. Should the dealer who is fortunately situated so that the volume of new-car business is naturally larger than the average, in proportion to capital employed and necessary operating expense and who therefore may enjoy abnormally high profit, be encouraged to allow more liberal prices for used cars taken in trade?
This subject was discussed at considerable length. It was generally agreed that the Ford policy, whereby the dealer is required to make money on the used-car end,

is unsound, at least as applied to our business. At the same time, it seemed to be the consensus of opinion that no definite policy could be established in respect to this general question.

The chairman stated that he would present a statement bearing upon the economics of the proposition at the next meeting, which might be helpful in removing apparent divergence of opinion on the matter.

4. Should the manufacturer recommend more strongly the careful appraisal of used cars?

Everyone agreed that more attention should be given to more dignified and thorough appraisals.

5. What should be the limit of the dealer's investment in used cars?

There was considerable discussion as to the principles covering the limit that should be set up for used-car stocks. Again it was pointed out that each instance must be dealt with in the light of its special conditions, not only with regard to the dealer's financial position but with regard to the status of the used-car market in his particular territory. There should be an attempt to establish definite limits as to the proper ratio of used-car stock to new-car stock, which would vary to some degree, due to seasonal conditions. Therefore, arrangements must be made and capital provided so that the dealer can carry the requisite number of used cars, as well as new cars, over the winter months.

Mr. Deane pointed out that it is difficult for General Motors Acceptance Co. to rate used cars as they do new cars, because of the variety of makes and the varying values represented by [the] same makes and the same models. He stated that the Blue Book prices do not afford a practical basis of appraisal, because these prices do not reflect the difference between the car that is in bad mechanical condition and one that has been thoroughly reconditioned.

6. To what extent should used cars be reconditioned?

It was generally agreed that as a matter of general policy the dealer should recondition used cars of the make which he represents but that he should not attempt to recondition the trade-ins of miscellaneous makes.

It was concluded that all used cars should be washed and tires cleaned, even though they are not to be mechanically reconditioned. If they are the dealer's own products, it is advisable to recondition them mechanically. Generally speaking, they should also be refinished. The most important thing is not to misrepresent the condition of the car.

7. Should a dealer's used-car business be separated from his new-car business?

It was generally agreed that this depends upon the size of the dealer. If the dealership is large enough, a separate used-car department should be maintained.

8. Should reliable reports be obtained periodically from dealers of their stocks of used cars? If so, what use should be made of such reports?

It was generally agreed that such reports would be very desirable because they would afford a good index to the trend of automobile demand. For example, if there were a business slump approaching, it would probably manifest itself through this data on used-car stocks.

It was pointed out, however, that such reports, to be of the greatest value, should be supplemented by reports covering the movement of used cars at retail. It was agreed that all divisions should include, with their regular periodical reports, reports of used-car stocks on hand and sales of used cars during each period.

Thus, in 1925, Ford and General Motors held radically different views respecting the policy that they desired their dealers to follow in the merchandising of used cars. Ford Motor Co. was taking the position that its dealers should so merchandise used cars as to yield a profit to dealers. General Motors Corporation, on the other hand, was formulating a policy respecting the handling of used cars by its dealers that related the volume of used cars to be handled to the problem of increasing sales of new cars, on the one hand, and, on the other, to the dealer's capital requirements to handle both new and used cars. The policies of both companies agreed to the extent that used-car reports from dealers were desirable.

In connection with the question of reconditioning only General Motors cars, the Buick Division, in 1926, was experimenting with the idea of making national in scope what was known as a "Buick gold-seal plan," under which Buick dealers would recondition and guarantee used Buick cars as a means of increasing sales of used cars. The general sales committee of General Motors Corporation discussed this matter, as indicated by the following from the minutes of that committee:

Mr. Strong [1] outlined the progress that is being made by Buick toward nationalizing the Buick gold-seal plan, which was developed by the Howard Automobile Co. on the Pacific coast. This plan contemplates a standardization of second-hand Buick cars of recent vintage. The gold-seal emblems will be issued by the factory organization.

.   .   .   .

The plan will be extended very cautiously in order to avoid abusive practices and only those dealers or distributors who are equipped to properly rebuild Buick cars will be qualified to participate in this plan.

Mr. Strong stated that he was properly protected on the plan from a copyright standpoint.

The point was raised as to whether or not the gold-seal plan might ultimately be extended through our other divisions, but it was the general feeling that this would be inadvisable or to say the least, it should be handled with great caution because of the difficulty of maintaining the proper standards if this plan becomes too wide spread among different General Motors organizations and their dealers.

Subsequently, other General Motors divisions as well as other manufacturers from time to time developed various used-car reconditioning and guaranty plans as evidenced by the Chevrolet red-tag plan, the Ford R & G (renewed and guaranteed) plan, the Studebaker certified used-car plan, the Hudson personally endorsed used-car plan, the used-car money-back guaranty of Chrysler, etc., all of which are intended to assist dealers in the sale of used cars as a means of increasing sales of new cars.

Eventually, also, the desirability of reconditioning used cars of other makes besides that handled by the dealer was recognized as a means of moving used cars more rapidly as a means of preventing the tying up of dealer capital in inventories of used cars that rapidly decrease in sales value if the cars are not promptly sold.

The adoption of used-car-selling plans and of definite used-car policies to be carried out with respect to their dealers has been the result of much

1 [General manager of the Buick Division.]

study and experimentation on the part of different manufacturers. In the making of such studies and the formulation of policies General Motors Corporation has taken a leading part, especially in studies of data bearing on the vital relationship of losses taken in used-car merchandising to the survival of dealers, and of what steps could be taken to aid dealers in the sale of used cars. For instance, in 1927, at the request of Alfred P. Sloan, Jr., president of General Motors, the advertising concern of Barton, Durstine & Osborne made a study of the used-car situation with the object of developing advertising that the company might run with the object of educating the public generally on the economics of trade-in allowances and [facilitating] the handling of used cars by General Motors dealers. Respecting this matter, the minutes of the general-sales committee of General Motors Corporation for March 16, 1927, state:

Mr. Bruce Barton presented some specimen ads resulting from their study, copies of which were supplied to members of the committee. After some discussion, it was generally agreed that the corporation could safely run this type of advertising and that, if done on a sufficiently extensive basis, it would accomplish much in facilitating the handling of trade-ins by our dealers. Mr. Barton also presented some ads which would follow this initial campaign, dealing with the value of General Motors used cars and pointing out the advantages of owning two cars. Mr. Grant called attention to the fact that this type of propaganda was, to some degree, inimical to the interest of Chevrolet sales, since Chevrolet would prefer to have the customer buy a Chevrolet car for his second car rather than a used Buick, Oakland, or Olds. It was the general feeling, however, that the idea was highly constructive.

After considerable discussion, Mr. Barton's proposals were tentatively approved, it being understood that he would present recommendations as to final copy, schedules, etc., at the next meeting of the general-sales committee, at which time the question of providing the necessary funds for the proposed campaign will also be decided upon.

It was the general feeling that we should base the amount of the appropriation on a $1,000,000-a-year rate.

.   .   .   .

PART III
The Challenge of Labor

THE READINGS

A New Type of Labor Force and Its Challenges

❨ THE COMING of the mass-produced automobile created as significant a revolution in labor organization and labor relations as it did in production, finance, management, and marketing. Indeed, by mechanizing heavy physical work and by eliminating many skilled tasks, Henry Ford and his imitators forced basic changes in American labor as profound as those forced by the coming of the factory in the previous century and by the automation of routine machine-tending work after the end of World War II.

The worker in the new mass-production industries was neither the skilled craftsman who "learned a trade," usually under some sort of apprenticeship, nor the unskilled worker who carried out heavy manual tasks. As a machine tender or assembler his tasks required neither skills nor brawn but did call for a certain amount of dexterity, quickness, and judgment. Yet unlike the skilled worker, the man on the assembly line never had the satisfaction of seeing how his efforts and talents helped build a finished product. He could find little psychic satisfaction from his work.

Prior to the mechanization of un-skilled and, indeed, many skilled jobs, the highly trained worker such as the "all-around machinist" dominated the American labor force. The trade-union movement, which brought the formation of the railroad brotherhoods and the craft unions of the American Federation of Labor, grew to meet the craft worker's needs. Also, in many American shops and smaller factories, the skilled men acting as foremen and superintendents were responsible for the hiring and firing of apprentices and other unskilled workers. Even in the larger factories the plant managers who had the final say in employment usually consulted carefully with senior shopmen as to wages, hours, and working conditions, and did so even when the skilled workers were covered by a contract with their craft union. As a result most American shops and factories were characterized by a great variety of wage scales and classifications based on the particular demand for different skills, the type and amount of union organization, local customs, and even historical accidents.

As a pioneer in mass production, Henry Ford was almost forced to innovate ways of handling the new type of mass labor. In the years when he was rapidly reducing the time required to build a car and just as rapidly expanding production facilities, he came to employ close to 24,000 men in the Detroit area alone. The mere volume of such employment demanded system and control. Moreover, the company was plagued by a very high turnover of personnel. To meet these needs Ford placed John R. Lee in charge of a new employee-relations department.

Lee moved quickly on several fronts. He reduced the number of job and wage classifications from sixty-nine to eight basic rates. These came to represent systematically specific experience and skills and not merely local conditions and practices. Such changes not only permitted a more equitable wage structure but also made it possible for Lee's department to transfer, promote, and fire on a more rational basis. This systematizing and institutionalizing of employment practices therefore removed hiring, firing, and promotion from the control of foremen and even plant managers and placed them in the hands of a central office staff.

Lee worked with Ford to make the company's factories among the cleanest, healthiest, and safest in American industry. Contemporary engineers and later-day historians were strongly impressed by their achievements. The Highland Park plant, for example, had superb lighting and ventilation, a wide variety of safety devices, and by 1916 even a model plant hospital.

More significant than the improved conditions of work were the wages and hours Ford offered his workers. In January 1914 Ford made his radical gesture of lowering the work day to eight hours and raising a day's pay to five dollars. While Henry Ford called the five-dollar day a profit-sharing scheme because of his belief that the wage

earner was "his partner," the innovation was really a high minimum wage made possible by high profits. In any case it was motivated by the logic of good business, for it helped cut down the high turnover of personnel and made it easier for Ford to obtain the most responsible workers in the Detroit area. To get such workers Lee and Ford were careful in applying the five-dollar day. A worker became eligible only after he had worked six months at Ford and then only if he had the good character traits and work habits that the company felt were so essential to the smooth operation of the assembly line. Lee then put together a band of investigators to check on whether employees met these qualifications. As the wages were high, the workers, over half of whom were immigrants from abroad, appeared little concerned by this check on their private lives. Moreover, these qualifications were apparently easily met, for by 1916 90 per cent of Ford's work force were, according to Lee, enjoying the new pay scale.

The readings in this first section on the challenge of labor begin with a perceptive article written by an industrial analyst, Charles Reitell, of the University of Pittsburgh, entitled "Machinery and Its Effects Upon the Worker in the Automobile Industry," published in 1924 in the scholarly *Annals* of the American Academy of Political and Social Science. Reitell describes with meaningful statistics the rise of a new type of worker in American industry and indicates how his needs and expectations differed from those of the earlier labor force. The second selection, written by John R. Lee, tells of Ford's initial response to the problems of recruiting, training, and keeping a huge labor force of semi-skilled workers. In studying these passages, the reader should try to determine exactly how the mass-production worker differed from his predecessors and how these differences critically affected the procedures and practices of two basic modern economic institutions —the large industrial corporation and the labor union. Which aspects of Lee's program were necessary to meet the needs of employing and maintaining a huge labor force and which were less than necessary? In evaluating Ford's employment policies and programs the reader might keep in mind the milieu of Aldous Huxley's *Brave New World* (1932) where a common piety was, "Ford's in his flivver, all's right with the world."

THE NEW LABORER

1] An Industrial Expert Analyzes the New Type of Worker

THE RECENT development of machinery in American industry has wrought definite changes in the nature of productive effort required of the workers. So pronounced have been the changes that they record definite influences upon the worker's wages, upon his mental actions and reactions, upon his physical being, and upon the whole social and industrial fabric of which he is a part.

Civilization stands before us proud of its achievements in the field of invention. Within a century the steam engine, the cottin gin, the typewriter, the rapid-fire gun, the telephone, the automobile, the turret lathe, the radio —all bear witness to a conquering [by] mankind of a blind nature.

But there is a backfire to all of this mechanical achievement. The workers by the millions in mills and factories are being shaped to meet the demands of these rigid machines. The requirements of dexterity, alertness, watchfulness, rhythmic and monotonous activities, coupled with a lessening of much of the older physical requirements, are registering results that portray a new type of worker in industry. Mankind has built this steel giant— the machine. He is finding the giant more powerful than its maker.

Literature contains much both in the way of appreciation and depreciation of our mechanical inheritance. Probably there is no bolder contrast in points of view than that shown in the following brief quotations: A most striking depreciation of machinery is expressed in George Moore's *The Confessions of a Young Man.*

FROM Charles Reitell, "Machinery and Its Effect Upon the Workers in the Automobile Industry," *Annals*, American Academy of Political and Social Science, Vol. 116 (November 1924), pp. 37–43.

The world is dying of machinery; that is the great disease; that is the plague that will sweep away and destroy civilization! Man will have to rise against it sooner or later . . . capital, unpaid labor, wage slavery and all the rest . . . stuff . . . Look at these plates; they were painted by machinery; they are abominable. Look at them! In old times plates were printed by the hand, and the supply was necessarily limited to the demand, and a china plate in which there was always something more or less pretty was turned out; but now thousands—millions of plates are made—more than we want, and there is a commercial crisis; the thing is inevitable. I say the great and reasonable revolution will be when mankind rises in revolt, and smashes the machinery and restores the handicrafts.

In contrast to this denouncement Oscar Wilde pictures the benefits of machinery in *The Soul of Man under Socialism.*

Under proper conditions machinery will serve men. There is no doubt at all that this is the future of machinery; and just as trees grow for the country gentleman while he is asleep, so, while Humanity will be amusing itself, or enjoying cultivated leisure—which, and not labor, is the aim of man—or making beautiful things or simply contemplating the world with admiration and delight, machinery will be doing all the unnecessary and unpleasant work. The fact is that civilization requires slaves. The Greeks were quite right there. Unless there are slaves to do the ugly, horrible, uninteresting work, culture and contemplation become almost impossible. Human slavery is wrong, insecure and demoralizing. On mechanical slavery, on the slavery of the machine, the future of the world depends.

In no industry has mechanical development been so rapid or so far reaching in its effects upon workers as in the automobile industry. Here is an absolutely new industry, free from all traditional methods, bringing into being a product which has the world as its market, and a product and a production that lends itself nicely to almost complete standardization. The outcome could be little else than a far reaching change upon those who do the work in this gigantic industry.

The aim of this paper is to list and briefly analyze the nature of the changes that the development of machinery has brought forth in the automobile and closely allied industries.

Before turning to the automobile industry proper, it should be noted that the antecedent industries of the automobile—the blast furnaces, the open hearths, the rolling mills and the foundries—have all passed through a definite revolution from hand to machine method during the last twenty-five years. The main results of this change in these industries regarding the worker are:

1. The elimination of physical labor formerly employed for the lifting and carrying and general handling of materials, product and equipment.

2. A great increase in the demand for machine operators and machine tenders whose chief requirements for successful operation are diligence, watchfulness, dexterity and such care as is necessary to direct moving machinery.

3. The effect upon wages. Wherever it has been possible to compare the old methods with the new, the results show a considerably higher, hourly

rate for a larger percentage of the workers under machine operations than under hand methods. Also, in contrast to the great increase in production of a given plant that comes with the machine, the total payroll is quite often less under the mechanical methods. This condition is due to the exit by the hundreds of common labor operations, which work is performed now by mechanical appliances.

Automobile Machine Shops and Assembly Plants

THE machine shops and assembly plants cover fairly accurately the operations that come within the narrower meaning of the term of the automobile industry. The analyses that follow cover these two divisions of the industry. . . .

The following constitute the more pronounced effects that machinery has made upon the workers in the industry.

The Coming of the Machine Tenders

THE "all around machinist"—the machinist who has gone through years of apprenticeship and has finally learned his trade—finds a falling demand in the automobile industry. So complete has become the expertness of the machine itself, and so standardized have become the operations that little of experience and skill is demanded of the machine operators. Only a few days of training are needed to fit the worker for many of the modern lathes, milling machines, drills, multiple punches, etc. This change makes more confusing than ever such terms as "skilled, semi-skilled and unskilled workers." In lieu of unskilled, semi-skilled and skilled there now exist *the tenders* who operate machines, *the technical force* who design, plan, schedule, route and cost the work, *the clerks, inspectors and foremen* who record all the miscellaneous activities of the shop, check the quality and quantity of production and who keep watch on the flow of material.

The ability to meet ("to hit") and maintain a constant machine pace; to be able to eliminate all waste and false motions; to follow without wavering printed instructions emanating from an unseen source lodged in some far off planning department—these constitute the requirements of a successful machine tender. The percentage that his actual production is below the standard production set for him is the measurement of the specific tender's inefficiency. And this percentage is more closely related to the conditions of his home life, his health, and his financial problems than to any academic classifications of skilled, semi-skilled or unskilled worker. As a superintendent in the Ford plant expressed it:

To obtain a normal day's production the worker is timed so as to keep up an energetic gait for eight hours a day—this can only be done when a well-regulated living is carried on by the worker in his home life. Worry, careless living, drunkenness and sickness must all be eliminated if the employe is to maintain his high grade production in this plant.

The following classification of the more important operations in the automobile industry is needed in order to obtain the proper perspective of machinery and its effects.

Group I. The Machine Tenders. This group embraces operators of boring mills, drill presses, lathes, milling machines, polishing machines, punch presses, screw machines, sewing machines, planers, shapers, sheet metal machines and a host of other miscellaneous machines. Roughly, it represents from 25 per cent to 40 per cent of the working force.

Group II. The Assemblers. This group, although not quite as highly paid as the men in Group I, must in the performance of their work carry on operations that are much like those of Group I. By the use of mechanical appliances and tools, working on standardized product according to definite and standardized motions, they follow very closely the activities of machine tenders. There is, however, more physical work connected with the assembly operations. This group totals from 10 per cent to 15 per cent of the working force.

Group III. "Skilled Workers"—Those Who Have a Trade. This group embodies machinists, blacksmithers, die sinkers, painters and varnishers. It includes somewhere between 5 per cent and 10 per cent of the workers.

Group IV. Inspectors and Testers. These men test and inspect the work at different stages of the operations and also test the finished cars. They will total about 5 per cent of the working force.

Group V. The Helpers. The duty of this group is to assist those workers embodied in the above groups. It covers varnish rubbers, trim bench hands, machinist helpers, blacksmith helpers, etc. This group represents about 15 per cent of the total working force.

Group VI. The Laborers. This group embraces those generally classified as common laborers. They are the lowest paid workers and are called upon to do such carrying, handling and clean-up work as is generally required of such workers. They will total around 10 per cent to 15 per cent of the workers.

Over a period of eleven years, 1912–1923, Groups I and II, the machine tenders and the assemblers, have increased considerably in the percentage of total workers. Groups III and VI, the skilled workers and common laborers, have greatly fallen off in percentage of total workers.

In one of the most modern of plants over two hundred different kinds of mechanical devices are found carrying and conveying materials and product. This same plant reported that the percentage of trade skilled employes had been more than halved during the last ten years.

Here, then, we find skill or long experience at the top and brawn at the bottom both greatly lessened. A lessening which has meant on one side a transfer of skill from the trained workers into intricate and complex machines; and on the other side the brute force of physical labor transferred into the powerful and gigantic lifting, carrying and conveying machines.

The natural concomitant of this is an increase in number and percentage of those who must operate or tend the machines and mechanical appliances.

Machinery and Wages

THE important development taking place in the automobile industry within the last twenty years and briefly suggested above, is:

a. The growth and development of automatic machines.

b. The growth of machinery for handling and conveying material and product.

This explains the entrée of machine tenders, assemblers and the corresponding displacement of both skill and common labor types. Changes in wages naturally are a part of changes in operations such as the above.

The following table gives the average hourly earnings of the different groups.

TABLE 1. GROUP CLASSIFICATION OF WORKERS AND AVERAGE HOURLY EARNINGS [a]
(*Male Employes only*)

GROUP NUMBER	TYPE OF OPERATION	NUMBER OF REPRESENTATIVE ESTABLISHMENTS	NUMBER OF WORKERS	AVERAGE HOURLY WAGE RATE	INCREASING OR DECREASING PROPORTION OF WORKING FORCE
I	Machine tenders	39	12,332	.68	Increasing
II	Assemblers	40	4,631	.66	Increasing
III	Skilled workers (trades)	34	2,360	.84	Decreasing
IV	Inspectors and testers	31	4,043	.61	No conclusive data
V	Helpers	23	653	.56	No conclusive data
VI	Laborers	24	2,307	.46	Decreasing

[a] *Wages and Hours of Labor in the Automobile Industry*, Bull. 348, U.S. Bur. Lab. Stat. Pub., Oct. 1923.

It should be noted that Groups III and VI represent the highest and lowest paid groups respectively and that Groups I and II are between these extremes. Also consider that Groups I and II are increasing in proportion to total working force, while Groups III and VI are decreasing. Therefore we can with fairness state that *the development of automatic and handling machinery has tended to level wages* by eliminating the high and low wage groups and increasing those who represent a middle grouping.

.   .   .   .

Approbation from fellow-workers and self-aggrandisement are denied the workers because of automatic machines and standardized operations. This constitutes the real bug-bear of the whole machine industry. The regular, rhythmic stride of the machine absolutely precludes the worker from showing off his individual ability in any definite field of activity. Automatic machines put padlocks on self-expression. The work of a modern machine-tender leaves nothing tangible at the end of the day's work to which he can point with pride and say *"I* did that—it is a result of my own skill and my own effort."

Practically all parts of the product have been so specialized in operations that no definite, tangible object can be shown as embodying the work of a specific individual. Man no more marvels at the nature of the labor effort expended in the automotive industry. He stands dumbfounded, however, before the complexity and intricacy of the machines. The author has guided hundreds of students through automobile plants. What interests them is the marvelous automatic machine. The labor effort scarcely arouses their attention. The words of Mr. Dexter Kimball find application in the modern automobile plant:

Automatic machines show a transfer of thought, skill or intelligence from person to machine. These principles of transfer of skill and transfer of thought lie at the bottom of modern industrial methods.

In contrast to the machine-tenders we notice the hand workers—men working at their trades—do gain an appreciation. The artisan is looked up to and admired by those who watch him and by his helpers and apprentices. The die makers, the hammermen, the painters doing the higher grade of work, the older type of machinists seldom fail to have their work commented upon. These workers carry a proud air of knowing all the "ins and outs" of their trade. With great pride a machinist showed me two steel blocks smoothed by hand tools to such an exactness that by cohesion one block lifted the other.

Even a casual survey of these "trade" or "skilled" workers in industry will quickly acquaint anyone with these—shall we call them—*psychic rewards* of appreciation that come to this smaller and fast-vanishing group of workers. Being human, they like this sort of thing. It constitutes a definite return for labor effort expended. It means much in the way of developing and maintaining self-respect. This definite return to workers the complex, automatic machinery denies. And just so long as automatic machinery holds from the worker the opportunity for showing or expressing to some degree his own individuality and ability, then just so long may we expect him to be unconcerned about his job save for the money he can get out of it. Time studies, measured production and portrayed unit costs may keep the workers energetic and nervously "on their toes," but it is with great difficulty that the workers can be aroused to wholesome interest or spirit.

Changes in wage systems come with automatic machines. The development of a uniform, standard production turned out by machines, whose capacity per day is measurable, lays the basis for paying on a standard production basis. This differs from the ordinary piece work. The standard job or day's work, which quite often is the machine's normal output, constitutes the base upon which all manner of premium, bonus and reward plans are built.

It is important to note that standard output under large scale production is the resultant uniformity that comes with automatic machinery, which, briefly stated, means that automatic machinery is the foundation for most of our successful time studies and methods of pay built upon such studies.

Automatic machinery has changed management method. By the introduction of machines whose operations and outputs have become uniform, standardized and automatic, the labor effort thereby is rendered measurable. In addition the growing speed with which metal can be cut and the machines operated, places emphasis upon the problem of quick dispatch of materials to and from the machines, and through the plant.

The first of these significant changes has resulted in placing upon management the responsibility of inaugurating measured production and pay plans for the workers. Once this is inaugurated the workers are controlled by a measured amount of work to be performed in a given time. Measured production tied up with adjustments in the pay envelope means that management needs little else to induce the worker to productive effort. The worker soon realizes that he is not only being measured but that this work is a link in a long chain of operations, which link, if it does not function properly, is quickly noticed by management and by other workers.

The need of quick material handling has led to many kinds of machinery for intra-plant transportation. As a result of this faster production, foremen are charged with the difficulties of having material flow smoothly and swiftly through the shop. But the measured production and the rapid flow of material through the plant call for the work of planning departments with their corp of technicians and clerks. This department plays an important part in the automobile plants as it originates the directions and instructions covering the productive operations.

The Onward March of Machinery

HE would be a rash and reckless prophet who would hold that the development of machinery in the automobile industry had reached its zenith. Automatic machinery so-called is not completely automatic until it has removed the necessity of all human effort. . . . In the automotive industry the direct operations of cutting, bending and shaping were the first to be transferred to the automatic machine. This was followed by the further transfer of feeding by hand to mechanical feeding. Soon a further development took place by the use of conveyers, endless belts, etc. And lastly a fourth development whereby machines are being built in batteries so that many machines are under one man control.

Regardless as to the ultimate place the machine method will take us—if there be an ultimate place—this important fact comes to our notice: Mechanical changes are taking place at an extraordinary rapid pace. The entire machine age comparatively speaking is indeed a very short one—not more than a hundred and fifty years and in America scarcely more than a hundred years. And in the last twenty years the growth of automatic machinery has made greater progress than it did in the preceding hundred years.

·   ·   ·   ·   ·   ·   ·   ·   ·   ·   ·   ·   ·

Quickly—over night as it were—the machine, gigantic, complex and intricate, has removed the need of muscle and brawn. As Frederick W. Taylor [1] puts it, "The Gorilla types are no more needed." Instead we have a greater demand for nervous and mental activities such as watchfulness, quick judgments, dexterity, guidance, ability and lastly a nervous endurance to carry through dull, monotonous, fatiguing, rhythmic operations.

Beyond these changed conditions, however, rests the larger problem, who shall share the results of this great advance in machinery? Shall it be a Mr. Ford, a Mr. Durant, or a Mr. Jordan? [2] Shall it be the consumer who constantly is buying a better car at a falling price? Or shall it be the workers who are being shaped physically and mentally by these machines? All of these interests perhaps in one way or another are now reaping some benefits from the progress of the industry. This much however seems clear and justifiable: That a first charge against the great productive increases that machinery has made possible are such costs as will fully and adequately reward the worker whose life is being rigidly shaped by this machinery. Shorter hours, higher wages, adequate insurance to cover death, accidents, [ill] health and old age are preferential charges to be met before profits and lower prices are made available.

Higher standards of living, shorter hours of labor, a further development of art and a greater degree of leisure are possible and near at hand as fast as man enslaves the machine for his welfare.

But the success of the machine must not only be measured by the goods it creates. We must see to it that those who build and operate it share in a greater happiness because of this master giant now in our midst.

1 [Engineer, management consultant, and father of the "scientific management" movement in American industry.]
2 [Edward S. Jordan, who formed the Jordan Motor Car Company in Cleveland in 1916.]

FORD'S RESPONSE

2] Ford's First Personnel Manager Describes the Five-Dollar Day and Other Labor Programs at Ford

.   .   .   .

IT WAS along in 1912 that we began to realize something of the relative value of men, mechanism and material in the threefold phase of manufacturing, so to speak, and we confess that up to this time we had believed that mechanism and material were of the larger importance and that somehow or other the human element or our men were taken care of automatically and needed little or no consideration.

During that year there were a number of things that happened that made their impression upon the minds of the executives of the company.

I recall a drop hammer operation that had gone along for a number of years at an even output, when somehow, the standard dropped off. The hammer was in good condition, the man who had operated the machine for years was on the job, but the finished output failed to appear in the old proportions that we were looking for and had the right to expect.

A superficial analysis of things brought no light, but a little talk with the operator revealed a condition of things entirely outside of business, that was responsible for our depleted production. Sickness, indebtedness, and fear and worry over things that related entirely to the home, had crept in and had put a satisfactory human unit entirely out of harmony with the things that were necessary for production.

This is the type of incident that played an important part in the conclusions that we reached.

Our first step was to reduce our working day from ten to nine hours and to give our men an increase of about 15 per cent for nine hours over what they had received for ten.

Following this we instituted a plan for grading employes according to skill, with the idea of eliminating, as far as possible, petty discrimination, misfits, and those unsatisfactory conditions which obtain now and then, possibly

FROM a speech by John R. Lee, published as "The So-Called Profit Sharing System in the Ford Plant," *Annals*, American Academy of Political and Social Science, Vol. 65 (May 1916), pp. 299–305, 308.

through the more aggressive making their worth felt and known than men of more retiring dispositions are wont to do, or to prevent the favoritism of a foreman for an employe, overstepping the bounds of merit or consistency in any case.

The details of this scheme are not hard of comprehension but would require a somewhat lengthy explanation.

Suffice it to say that when we undertook this work we had in the shop some sixty-nine different rates of wage and were employing men at their face value in the employment department, trying them out, and if they did not fit, letting them go.

In the turn-around we established some eight different rates of wage. We classified our men into six groups, which were further subdivided into three each, and a definite wage was applied against every skill rating, so that a man might understand when he came with us just exactly to what extent his developed ability would earn and furthermore, by a very simple means, we put a check upon each individual case, so that he would not have to wait for an increment in recognition of his ability and worth through any one agency, but was automatically looked up in case his advancement did not come within an average time set for such development.

Moreover, we laid down a rule whereby a foreman might eliminate a man from his particular department but could not discharge him from the employ of the company.

If Jones, somehow or other, was a misfit in Smith's department, Smith could send Jones to our employment office where his case would be looked into impersonally. If we found that Jones, in his zeal and desire to obtain a position had done so by misrepresentation (and this occurs very often), we would question him carefully as to his ability and possibly find that in Jones we had put a tailor or tinsmith in our machine shop or heat treat department because Jones, when he stood in line at the employment office door, repeated parrot fashion what the man ahead of him said and secured a job, on the theory that we were needing machinists or help in the heat treat department and hoping that he could somehow make good and take care of his family, even though he knew he was not fitted for that work.

Now, we have found in these cases that by giving a man a second chance and placing him where he will fit in that we apparently get better men on the second analysis than we have in the first; furthermore, we have found that in teaching a man in any department certain of our *modus operandi,* it is a great deal cheaper for us to take him from one department and transfer him to another than it is to discharge him.

However, if we find that the man is absolutely out of harmony with the work in general, belligerent and unfit, he can, with the approval of our general superintendent and general manager, be dismissed from the company's service.

It may be startling for some of you to know that in the last six months there has been but one man discharged from the Ford organization.

. . . Suffice it to say that the good things and the substantial increases that came to the company through their efforts in the directions indicated gave rise to a further consideration of the human element which has resulted in our so-called profit sharing plan.

Now, I should like to impress upon you the fact that this profit sharing work was in no sense instituted as a spasmodic thing, was not designed or conceived for the sake of business expedient or advertising. We were perfectly satisfied with what each man was giving us, as far as daily return was concerned. We did not seek to advertise the car nor the company through this plan, but rather we felt that we owed it to our men at that time to give them all the help we consistently could to better their financial and their moral status, and to insure, as far as we could, a life worth while, and not merely a bare living.

It was established some time prior to this work that a man who comes out of a home well balanced, who has no fear for the necessities of life for those he is taking care of, who is not in constant dread of losing his position for reasons beyond his control, is the most powerful economic factor that we can use in the shape of a human being.

The profit sharing plan of the Ford Motor Company gives unto every man who can use it within limitations which I shall state, in addition to his wage, a certain amount, according to his worth and what his skill and ability merit for him, to have and to use according to his individual needs for his health and happiness in youth and in old age.

Now, over against each of the eight rates of wage we have set a profit sharing rate, and the lowest total daily income that a worker receives under the profit sharing plan is $5 a day.

This $5 a day, or 62½ cents an hour, is not the lowest minimum wage of the Ford worker; 34 cents is the minimum hourly wage and 28½ cents the minimum share of profits, totaling 62½ cents, which makes a total daily income of $5.

There are three groups under which each employe is considered for profit sharing—these, practically, are all the rules and regulations in connection with the work.

1. All married men living with and taking good care of their families.
2. All single men, over twenty-two, of proven thrifty habits.
3. Men, under twenty-two years of age, and women, who are the sole support of some next of kin or blood relative.

It was clearly foreseen that $5 a day in the hands of some men would work a tremendous handicap along the paths of rectitude and right living and would make of them a menace to society in general and so it was established at start that no man was to receive the money who could not use it advisedly and conservatively; also, that where a man seemed to qualify under the plan and later developed weaknesses, that it was within the province of the company to take away his share of the profits until such time as he could rehabilitate himself; nor was any man urged against his own judgment, likes or dislikes, to change his mode of living and to qualify under that plan if he did not willingly so elect.

The company organized a band of thirty men who were chosen because of their peculiar fitness for the work to act as investigators. The whole work was put into effect and supervised by the employes of the company—no outside talent or assistance was asked. We have worked out the whole scheme with Ford men.

This band of thirty men was commissioned to see each individual employe and to report as to whether, in their judgment, a man was eligible for a share in the profits. These reports were in turn reviewed by a committee and each case passed upon individually.

As a result of this work our employes were grouped as follows:

First Group.   Those who were firmly established in the ways of thrift and who would carry out the spirit of the plan themselves were catalogued as one group.

Second Group.   Those who had never had a chance but were willing to grasp the opportunity in the way every man should, were catalogued in the second group.

Third Group.   Those who had qualified but we were in doubt about as to their strength of character to continue in the direction they had started in, were placed in the third group.

Fourth Group.   And the men who did not or could not qualify were put into a fourth group.

The first group of men were never bothered except when we desired information for annual or semi-annual reports or something of that kind.

The second group were looked up as often as in the judgment of the investigation department, so called, we could help them or strengthen their purpose by kindly suggestion.

The third group were dealt with in much the same fashion, although some detailed plans had to be laid for them.

The fourth group were very carefully and thoroughly studied in the hope that we might bring them, with the others, to a realization of what we were trying to accomplish, and to modifications, changes and sometimes complete revamping of their lives and habits, in order that they might receive what the company wanted to give them.

During the first six months 69 per cent of our force qualified. At the end of the first year about 87 per cent were on a profit sharing basis, and at the present time about 90 per cent are receiving the benefits under this plan.

.   .   .   .

The profits are paid to each employe with his wages in his pay envelope every two weeks. He is not influenced or coerced to spend his money for any one especial thing. The policy of the company is not to sell its men anything or influence them to buy anything—with the exception of Ford cars.

Our legal department has been enlarged so that men may come for counsel and suggestion as to ways and means for employing professional help.

As a part and parcel of the legal department also, we have a committee that makes appraisals of property for employes. A man who has picked out a home and gotten a price upon it, may submit the facts to our legal department, and without charge get from them an idea as to the worth of the property in connection with the price asked, also a general report as to the worth of the house, from the standpoint of construction, finishing and equipment.

We are also doing, in connection with the investigation work, something that is of great benefit both to the men and to the company.

Every morning there is turned over from the time department to our investigation staff a list of the absentees of the day previous, which is carefully looked up. If a man is in trouble he gets help; if a man has been wasting his time and himself, he is reminded of the fact quite forcibly, and is made to feel that to hold his position he must realize the necessity of coöperation.

This little scheme, which is merely eternal vigilance, has cut the number of our daily absentees from 10 per cent to less than one-half of 1 per cent, exclusive of the times when epidemics of grippe, cold, and other human ills prevail, and then it is increased by just the proportion that our men bear to the number afflicted.

It has been no easy task to add to the number of men we originally had, twenty more of the same type and calibre to act as investigators as our forces grew.

Two years ago we were employing some thirteen thousand men; today we have some twenty-four thousand, but we have gained rather than lost in the kind of men and in the spirit and energy shown, as far as this force is concerned.

At the present time we have divided the whole number so that those especially gifted in cases of domestic infelicity might tackle jobs of this type; those who have evidenced unusual skill in handling men with criminal records, are detailed to such cases, and so on.

As you probably know, of necessity rather than choice, a large part of our working force is made up of non-English-speaking men.

It was utterly impossible to reach these men with an explanation of our work through the medium of interpreters, and besides, we found a mercenary unwillingness, if you please, on the part of sophisticated fellow countrymen to aid us in helping this great army of men, which comprised 50 to 60 per cent of the entire number of Ford employes.

.   .   .   .

We sought out Dr. Roberts—he came to Detroit, and there was organized the plan for giving all non-English-speaking employes a good basic knowledge of the English language through this system.

At the present time we have enrolled in our shop some 1,500, who are taught by volunteer teachers,—foremen, sub-foremen and graduates of the school, who receive in six or eight months, not a lot of grammar or mathematics, or geography, but the ground work of the English language, which enables them to read, write, speak and understand our tongue.

In our motor department there has been a gradual voluntary increase of production (the general layout and operations being practically the same as before with the same number of men), of from 6,125 motors in a 9-hour day to 7,200 in an 8-hour day.

The assembly of radiator cores, for example, has jumped so that a unit of men, previously putting together 750 in nine hours, now assemble 1,300 in eight, and a single group in the fender department heretofore making 38 fenders in nine hours are today producing 50 in eight.

In the making of gasoline tanks 1,200 for 60 men is the output in eight hours versus 800 by 65 in nine hours.

Many of the methods and schemes used in our factory which have lately helped us so much in cutting out waste motion and lost time, are the direct results of the new spirit in the men and come to us from the rank and file of our employes.

We are finding additional capacity that is willing and always available if justly recognized and amply rewarded.

We used to hire from 40 to 60 per cent of our force each month to maintain it. In the year 1913 between 50,000 and 60,000 people passed through our employment office. In the year 1915 we employed about 7,000, of which number only 2,000 can be used in contrast with the 50,000 mentioned, because the 5,000 were for new jobs and for the enlargement of forces.

As I have previously stated, our daily absentees have decreased from 10 per cent to less than one-half of 1 per cent.

.   .   .   .

The Unionizing of
the Industry

❰ UP TO 1920 the Ford Motor Company responded quickly and effectively to the challenges raised by the coming of the new labor force. And General Motors and the other automobile companies quickly adopted many of its innovations. After 1920 Ford's labor policies, like so many of his other programs, went awry. By the mid-1920's Ford's name was already becoming synonymous with many of the most notorious of labor malpractices, such as the speedup of work, the dropping of the older, higher-paid men, arbitrary discharges, and so on. Lee had left the company. His successor and disciple, Dean Marquis, was soon fired. The tough Sorensen and then the sinister Harry Bennett took charge of the employee-relations department. They drove the men instead of leading them. Moreover, as competition intensified, the pay differential between Ford and the other companies decreased. At the same time "frills" like company commissaries and the model hospital were dropped.

The Ford employees had no place to turn for a redress of their grievances. As yet there were no unions for automobile workers. The craft unions of the American Federation of Labor were fully aware of the importance to their own organization of unionizing what had so quickly become one of the nation's largest industries. They also appreciated the difficulties involved. The workers were among the highest paid in the nation. Many were immigrants who, with the possible exception of those working at Ford, as yet had little incentive to join and pay dues to a union.

The greatest difficulty facing the AF of L, however, lay in the nature of the work carried on by the new type of labor force. Only 5 per cent of the automobile workers were skilled men with a trade. The assemblers and machine tenders could hardly be considered trained craftsmen, while the makers of multipurpose tools and dies did work that came under the jurisdiction of several craft unions. As James O'Connell, president of the AF of L's Metal Trades Department, suggested in 1925, the "automobile industry [was] so highly and scientifically specialized as to produce a jumble of jurisdictional claims and disputes that would be almost impossible of unravelling." Even so O'Connell did urge the AF of L to organize the industry through an industrial union or through the parent organization itself rather than through existing craft unions. Yet the opposition of several of its members, particularly the International Association of Machinists, was so strong that the AF of L

had almost no success in finding recruits in the automobile industry during the 1920's.

The agonizing experience of the great depression created economic and political conditions increasingly favorable to expanding union membership. The swift decline in production after 1929 brought layoffs, wage cuts, and long periods of unemployment. As rising demand after 1933 slowly but steadily returned the automobile workers to their jobs, they were much readier than they had been in the 1920's to join organizations that could protect their economic security and permit them to have some say in their economic destinies. In addition, the Democratic Administration of Franklin D. Roosevelt was sympathetic to labor. Section 7a of the National Industrial Recovery Act guaranteed to workers the right of collective bargaining through their own agencies. The National Labor Relations Act (the Wagner Act) passed in 1935 strengthened these guarantees by defining unfair labor practices and by setting up the National Labor Relations Board to prevent employers from using them.

Despite this favorable situation, the automobile industry remained unorganized until 1937. This delay occurred partly because the Automobile Board formed under the NRA had tended to favor the employers who met the terms of Section 7a by setting up company-dominated unions, and partly because Ford and General Motors took strong internal police action to prevent outside unions from getting a foothold in their plants. But the AF of L's continuing inability to agree on how to organize the industry was probably an even more powerful cause of delay. For the AF of L the basic problem remained that of adjusting older institutional patterns to new needs. William Green, president of the AF of L, energetically supported by John L. Lewis, the head of the United Mine Workers, continued to insist that "if organization is to be established in the automobile industry it will be on the basis that the workers employed in this mass-production industry must join an organization en masse. We cannot separate them." Only through a united front could any union win concessions from industrial giants like Ford and General Motors. Green and Lewis argued that even where jurisdictional lines were clear, and this was rarely the case, the signing of contracts with different craft unions at different times could only give the employers an unnecessary advantage. John P. Frey, William Hutcheson, Matthew Woll, and other conservative craft-union leaders admitted the validity of these arguments. They would go along, but only if the interests of existing craft unions were fully protected.

The conflict over the role of the older craft union versus the new industrial union in the organizing of mass-production industries finally had to be fought out on the floor of the AF of L's annual conventions. In 1934 the AF of L, meeting in San Francisco, passed a resolution urging the organization of mass-production industries by industrial unions in a way that would fully protect the jurisdictional rights of craft unions. In order to ensure this protection, the resolution stated that the AF of L "for a provisional period direct the policies, administer the business and financial affairs of the newly organized unions." At the next convention held at Atlantic City in October 1935, Lewis, Charles P. Howard, and other advocates of industrial unions pleaded for the elimination of this last clause. They insisted that unrestricted charters were essential if the new unions were to have any success in organizing the automobile, rub-

ber, petroleum, and other mass-production industries.

Lewis and Howard stressed that control by the craft-oriented Executive Council of the AF of L would lead to constant interference by existing unions and so handicap any aggressive organizing drive. The workers were impatient, they added, and if the AF of L failed to act quickly, they would move ahead on their own under the protection of the recently passed Wagner Act. Frey, Hutcheson, and other defenders of tight AF of L control of the new unions again explained their preferences, and in so doing revealed their continuing bias against the industrial union. They pointed to the success of the craft unions over the past fifty-five years and the failure of earlier industrial unions. They indicated the difficulties of defining an industry and therefore of defining jurisdictional lines of an industrial union. The defenders of the old order further argued that mass-production workers were not really interested in joining unions, and they expressed their fears that the new unions would be "plant organizations" in which the skilled worker would be greatly outnumbered (and therefore on many issues outvoted) by the semiskilled. After a long and heated debate the convention defeated the proposal to give the new industrial unions unrestricted charters by a vote of 18,024 to 10,933.

Before the Atlantic City Convention adjourned, a fist fight between Lewis and Hutcheson sharpened the break between the two groups. The dissenters, led by Lewis, then formed the Committee for Industrial Organization to coordinate and supervise the work of unions interested in organizing the mass-production industries. In May 1936 the United Automobile Workers, set up by the AF of L in August 1935, held its first convention, where it immediately voted to join the new CIO. During the year the young UAW, with Lewis' strong support, began energetically to organize unions in the industry's many plants and factories.

As the UAW and the CIO began preparations for battle, so did the giant automobile companies. Henry Ford, Walter Chrysler, and the members of the Executive Committee of General Motors were, like most American industrialists, determined to have no dealings with outside labor unions. They agreed that to bargain collectively with a national union meant turning over a critical part of the production process to "outsiders" whose objectives were very different from their own. To prevent unions from recruiting men in its factories and offices, General Motors hired Pinkerton detectives to spy and report on union activities, while Ford characteristically relied on his own organization. The Ford Service Department, normally used to police Ford property, was enlarged to act as an anti-union brigade. It spied on union meetings, actively prevented the calling of workers' meetings, and even forced organizers off the property. Servicemen also passed out anti-union propaganda, and their reports led to the discharge of union sympathizers. All these activities were carried on in direct violation of the Wagner Act.

The showdown between labor and management began shortly after Christmas of 1936 when sitdown strikes closed General Motors plants in Cleveland and in Flint. The sitdown strike was already proving itself an eminently effective labor weapon, even though the courts had declared it illegal. Under the guidance of the UAW and the personal supervision of John L. Lewis, the strike spread to other General Motors plants.

General Motors then obtained an injunction to evict the strikers. But Frank Murphy, governor of Michigan, and Franklin D. Roosevelt hesitated to intervene directly to enforce the injunction until all peaceful means of settlement had been tried. Both repeatedly urged General Motors to negotiate with the union. Finally on February 11 the corporation capitulated to these many pressures and agreed to recognize the UAW as the collective-bargaining agency for seventeen of its plants. Chrysler soon followed suit. By 1940 both General Motors and Chrysler had accepted the union as the exclusive collective-bargaining agency for all production and maintenance workers in plants where elections under NLRB supervision had legitimized the union's power.

Ford proved a tougher nut to crack. Harry Bennett had little compunction about using force to keep organizers out of Ford plants and to prevent any concerted action among the men. Moreover, the recession of 1937 had struck just as Walter Reuther and the union turned their attention to Ford. A decline in demand made it easier for Ford to withstand a strike. Then an internecine political conflict within the UAW, involving among other things Communists versus non-Communists, distracted its energies and prevented a coherent strategy of attack. By 1941 American defense production for the war in Europe and domestic rearmament had revived the economy and created a high demand for cars. In addition, the union, having purged its Communist element, was no longer divided by then. Aided by its parent organization, the CIO, the UAW fought hard and effectively. In the election held late in May 1941 the UAW received 58,000 out of 80,000 votes cast.

Of the remaining 30 per cent, five-sixths voted to join the AF of L while less than 5 per cent went on the ballot as favoring no union at all. In June, Ford and the UAW signed a contract that gave the union even more power and influence than it had in the other automobile companies.

The readings in this section begin with extracts from the *Proceedings* of the AF of L's Atlantic City convention in October 1935. These record the debate over the demands of Lewis and others for unrestricted charters for the new industrial unions and so present the arguments of both craft and industrial unionists on the issue of organizing the automobile industry. They are followed by selections that indicate how General Motors and Ford tried to combat the organizing activities of the UAW. The first, from the testimony of Senator Robert M. La Follette, Jr., chairman of a Congressional committee that investigated "oppressive labor practices" in American industry and commerce, describes how General Motors used the Pinkerton Agency for labor espionage. The second is from one of the many cases in which the National Labor Relations Board decided against the Ford Motor Company for violating the Wagner Act. It illuminates the activities of the Ford Service Department. The last set of selections deal with the victory of the CIO over General Motors and Ford. The first reading on the General Motors strike and its results, taken from the *Monthly Labor Review* published by the United States Department of Labor, may not indicate the strife and the passionate feelings raised by the strike, but it does pose clearly the issues and the nature of their outcome. The second selection, from an article by Edward Levinson, the labor editor of

the New York *Post*, describes that powerful weapon, the sitdown strike, that contributed so much to General Motors' defeat. The initial reading on Ford describes Bennett's early response to the efforts of the UAW to organize the Rouge. It is followed by a short article written by James A. Wechsler shortly after the beginning of the union's final campaign against Ford. The final selection is from *Business Week* and tells of Ford's complete capitulation after 70 per cent of the Rouge's workers had voted for the CIO in the election held by the National Labor Relations Board.

Numerous questions are raised by these readings. Was the open split in the ranks of organized labor necessary? Could a formula have been devised on which Lewis and Frey or Howard and Hutcheson could agree? If this had been achieved, how might the organizing of the industry have been different? What other policies might have General Motors and Ford adopted toward the union? Why did they not? How might Ford's strongarm measures reflect his belief that workers were his "partners?" Why did the unions and the companies ignore the law of the land? And what does this recourse to illegal methods suggest about the temper of the times? What was the most critical issue of contention between General Motors, Ford, and the UAW? Was it hours, wages, conditions of work, or recognition of the union? Did the UAW get more from Ford than from General Motors? If so, why? What do the actual events of the organizing of the industry suggest about the validity of the arguments for and against unrestricted charters made at the Atlantic City convention?

UNION CONFLICTS OVER ORGANIZATION

1] The American Federation of Labor Debates the Organization of the Automobile Industry and the Merits of the Industrial Union

Report of Committee on Resolutions

SECRETARY FREY continued the report of the committee as follows:

The introducers of Resolutions No. 99 and No. 226 asked to have them withdrawn. I move that the request be complied with and the resolutions withdrawn.

The motion was seconded and unanimously adopted.

SECRETARY FREY: There were a number of resolutions in connection with industrial unionism referred to the committee. Some of these ask for the granting of a charter along industrial lines in some industries. Some of them dealt with changing the policy of the American Federation of Labor in connection with industrial unions. The committee decided that the resolutions which called for the issuing of charters along industrial lines would be held over until such time as those resolutions which called for a change in organization had been reported on. In attempting to reach accord in a report it was found that some members of the committee favored resolutions providing for a change in form of organization. The majority of the committee were informed that a minority report would be prepared and introduced by those in favor of these resolutions. It was the understanding of the committee that the minority, after preparing their report, would follow the usual rule —as well as the courtesy included—and present their [report] to the full committee so that the committee would be familiar with the report which the minority desired to present. Up to this moment the majority of the committee have no knowledge whether the minority intend to submit a report, and if they do, the majority of the committee is without any knowledge whatever of what the report may be.

FROM *Proceedings of the Annual Convention of the American Federation of Labor* (1935), pp. 521–30, 533–34, 554–58.

Majority Report

YOUR committee had referred to it 21 resolutions dealing with the subject of Industrial Unionism; nine of these resolutions—Nos. 24, 27, 31, 74, 79, 93, 107, 126 and 222—call for the issuing of a charter establishing an industrial union for a specific industry. One of these resolutions—No. 24—was withdrawn upon the request of the delegate introducing it. These resolutions will be reported upon individually.

The remaining resolutions call for the setting up of industrial unions to replace existing National and International Unions, these are Resolutions Nos. 30, 36, 40, 50, 51, 73, 105, 112, 120, 133, 163, 189 and 231. Two of these were introduced by International Unions—The International Union of Mine, Mill and Smelter Workers, and the Textile Workers of America. Two were introduced by the delegates of State Federations of Labor of California and of Wisconsin. The others were introduced by Federal Labor Unions, in some instances by a single delegate, and in one instance by delegates representing some forty-two Federal Labor Unions.

Your committee finds, upon examining these resolutions, that the introducers either misunderstood the Declaration adopted last year by the San Francisco Convention, or desire that the policy established in that Declaration should be set aside and existing International Unions merged into industrial organizations organized for the several industries.

The Declaration adopted by the convention last year was specific upon the question involved. It was recognized that in many industries large numbers of so-called mass production workers were employed. The skill they required being of an entirely different character from that of those who became craftsmen through years of apprenticeship. In many mass production industries, the newly employed workers within a few months become as competent to perform the specialized operation required to do the work, as they ever will be. This is in marked contrast to the skill required of craftsmen who, in addition to their years of apprenticeship, require additional time before they master all of the knowledge required to round out complete mastery of their craft.

The Declaration of the San Francisco Convention provided that the workers classified as "mass production employes" should be granted charters in the mass production industries which would include all of the mass production workers employed in such industries. So that there might be no misunderstanding, and for the purpose of differentiating between craftsmen and mass production workers, the Declaration adopted last year included the following language:

The American Federation of Labor is desirous of meeting this demand. We consider it our duty to formulate policies which will fully protect the jurisdictional rights of all trade unions organized upon crafts lines and afford them every opportunity for development and accession of those workers engaged upon work over which these organizations exercise jurisdiction. Experience has shown that craft organization is most effective in protecting the welfare and advancing the interests of workers where the nature of the industry is such that the lines of demarcation between crafts are distinguishable.

So that there might be no infringement upon the rights of the National and International Unions affiliated with the American Federation of Labor, provision was made in the Declaration to protect these rights. The final paragraph of the Declaration reading

That in order to protect and safeguard the members of such National and International Unions as are chartered, the American Federation of Labor shall for a provisional period direct the policies, administer the business, and designate the administrative and financial officers of the newly organized unions.

The convention could not have done otherwise than reaffirm the rights and the jurisdiction given to the National and International Unions which had been chartered by the American Federation of Labor, many of which had become International Unions before the Civil War and had maintained a continuous existence since that time.

It was principally these great International Unions which had brought the American Federation of Labor into existence. When the American Federation of Labor was organized, and these Unions accepted charters, and when National or International Unions have been organized since 1881, a contract was entered into between the American Federation of Labor and the National and International Unions.

This contract called for loyalty to the purposes and policies of the American Federation of Labor. In return the National and International Unions were guaranteed two specific things: first, jurisdiction over all workmen doing the work of the specific craft or occupation covered by the organization; secondly, guaranteeing to the National or International Unions complete autonomy over all of its internal affairs.

The American Federation of Labor could not have been organized upon any other basis of relationship between the National and International Unions and the Federation. It is recognized that where a contract is entered into between parties, it cannot be set aside or altered by one party without the consent and approval of the other.

For these valid and vital reasons, your committee recommends non-concurrence with Resolutions Nos. 30, 36, 40, 50, 51, 73, 105, 112, 120, 133, 163, 189 and 231, and reaffirmation of the Declaration of the San Francisco Convention upon this subject.

DELEGATE HOWARD, International Typographical Union: . . . The report of the minority of the committee is presented because the report of the majority of the committee was not acceptable, after hours of debate upon this question. The minority report says:

Minority Report of Resolutions Committee on Organization Policies

DURING the fifty-five years the American Federation of Labor has existed its declared purpose has been to organize the unorganized industrial workers of the nation. The contributions from its numerous affiliates have been made in the belief that organization would be advanced for the purpose of adding economic strength to the various units and that the organization policies would at all times be molded to accomplish the main purpose of organizing the unorganized workers in the industrial field.

During the existence of the American Federation of Labor and since the date many of the charters were granted to National and International Unions upon craft lines, the changes in industrial methods have been such that the duties of millions of industrial workers are of a nature that did not exist at the time many National and International charters were issued. This makes it apparent that jurisdiction over these new classes of work could not have been anticipated and included in the jurisdictional outlines of charters issued to National and International Unions at a time when the work that is now performed by these millions of industrial workers did not exist.

We refuse to accept existing conditions as evidence that the organization policies of the American Federation of Labor have been successful. The fact that after fifty-five years of activity and effort we have enrolled under the banner of the American Federation of Labor approximately three and one-half millions of members of the thirty-nine millions of organizable workers is a condition that speaks for itself.

We declare the time has arrived when common sense demands the organization policies of the American Federation of Labor must be molded to meet present day needs. In the great mass production industries and those in which the workers are composite mechanics, specialized and engaged upon classes of work which do not fully qualify them for craft union membership, industrial organization is the only solution. Continuous employment, economic security and the ability to protect the individual worker depends upon organization upon industrial lines.

In those industries where the work performed by a majority of the workers is of such nature that it might fall within the jurisdictional claim of more than one craft union, or no established craft union, it is declared that industrial organization is the only form that will be acceptable to the workers or adequately meet their needs. Jurisdictional claims over small groups of workers in these industries prevent organization by breeding a fear that when once organized the workers in these plants will be separated, unity of action and their economic power destroyed by requiring various groups to transfer to National and International Unions organized upon craft lines.

To successfully organize the workers in industrial establishments where conditions outlined herein obtain there must be a clear declaration by the American Federation of Labor. It must recognize the right of these workers to organize into industrial unions and be granted unrestricted charters which guarantee the right to accept into membership all workers employed in the industry or establishment without fear of being compelled to destroy unity of action through recognition of jurisdictional claims made by National or International Unions.

It is not the intention of this declaration of policy to permit the taking away from National or International craft unions any part of their present membership, or potential membership in establishments where the dominant factor is skilled craftsmen coming under a proper definition of the jurisdiction of such National or International Unions. However, it is the declared purpose to provide for the organization of workers in mass production and other industries upon industrial and plant lines, regardless of claims based upon the question of jurisdiction.

The Executive Council of the American Federation of Labor is expressly directed and instructed to issue unrestricted charters to organizations formed in accordance with the policy herein enunciated. The Executive Council is also instructed to enter upon an aggressive organization campaign in those industries in which the great mass of the workers are not now organized, issue unrestricted charters to workers organized into independent unions, company-dominated unions and those organizations now affiliated with associations not recognized by the American Federation of Labor as bona-fide labor organizations.

> Submitted by:
> CHARLES P. HOWARD,
> DAVID DUBINSKY,
> FRANK B. POWERS,
> JOHN L. LEWIS,
> A. A. MYRUP,
> J. L. LEWIS.

DELEGATE HOWARD: I move you, Mr. Chairman, that the minority report be substituted for the majority report and adopted by this convention.

. . . .

Conditions as they exist at this time make it more necessary, in my opinion, for effective organization activity than at any time during the life of the American Federation of Labor. In response to the demands of labor there has been adopted by the Federal Congress what is known as the Wagner Act. Many of us understand that the Wagner Act does not give the workers of this country any right or privilege that could not have been exercised under the Constitution of the United States. The one particular difference is that it makes it the duty of the Government to protect the rights of workers engaged in industries devoted to interstate commerce, to bargain collectively, choose their own representatives and form an organization of their own choice.

Now, let me say to you that the workers of this country are going to organize, and if they are not permitted to organize under the banners of the American Federation of Labor they are going to organize under some other leadership or they are going to organize without leadership. And if either of those conditions should eventuate, I submit to you that it would be a far more serious problem for our Government, for the people of this country and for the American Federation of Labor itself than if our organization policies should be so molded that we can organize them and bring them under the leadership of this organization.

I contend that the success of an organization campaign depends upon molding the policies of the American Federation of Labor to meet the desires of those whom we decide to organize, rather than to attempt to mold the desires of the millions of workers who are unorganized to accept the policies that we would impose upon them.

That is one of the principal, fundamental reasons that I am presenting to this convention in a minority report an organization policy which I believe will accomplish that result. I represent in this convention what is usually referred to as strictly a craft union. I cannot be charged with having a personal or organizational interest in this matter other than the general welfare of the workers of my country. I understand, because of contact during the past three or four years, the reasons why we have failed to organize the workers in these mass production industries. First, there is involved the question of continuous employment. Any one who is familiar with the situation knows that under the system for the operation of these industries the workers are required, perhaps within the limit of one day, to perform work that would come under the jurisdiction of more than one national or international craft union. Now these workers are sufficiently intelligent to know that immediately they are directed to step across jurisdictional lines by their supervisors that there is the possibility of a jurisdictional controversy which will affect their opportunity for continuous employment. I am told by some of those who are employed in the type of craft that we seek to organize that there are times when a worker will be engaged upon work that would come under the jurisdiction of three or four craft unions within a single day. I submit to you that it is not possible to induce those men, with their inexperience, to organize upon craft lines.

I am one of those who are willing, first to organize them, and to organize them with the assurance that their continuous employment is not going to be affected by jurisdictional controversies. And I am willing to believe that their experience in organization in the future will indicate the class of organization that will most effectively protect and advance their interests.

Now there is another condition that interferes with the organization of workers in these plants. And it is not a theoretical fear, it is one that has been experienced in many places and it is one that is real in the minds of these workers. They believe—and not without cause—that if they be organized in a Federal Union without the drawing of jurisdictional lines, that as soon as some national or international union makes a jurisdictional claim for a small block of these workers, that the unity of action will be destroyed and that this group will be forcibly removed from the Federal organization on industrial lines and set over into a craft organization that cannot protect them under the existing conditions.

I was told since I came into this hall where there is a plant that employs about 2000 workers. Those interested in organization work in that particular city set out upon an organization campaign for the purpose of organizing those employed by this plant. They succeeded to a marked degree and they secured from the American Federation of Labor a charter. And after they secured that charter jurisdictional claims were made by national and international unions for some of those in the group who were organized, with the result that the charter was recalled and in that plant today there is no semblance of an organization. Now that story can be repeated as applying to numerous places in this country.

I ask you if it be the policy of the American Federation of Labor to organize the unorganized workers, where is there common sense in making requirements that cannot be and will not be met? And where is there common sense in continuing to make organizational lines which defeat the very purpose of this organization?

When we go into the practical application of our present organizational policies, what is the condition with which we are confronted? Here is a plant in which there may be 600 or 6,000 workers. Nobody outside of those who have access to the payroll are fully informed as to the nature of the duties the workers perform, but for some reason or other, because they have read in the public press that the workers have a right to organize, or because they have heard an inspirational address upon the subject of organization, or because they have read something that the President may have said, there is inspired in some of those workers a desire to organize.

Of course they are inexperienced, they know nothing about the process of forming an organization, and perhaps through inquiry they learn that the information could be secured from the American Federation of Labor and they endeavor to seek information as to whether or not a charter could be secured. I say to you that nobody this side of Heaven could answer that question under the present conditions. You have got to know the classification of work, you have got to know the duties these workers are performing, you have got to be able to judge how many of the national and international craft unions might claim jurisdiction, and after you have secured that information any one of the national or international craft unions that is inclined to object to the issuance of a charter to that group can prevent the issuance of a charter. I submit to you that that is not a common sense policy if we desire or intend to organize the unorganized workers in this country.

I don't know, there is no one in this convention knows, and I don't know that there is a man in the United States who knows, how many workers have been organized into independent unions, company unions, unions and associations that may have some affiliation with subversive influences during the past few years. However, I am inclined to believe that the number of members in these classes of organization is far greater than any of us would grant. If that be true, I submit to you that there is a menace rapidly growing, a menace to the American Federation of Labor, because if some one or some agency interested in creating a movement that is dual to the American Federation of Labor, they have a fertile field and a very fine basis upon which to work, and I am sure that that is a condition that no delegate in this convention desires should arise or a condition with which the American Federation of Labor should be confronted at any time in the future.

In discussing the question of organizational policies I have been asked many times as to how they were to be applied. The minority report says it is not the purpose to take from any national or international union any part of their present membership, or any part of their potential membership employed in certain types and plants of industry. Certainly that should be accepted as protecting their craft and national or international unions. I do not believe there should be such a degree of selfishness or organizational interest that would inspire an objection to the issuance of a charter to a large number of workers in a plant simply because one or more organizations might have workers employed in there who would be eligible to membership in our craft unions.

I believe the organization of these workers is far too important to permit objections of that kind to prevent the issuance of charters to industrial and plant unions in the types of industries which we have referred to.

.   .   .   .

I heard an address from this platform this morning upon the subject of industrial peace. I bow to no delegate in this convention in the matter of industrial peace. I do not believe that the workers in any line of industry profit as a result of industrial warfare. I submit to you that the only way we can have industrial peace in the industries of this nation is to organize the workers to a sufficient extent that those who manage and operate and own the industries and the tools of production of the country will not dare to invite a conflict of that kind. My interest in this matter is to provide an organization policy that will bring about that condition.

I think no truer words have been said than the statement . . . this morning that it has been the policy of the industrial kings of this country to divide and conquer, and so long as they are permitted to continue that policy they will continue to divide and conquer, and it is my belief that the American Federation of Labor cannot stand still upon a question of this kind, that it should not be wedded to the policies that were made a half a century ago, or even a year ago, but that we must go ahead and perform our full duty in organizing the unorganized workers of this country.

I thank you.

PRESIDENT GREEN: The Chair recognizes Chairman Woll of the committee.

VICE PRESIDENT WOLL: Mr. Chairman, . . . I have carefully listened to the reading of the report as submitted by these six delegates who are members of the committee. I wish that I might reconcile the presentation of Delegate Howard on the subject of organization, the need, the assurance of protection to the various national and international unions when compared with the document presented for adoption by the committee's report. At first it had been my belief until I heard the document read and very carefully viewed it—and frankly I have not yet had the time to carefully analyze all phrases contained in there—that the difference of opinion between the majority and the minority today was not a question of the report adopted at the San Francisco convention upon the unanimous recommendation of all concerned, in a divided report, that it was purely a matter of interpretation of a matter of enforcement. The delegate in one part of his statement practically reaffirmed that point of view. It is difficult, however, to reconcile the report with that. I wish that that might be the clear cut issue, that other extraneous issues might not become involved, but I cannot help, in reading this report of the six delegates, referring to the fact that throughout the report it speaks of industry establishments, plants and industries.

I think a great menace and a great danger is involved in speaking of plant organization, in connection with industrial organization. I don't think the delegates had in mind endorsing plant organization, but certainly the document throughout gives that clear cut indication.

Then we read further that

it is not the intention of this declaration of policy to permit the taking away from national or international craft unions any part of their present membership or potential memberships in establishments where the dominant factor is skilled crafts-men coming under a proper definition of the jurisdiction of such national or inter-national union[s]. However, it is the declared purpose to provide for the organization of workers in mass production and other industries upon industrial and plant lines, regardless of claims based upon the question of jurisdiction.

Is that to be the policy of the American Federation of Labor, and are the advocates who believe that our members should be organized, in a more broadly defined term of industry, . . . into one industry? Do we understand likewise that this committee intends that we shall go into a process of plant organization?

Reading further, the final recommendation of the committee:

The Executive Council of the American Federation of Labor is expressly directed and instructed to issue unrestricted charters to organizations formed in accordance with the policies here enunciated. The Executive Council is also instructed to enter upon an aggressive organization campaign in those industries in which the great mass of the workers are not now organized, issue unrestricted charters to workers organized into independent unions, company-dominated unions and those organiza-tions now affiliated with associations not recognized by the American Federation of Labor as bona fide organizations.

What is the implication? What is the meaning? What is the interpretation to be placed upon these directions and instructions where no volition, no discretion, is given to your Executive Council? Is it that the American Fed-eration of Labor, where there is a company union and their organization so decides, shall issue a charter to it? Or here is an independent or dual or-ganization—shall we issue a charter to it? The instructions are clear. The language would imply that. And yet we are asked to adopt declarations of that kind and type and character.

.   .   .   .

Might I say this question of organization of labor is of the utmost im-portance to all of us. Delegate Howard has referred to the Industrial Labor Disputes Act. Bear in mind that we now have legislation on our books which does not make us the sole factor in determining the form and character of organization that shall hereafter prevail in the labor movement. That power, to a large degree, has now been lodged in a Federal government agency. Of course it is hoped that in its administration we may not find the full vigor and rigor of this law applied against our respective organiza-tions, industrial or craft, whatever designation we might give to our own particular organization.

That that power has been vested and that it leaves out the question of industrial organization as we understand it is clearly indicated by merely a cursory review of the Act itself. On the question of organization it means that regardless of what our point of view is, regardless of what difficulties we may have in our convention, it is one of the most important things we must consider. We must not be guided by sentiment but by cold logic and reasoning and by no political preferment or otherwise in reaching conclusions on this matter.

Section 7 of the Act, first of all, gives the employes the right of selecting their own representatives and we know, of course, interpreted rigidly it would mean entirely an employe or plant organization and not groups of organizations within an industry, trade or calling. We have sought to safeguard that by the exception in Section 3 by saying:

Nothing in this act or in any other Federal statute shall preclude an employer from making an agreement with a labor organization (not established, maintained, or assisted by any action defined in this act as an unfair labor practice) to require as a condition of employment membership therein, if such labor organization is the representative of the employes as provided in Section 9.

While of course we seek to safeguard our collective agreements requiring every member in the industry or craft to belong to our respective organizations, the question of the validity of our organization finally in its right to represent employes rests with the Labor Board—to be determined how? Not as it may please, but as it is prescribed in the law itself.

When we get to Section 9 what does it say:

Representatives designated or selected for the purposes of collective bargaining by the majority of the employes in a unit appropriate for such purposes, shall be the exclusive representatives of all the employes in such unit for the purposes of collective bargaining in respect to rates of pay, wages, hours of employment or other conditions of employment.

In addition this section provides that the individual employes or groups of employes shall have the right at any time to present grievances to their employers.

Realize that here is the enactment of law—that a majority in the plant may bind all within that plant as to right of representation.

Now Charlie Howard and I might differ as to philosophies of organizations. Better that we come to an understanding and forget our present difficulties and differences of opinion and look more to the greater danger that would seek to disrupt our entire movement.

But then how is the Board to make its decisions: "The Board shall decide in each case whether in order to insure to employes the full benefit of their right to self organization"—we may issue charters all we want, we are not the supreme body in this matter, self-organization is not to be determined in the councils of the American Federation of Labor. We may issue a charter, we may seek to grant the claims of jurisdiction and seek to safeguard those claims from the invasion of any other group of workers, but we are not the ultimate judges. This Board shall be the Judges.

Let me quote again:

The Board shall decide in each case whether in order to insure to employes the full benefit of their right to self-organization and to collective bargaining and otherwise to effectuate the policies of this Act, the unit appropriate for the purposes of collective bargaining shall be the employer unit, craft unit, plant unit or subdivision thereof.

There is no industrial unit provided for in the law. Can there be any doubt about that? And it is not for us to interpret that, because it is to be interpreted by the Board. Unconsciously, I am sure, this report of the committee in emphasizing plant organization and charters to independent unions and company-dominated unions, regardless of claims of affiliated national and international unions, will be supporting the decisions and enactments of a Board that is confined in the nature and character of its decisions that it is delegated by the Government to render.

.   .   .   .

So you see throughout this report it was clearly understood that it laid down a policy of organizing the unorganized, of issuing charters of broader jurisdiction in the three specific instances, and then a general delegation of power in miscellaneous trades, with the assurance and understanding had by the convention, regardless of the understanding Delegate Howard might have had as to the language used, that the Executive Council would ultimately be the determining factor in defining the jurisdictions of charters to be granted, so that every organization, craft, trade or industry might have the opportunity of laying its difficulties or its claims of infraction upon its rights before the Executive Council and thus have its day in court.

This report would now destroy that discretionary power, in addition to the enlargement and the changing of the fundamental character of the issuance of charters in the American Federation of Labor.

I have confidence in the Executive Council, no matter who may be its personnel, whether I am on that Council or not, for it is the only efficient method we have in dealing with problems arising from day to day, yes in the matter of form of organization, and we cannot wait from year to year and merely outline a strict course wherein no discretion is permitted.

Now the fact that that is true and that the report of a year ago was sound is best illustrated in several resolutions which have been presented to your committee and which the committee is not now reporting on, but as stated by the secretary of the committee, will be reported on later on. One of them is an appeal to the convention that the jurisdiction as defined by the Executive Council in the automobile industry shall be enlarged and that limitations placed upon that charter be removed. The question is a valid one in this way: That it does present the opportunity of the organizations and the workmen affected to differ with the Executive Council and to come to a convention of the American Federation of Labor and to indicate to the delegates, if they can, that the Executive Council was in error in its judgment. That is as it should be. . . .

If we don't trust the Executive Council, if we have no confidence in their judgment, if we feel they are biased, then pray let us change the Executive Council, but let us not adopt a policy of straitjacket judgment and decisions that permit of no flexibility. That, I dare repeat, will lead us into a channel that will strengthen the forces within industry and government that would force labor to submit to its judgment and deprive organized labor of America of its voluntary character, with all of its difficulties, with all of its conflicts, with all of its travail—a self-formed organization, founded upon the basis of volunteerism.

I hope the majority report will be substantiated and approved by this convention.

DELEGATE LEWIS, United Mine Workers: Mr. Chairman and delegates of the convention—I rise to support the minority report as presented to this convention by Delegate Howard. . . .

Then, as now, the American Federation of Labor offered to the workers in these industries a plan of organization into Federal labor unions or local trade unions with the understanding that when organized they would be segregated into the various organizations of their respective crafts. Then, as now, practically every attempt to organize those workers broke upon the same rock that it breaks upon today—the rock of utter futility, the lack of reasonableness in a policy that failed to take into consideration the dreams and requirements of the workers themselves, and failing to take into consideration the recognized power of the adversaries of labor to destroy these feeble organizations in the great modern industries set up in the form of Federal labor unions or craft organizations functioning in a limited sphere.

For twenty-five years or more the American Federation of Labor has been following this precise policy, and surely in the absence of any other understanding of the question, a record of twenty-five years of constant, unbroken failure should be convincing to those who actually have a desire to increase the prestige of our great labor movement by expanding its membership to permit it to occupy its natural place in the sun.

What is the record? Delegate Howard expressed it when he said that we laid claim to a membership of approximately three and a half million, out of an organizable number of approximately thirty-nine million. There is the answer. If we know nothing else on the question we can at least read the results, and in reading the results we surely understand that our influence is less great, that our activities are more circumscribed, and that our power is more limited to achieve our natural and desirable and virtuous objective than it would be if we had those twenty-five million workers that President Green, in his public address in 1934, talked of organizing. Where are they? Where are those twenty-five million that in a moment of exuberance we were going to organize? Perhaps President Green's arithmetic was wrong and he meant twenty-five thousand, because the total results are nearer the twenty-five thousand than the twenty-five million.

.   .   .   .

[JOHN P. FREY:] When Mussolini gained control in Italy he destroyed all the free trade unions, and in their place organized three industrial unions to which every one must belong who worked for wages. And I submit to you that while this has no direct bearing upon the question we are considering, that the only thoroughly industrial unions in the world are the company unions or the type of organization forced upon the workmen in Russia, in

Italy, and recently in Germany, by dictators brought into existence only after free institutions and free expression had been suppressed.

We have been organized as we are up to the present time for fifty-five years. During all of these years so-called industrial unions and so-called craft unions have co-operated as best they could. We have made some progress. I have heard our trade union movement condemned for ineffectiveness. Employers have done that, the press has done that, and I am not altogether disheartened after listening to some of the remarks that have been made here. I believe that the American Federation of Labor is going to carry on just as it has in the past.

Now, when men propose that an organization such as ours shall change its entire construction, shall alter all that it has been acquainted with and use a new method, so far as I am concerned, they must bring to me something much more effective and convincing than either eloquence or sarcasm. And, as a number of international unions support the change in our form of organization, it seems to me that we have a right to put some searching questions to them.

There are a number of delegates in this hall with whom I have had the privilege of associating for many years. The newer ones can easily learn the record. We have had for fifty-five years so-called industrial unions which never, by the wildest stretch of imagination, covered the entire industry; and we have had the so-called craft unions, many of which are more industrial than those so called. We have worked with them side by side, and I want to ask those who have had more of an industrial form of organization than others whether their form of organization has enabled them, during the years, to show a better record of accomplishments than the so-called craft unions which now are accused of standing in the way of progress. Those who come in and accuse one type of union of standing in the way of progress must be prepared to answer those questions, and those of us who reply must be willing to ask certain questions that cut to the bone.

I want to ask some organizations which favor this complete change, and which for years have been affiliated with the American Federation of Labor, whether they can show a better record of accomplishments than the craft unions? I want to ask them whether it is the craft unions that have come into these conventions year after year for all of the assistance which we were generously willing to give? Or which have been coming into these conventions with such a problem on their hands that they dumped it into our laps and we were called upon, not only to finance them, but to turn over our organizers to help them to organize.

Is it the craft unions that have done that? Is it some of the so-called industrial unions which now ask us to throw overboard the type of organization we have built up, without which they would have passed out of existence many years ago? If an organization wants to convince me that the form they have adopted is more effective than my own International Molders' Union they will have to show me that they made more progress.

I want to analyze for a moment the proposition which has been presented in the arguments of the two members who submitted a minority report that, to my mind, would throw the trade union movement or even the industrial movement into such confusion that no one would be able to straighten out the tangle. Let us look at facts and facts alone.

.   .   .   .

Last year there was the intention that a sincere effort would be made to organize the automobile [industry]. Let us look at the problem as it really is, which has nothing to do with anything except cold facts. What is the automobile industry? There are plants which do little more than assemble parts that are made in other manufacturing plants not owned by the automobile company. There is a great automobile company in this country which manufactures all the parts. Not only do they manufacture the parts, but they make their own steel; they have their own blast furnaces, they make their own sheet iron, they have their rolling mills and their drawing mills and they do the same work which the men in the steel industry do for the other automobile plants.

Now, what kind of an industrial union shall be established in the automobile industry? Shall we place in the automobile industry all of the iron and steel workers who are employed by that industry? Or will we be compelled, in organizing the steel industry along industrial lines, to say to the automobile workers: "The logic of the situation makes it impossible to turn over the steel workers to the organization to which you belong because they belong to another organization which we have set up?"

.   .   .   .

Now I submit to you that I might look upon the question a little differently if, in the interest of thorough-going industrial unionism, the eloquent gentleman who preceded will say:

To prove my sincerity and my deep conviction in this matter, and my conviction is that the only way to organize industry is to organize along industrial lines, I am going to assert that the coal miners working for the automobile industry shall belong to the automobile industrial union and that the coal miners working for the steel industry, in order that they may have an industrial union, shall also belong to the steel workers' industrial union.

There is nothing new about this question we are discussing, but it seems to me that every generation has to learn its own lesson over, and that the experience of the past is either meaningless or is forgotten. We have heard this form of organization advocated in the past, and not only that, but the very organizations which applied it, and there is only a tombstone now to mark the fact that they existed.

Now, I want to go into this for a moment, because if we are going to pass on this question we want to know what we are doing. I will make the history very brief. . . .

[Frey then reviews the history of the American labor movement, pointing to the failure of earlier industrial unions like Eugene V. Debs's American Railway Union, the Western Federation of Miners, and the Industrial Workers of the World.]

. . . And so the advocates of the One Big Union endeavored to show that the American Federation of Labor didn't know what it was doing, that its leaders were incompetent to provide the form of organization that would protect the workers' interests. They, too, are in the graveyard of those labor movements launched in this country which had high ideals, which desired to serve the workers, as we know, but who lacked the capacity to build up a practical organization that would stand the test of good times and bad times alike.

I realize that the delegates would not care to listen to one speaker too long. I don't want to impose upon you too long. I want to mention one or two things. In the first place the organization I have the honor to belong to, the Molders' International Union, was an international union in 1859. It helped organize this Federation of Labor. It did not need at that time any help. It came to be of assistance. It desired a charter from this Federation. It was given that charter, given jurisdiction over those who had been in it since 1859. That is true of all international unions.

Now, when we receive a charter something definite has taken place. A contract has been entered into between that international and the rest of us, calling ourselves the American Federation of Labor. It is a contract the same as a contract with an employer, something mutually agreed to. We do not permit an employer, after we have entered into a contract with him, to call us into the office and say, "I have changed my mind, the terms of this contract are going to be altered." When we do that we are resisted. When any contract is entered into, neither party can have a moral right or a legal right to change the terms of that contract without the consent of the other. I want to remind you that these contracts, these charters we have, are something the terms of which cannot be altered by a mere vote. Something much more fundamental than that is required.

Now as to the difficulty we have had to contend with. Corporation attorneys in the state legislatures and in Congress, corporation attorneys sitting on the judge's bench, corporation attorneys securing injunctions from those on the bench who a short time before have been corporation attorneys. I need not refer to the powerful structures that have been built up in this country.

I merely want to say that no trade union movement in any country at any time except when it encountered armed forces has had to contend with the problems we have had to face, and going through the battle, the so-called craft unions were at least able to hold their own.

.   .   .   .

ANTI-UNION ACTIVITIES

2] Pinkertons at General Motors

THE COMMITTEE first turned its attention to the dirty business of labor spying, which is described in its report on Industrial Espionage. This practice, which is so abhorrent to the American concept of a free society, was found to be flourishing in every quarter. Organized businesses were taking in millions of dollars for dealing in labor spies. National and local employers' associations regarded labor espionage as a regular part of their services to their members. Great interstate corporations maintained private espionage systems which rivaled the detective agencies in scope and in ruthlessness. The poison of espionage was spreading throughout industry, creating strife, and corroding mutual trust between management and labor.

The leaders in the detective-agency field were summoned to testify. Pinkerton's National Detective Agency, Inc., with offices in 27 cities, was the most powerful dealer in the labor-spy traffic. The firm was grossing well over $2,000,000 a year. Robert A. Pinkerton, president of the agency, who in 1935 held 70 per cent of its stock, received in that year $129,500 in dividends. The agency had influential connections. From 1930 until the first part of 1936, Carl de Gersdorff, partner of Cravath, de Gersdorff, Swaine & Wood, a prominent Wall Street firm of attorneys, served on the board of directors of the Pinkerton agency. The clients of Pinkerton's figured among the most powerful corporations in the country. Between 1933 and 1936 Pinkerton had 309 industrial clients, many of them giants in their respective fields of industry, such as the General Motors Corporation, Bethlehem Steel Corporation, Pennsylvania Railroad Co., and Baldwin Locomotive Works. . . .

To anyone versed in the affairs of unions it is at once obvious how dangerous these spies can be to the union. To take a comparable situation, if detective agencies had sent a number of operatives into business houses and one had become vice president of a large national corporation, others had become presidents of small firms and others had worked their way into positions of confidence and power of various kinds throughout the corporate set-up of the country, their capacity for wrecking would be practically limitless.

The Pinkerton Detective Agency refused to reveal the identity of its spies. It was not protecting its operatives; it was hiding the history of their union-wrecking activities. Nevertheless, the committee was able to secure proof that

FROM Testimony of Senator Robert M. La Follette, Jr., Hearings, Subcommittee of the Senate Committee on Education and Labor on S. 1970, the Oppressive Labor Practice Act (Washington, D.C., U.S. Government Printing Office, 1939), pp. 14–16.

the agency has used its power and ability to frustrate the exercise by workers of fundamental, constitutional, and statutory rights. The garbled and fragmentary records which the Pinkerton agency produced in connection with its service for the General Motors Corporation showed that few labor leaders had escaped the surveillance of the Pinkerton Detective Agency. William Green, president of the American Federation of Labor, John P. Frey, of the Metal Trades Council, Adolph Germer, Homer Martin, T. N. Taylor, and Walter Reuther were among the names of union leaders who appeared in the records as having been shadowed by Pinkerton agents pursuant to its arrangement with the General Motors Corporation.

This private spy system is even used to interfere with the processes of government. When Edward F. McGrady, Assistant Secretary of Labor, was dispatched to Toledo in the spring of 1935 to act as mediator in the strike at a General Motors plant, he was surrounded by Pinkerton agents. They followed him about town, took rooms adjacent to his room in the hotel, and attempted to eavesdrop on his conversations. Thus the General Motors Corporation, through its informers, sought to penetrate the confidence of an impartial conciliator, ruthlessly pursuing its private advantage without regard to the public interest in terminating the strike, and contemptuous of the governmental authority involved. Callous to such consideration, Robert A. Pinkerton, president of the company, said on the witness stand: "I certainly never looked at it that way."

Dishonesty is the basis of the labor espionage trade. Burglary, larceny, false pretenses are the techniques of the labor spy. The agencies cheat their employees and their clients. The spies write false and inflammatory reports to create a continued demand for their services. But the final victims of the whole sorry business are the workmen who, in an effort to raise their living standards, innocently join a labor organization infested with spies. The committee found union after union reduced from a healthy collective-bargaining agency to a skeleton organization dominated by the employer, its former leaders fired and blacklisted through the reports of the spy. In Lansing, Mich., a local of the United Automobile Workers embraced in its membership all the employees of the Fisher body plant of General Motors. Pinkerton agents wormed their way into the leadership. After several months the union had lost all its membership except for five officers, and the five officers were all paid stool pigeons on the pay roll of the Pinkerton agency.

·   ·   ·   ·   ·   ·   ·   ·   ·   ·   ·   ·   ·   ·

3] "Servicemen" at Ford

WE HAVE already described the important participation of certain servicemen in the banner incident [in which an announcement of a UAW meeting was torn down] and the espionage at the early meetings of the Union. These events, together with numerous other activities of service-

FROM *Decisions and Orders of the National Labor Relations Board,* Vol. XXIII (Washington, D.C., U.S. Government Printing Office, 1941), pp. 556–60.

men to be discussed presently, raise the question of the respondent's [the Ford Motor Company] responsibility for the actions of these men, a matter requiring discussion in some detail.

The head of the service department is Malone, who is responsible directly to Yule, the plant manager. Malone testified that the men in his department have a variety of functions, such as inspecting fire equipment, keeping the aisles and passageways clear, and so forth. The men who patrol the plant make hourly reports from various telephone stations in the plant. By staggering the shifts of the men, the plant is kept under their surveillance 24 hours a day. In the event of damage to equipment, the servicemen in the plant undertake to track down those responsible for it. In April 1937 there were 46 men in all in the factory-service department, of whom 23 were designated as "watchmen" and were assigned to patrol the plant.

Sometime in April 1937 the respondent added 11 servicemen to its staff. Yule explained that this was due to current reports of an impending attempt to organize a union at the plant. He stated that extra men were deemed necessary "to protect our property" and "to prepare ourselves for whatever might arise." Most of these extra men were former railroad police, sent to Malone by a friend of his who was Captain of Police at the Pennsylvania Railroad.

There is considerable testimony in the record as to interference by these servicemen with the organizational efforts of the employees. Without setting forth all of it, several examples in addition to the banner incident and the espionage at union meetings are worth noting. Numerous witnesses testified that during May 1937 the servicemen became very active, keeping the employees under close surveillance. One witness testified that shortly after he joined the Union in June, "they kept spying on me and they watched me as I would eat during lunch." He continued: "Some worked and they walked and some swept five to ten yards up and back and back and forth, and some kept on gazing and watching." Another witness testified that the servicemen gathered around the men when they were eating lunch, and otherwise would "just stand around and keep behind the boxes and spying on the men." Another witness stated: "Well, they would be walking up and down the line and probably two of them would get together and say something, get behind the stock bins and just watch back and forth and if they could see two or three men that were talking together, sort of listen to the conversation." The men often discussed unionization during the lunch periods. One of the witnesses, referring to the influx of new servicemen after the decisions of the United States Supreme Court in April 1937 sustaining the constitutionality of the Act, testified: "I noticed there were at least three strangers parading up and down the line in the body shop. When I first noticed, I thought someone had got away from the guide. It was total strangers." Another witness, who had joined the Union, on one occasion had a serviceman sitting on either side of him as he ate lunch. There was other testimony that servicemen stood around the fountains when the men would go for a drink, followed members of the Union into the lavatory, and accompanied the men when they went outside to smoke.

Another witness testified that "they would stand there and watch the fellows and when they talked they would come right up behind them." Another observed: "Never saw them do any work but I saw them do plenty of spying on the men." It is evident from the whole record that John Clark, one of the employees, voiced the sentiments of the employees generally when he testified: "That is a known fact; the conditions out there of the service men are just a police department."

It is clear from the above testimony, which was corroborated by many other witnesses, that the servicemen were engaged in keeping the employees at the plant under close surveillance. That this was in substantial part for the purpose of ascertaining who were members of the Union and was also directed toward ridding the plant of union men is indicated by other testimony. Vincent Lipira, a union member who was subsequently discharged, was accosted at his bench one day late in June by a serviceman who attempted to draw him out on the subject of a strike then in progress in Detroit. Lipira parried the questions of the serviceman, however, and did not admit any sympathy for the strikers. Otto Otte, another union member, also successfully withstood an attempt by a serviceman to draw him into a conversation about a sit-down strike.

Lawrence Lawler, an employee, had attended the union meeting on May 15 at Marr's Hall at Broadway and Ash Streets in Buffalo. A week or two thereafter, Klump, assistant head of the service department, came to the cushion department where Lawler worked and, together with Foreman Maue of the department, passed among the men looking at the badges of some of them. Passing up several of the men, they stopped and looked at the badge of Harry Strash, who had been at the union meeting on May 15. Skipping another man, they came to Lawler and looked at his badge, after which they left. As set forth below, both Strash and Lawler subsequently were discharged.

Frank Snyder, an employee who had attended the first union meeting at the Root Building on May 8, worked on the trim line. Snyder is somewhat lame. Previous to Snyder's discharge, discussed below, a serviceman approached Joseph Malecki, a subforeman, and said, referring to Snyder: "There is a lame man working on the trim line. I would like to get something on him." However, Malecki refused to cooperate in this endeavor.

William Kalman, an employee, testified that during August 1937 Malecki, accompanied by a serviceman, obtained his number. Malecki testified that the serviceman ordered him to obtain the number and that the serviceman then told him, "Get him [Kalman] out."

About the middle of May 1937 Bernard Czarnecki, an employee in the trim department, had some tickets to a dance and undertook to sell a few during his lunch hour. He was talking to some of the men on the matter and upon removing the tickets from his pocket heard a noise overhead. He looked up and saw a serviceman watching him through a "transom." Seeing the tickets, the serviceman "almost fell out of the transom." He immediately came down and demanded to know of Czarnecki, "What have you got?" Czarnecki testified further: "He thought I was signing up members and I told him I got tickets to a dance." In view of the activities of servicemen shown by the whole record, it is plain to us, and we find, that the serviceman here was attempting to catch Czarnecki in the act of distributing union cards.

During June or July 1937 Weldon Farnish, an employee in the body shop, was asked by his foreman, one Holden, "Who is passing out these cards out here?" Farnish replied: "What kind of cards do you mean?" Holden explained: "Union cards are being passed out. Factory service know they are in here." Upon Farnish's assertion that he knew nothing about it, Holden said: "You should. I understand you are in it."

   .   .   .   .

All the above facts take on added significance when considered in the light of the discharges and other discrimination against union members, treated below. On the whole record, we find that the servicemen by their activities described above were actively engaged in identifying union members and combatting union activities, that the activities of the servicemen had the sanction of Klump, assistant head of the department, that the respondent made no effort to prevent such activities, and that the respondent through its officials, pursued a consistent course of anti-union action, which paralleled closely the activity of the servicemen. The respondent, having hired the servicemen as representatives of the management to engage in general surveillance of the plant, stood responsible when the actions of the servicemen took the form of unlawful interference with organizational activities. In addition, in view of the above facts and on the whole record, we are convinced that at least one of the purposes for which the servicemen were employed was to effectuate the prevention of organization at the plant, and we so find.

   .   .   .   .

THE VICTORY OF THE CIO

4] Success at General Motors, February 1937

a] THE GENERAL MOTORS STRIKE

A 6-WEEKS' strike called by the United Automobile Workers of America against the General Motors Corporation was terminated on February 11, 1937. While the strike was confined to 18 plants, employing 48,000 workers, lack of automobile parts seriously impaired or tied up operations in 50 of the company's plants employing 126,000 workers in 25 cities.

FROM "The General Motors Corporation Strike," *Monthly Labor Review* (March 1937), pp. 666–70.

Although the large majority of these employees did not cease work until after the first of the year, the strike was an outgrowth of certain incidents which had developed late in 1936. . . .

On December 28 operations ceased at the Fisher Body plant in Cleveland, Ohio, when workers objected to the postponement of a conference to discuss certain wage adjustments and lay-offs.

When the union attempted to negotiate directly with officials of the General Motors Corporation for the settlement of these scattered strikes, the company took the position that all negotiations and collective bargaining was to be carried on with local managers of individual plants. The union maintained that general labor policies were determined, not at the local plants, but at the headquarters of the corporation. When the corporation continued to refuse direct negotiations, strikes at other plants were called. At the two Fisher Body plants in Flint, Mich., strikers refused to leave the plants when they became suspicious that the company was attempting to remove dies. These "sit-down" strikes continued throughout the dispute.

On January 3 representatives of the United Automobile Workers of America, with the assistance of the Committee for Industrial Organization, created a board of strategy and authorized this board to call a general strike against all plants of the company if the refusal to bargain on a national scale was maintained. The board immediately demanded a national conference between responsible heads of the General Motors Corporation and chosen representatives of the United Automobile Workers of America to discuss and bargain collectively on the following points as a basis for a national agreement:

Abolition of all piecework systems of pay and the adoption of straight hourly rates.

Thirty-hour workweek and six-hour workday and time and one-half for all time worked over the basic workday and workweek.

Establishment of a minimum rate of pay commensurate with an American standard of living.

Reinstatement of all employees who have been unjustly discharged.

Seniority, based upon length of service.

Recognition of the International Union, United Automobile Workers of America, as the sole bargaining agency between the General Motors Corporation and its employees, and the establishment of joint tribunals and joint rules of procedure for the adjusting of any or all disputes that may arise from time to time between employees of General Motors Corporation and the management.

Speed of production to be mutually agreed upon by the management and the union committee in all General Motors plants.

On January 5, General Motors posted on the bulletin boards of its various plants a statement explaining its position:

1. General Motors will not recognize any union as the sole bargaining agency for its workers, to the exclusion of all others. General Motors will continue to recognize, for the purpose of collective bargaining, the representatives of its workers, whether union or nonunion.

2. Work in General Motors plants will continue to depend on the ability and efficiency of the worker—not on the membership or nonmembership in any labor

organization whatsoever. This means that you do not have to pay tribute to anyone for the right to work.

3. General Motors will continue to pay the highest justifiable wages in the future, as it has in the past, and just as it is doing at the present. It believes in high wages. It is justly proud of its record in that respect.

4. General Motors standard workweek will continue to be 40 hours. Time-and-a-half will be paid for overtime.

5. Seniority rights will be observed under the rules laid down by the Automobile Labor Board appointed by the President of the United States in March 1934. These rules are recognized as fair and just to all workers and permit no discrimination against any worker on account of any organization membership.

The Governor of Michigan and the conciliators from the Department of Labor had tried from the beginning of the strike to bring representatives of the two sides together to discuss the disputed issues but officials of the company refused to meet with the union until the sit-down strikers evacuated the plants. On January 9 the union agreed to the "withdrawal of the sit-down strikers if negotiations are immediately opened, with recognition of the United Automobile Workers of America; with an agreement that all plants remain closed, without movement of equipment or resumption of activities, until a national settlement is effected; and with the further agreement that all activities, such as circulating petitions, organizing vigilante activities, threatening or coercing employees, be immediately stopped."

A few days later company and union representatives met in the Governor's offices for a joint conference and agreed that negotiations for settlement should begin on January 18. It was agreed that the union would evacuate all plants held by sit-down strikers and the company would not remove any dies, tools, or equipment from any plants involved in the strike.

When time for the conference arrived, the company officials refused to proceed with negotiations because strikers had not withdrawn from the two Fisher Body plants in Flint. The union had evacuated several plants the day before but had retracted orders for evacuation of the Flint plants, charging that the company had violated its agreement with the union when it answered a request from the Flint Alliance for a conference by saying: ". . . No man's right to be represented by whomsoever he chooses will be denied. . . . We stand ready always to discuss with your group or any group of our employees any question without prejudice to anyone. We shall notify you as soon as possible as to time and place for meeting." The Flint Alliance had been organized a few days previously by nonunion workers under the leadership of an ex-mayor of Flint who at one time had been a paymaster for General Motors.

After the stalemate in negotiations, the Secretary of Labor invited company officials, representatives of the union, and the C.I.O. to meet with her in Washington. The labor representatives accepted the invitation but company officials refused to meet with the C.I.O., stating, ". . . we must decline to negotiate further with the union while its representatives continue to hold our plants unlawfully." The Secretary of Labor met with each side on several occasions, but the company would not agree to a joint meeting to discuss a settlement of the dispute.

Early in the strike the company had obtained an injunction to have sit-down strikers evacuate the plants. When it became widely publicized that the judge granting the injunction owned considerable stock in the General Motors Corporation, no attempt was made to enforce his order. On February 2 a second injunction was granted by the circuit court at Flint ordering the sit-down strikers to vacate the plants within 24 hours. The strikers refused to obey the order. The sheriff was unwilling to attempt forcibly to eject them without the aid of the National Guard. The Governor, fearing bloodshed, ordered the Guard, which had been on duty in Flint since early in the strike, to stand by.

A few days previously Governor Murphy of Michigan had sent a letter to the General Motors and union officials directing that they meet with him and a representative of the Department of Labor on February 3. Both sides accepted. Negotiations were carried on for 10 days, and on February 11 an agreement was signed which settled the strike. The terms of settlement took the form of the following agreement with the United Automobile Workers of America . . . .

AGREEMENT ENTERED INTO ON THE 11TH DAY OF FEBRUARY 1937, BETWEEN THE GENERAL MOTORS CORPORATION (HEREINAFTER REFERRED TO AS THE "CORPORATION"), AND THE INTERNATIONAL UNION, UNITED AUTOMOBILE WORKERS OF AMERICA (HEREINAFTER REFERRED TO AS THE "UNION")

1. The Corporation hereby recognizes the Union as the collective bargaining agency for those employees of the Corporation who are members of the Union. The Corporation recognizes and will not interfere with the right of its employees to be members of the Union. There shall be no discrimination, interference, restraint, or coercion by the Corporation or any of its agents against any employees because of membership in the Union.

2. The Corporation and the Union agree to commence collective bargaining negotiations on February 16 with regard to the issues specified in the letter of January 4, 1937, from the Union to the Corporation, for the purpose of entering into a collective bargaining agreement, or agreements, covering such issues, looking to a final and complete settlement of all matters in dispute.

3. The Union agrees to forthwith terminate the present strike against the Corporation, and to evacuate all plants now occupied by strikers.

4. The Corporation agrees that all of its plants, which are on strike or otherwise idle shall resume operations as rapidly as possible.

5. It is understood that all employees now on strike or otherwise idle will return to their usual work when called and that no discrimination shall be made or prejudices exercised by the Corporation against any employee because of his former affiliation with, or activities in, the Union or the present strike.

6. The Union agrees that pending the negotiations referred to in paragraph 2, there shall be no strikes called, or any other interruption to or interference with production, by the Union or its members.

7. During the existence of the collective bargaining agreement contemplated pursuant to paragraph 2, all opportunities to achieve a satisfactory settlement of any grievance or the enforcement of any demands by negotiation shall be exhausted, before there shall be any strikes or other interruption to or interference with production by the Union or its members. There shall be no attempts to intimidate or coerce any employee by the Union and there shall not be any solicitation or signing

up of members by the Union on the premises of the company. This is not to preclude individual discussion.

8. After the evacuation of its plants and the termination of the strike the Corporation agrees to consent to the entry of orders, dismissing the injunction proceedings which have been started by the Corporation against the Union, or any of
its members, or officers or any of its locals, including these pending in Flint, Mich.,
and Cleveland, Ohio, and subject to the approval of the courts to discontinue all
contempt proceedings which it has instituted thereunder.

.   .   .   .

b] THE SITDOWN STRIKE

THE DEFIANT sit-down strikers who held captive a mile-square Fisher
Body Plant in Flint, Michigan, read in their official, mimeographed
newspaper late in February that there were atmospheric disturbances of
serious proportions. "A tornado burst on Detroit at eight o'clock this morning," the paper announced. "John L. Lewis arrived after traveling all night
on the Ambassador express." Mr. Lewis had come, said the strikers' paper
with complete assurance, "to see that the union men are given their full
civil and legal rights." Mr. Lewis himself appeared to have no illusions concerning the portentous nature of his mission.

"Let there be no moaning at the bar when I put out to sea," said the
miners' leader as he boarded the Ambassador Express.

The tornado discerned by the sit-down strikers' editor had been gathering
for something more than a year. The experts saw it coming in the declaration of war which Mr. Lewis delivered in November, 1935, to the elders of
the American Federation of Labor and, through them, to the masters of
steel and automobiles and other open-shop domains of American industry.
The storm was to break first, by schedule, over the steel-smoked skies of
Pittsburgh, Gary, and South Chicago. But, as if to prove the authentic social
and economic compulsions behind the new labor movement, it manifested
itself first where mass pressure was strongest—in the automobile industry.

.   .   .   .

Mr. Lewis took up the gage of battle. His method of attack included one
new technic—the "sit-down" strike—and one older, if untried, policy, the
industrial unionism idea which has been driven from the door of the
American Federation of Labor every year since Samuel Gompers launched
his craft union group in 1881.

.   .   .   .

Since it was the Flint sit-downs which broke the back of General Motors'
resistance to unionism and, incidentally, held the fate of the steel unionization drive in their grasp, this departure in labor technic deserves a leading
position in any inventory of the events of the "tornado." More so since the

FROM Edward Levinson, "Labor on the March," *Harper's Magazine*, Vol. 174 (May 1937),
pp. 642 ff.

sit-downs of which they are the outstanding examples are not historic facts but current realities. A news service recently counted up the twenty-four strikes of a single day and found that sixteen of them were of the sit-down variety. After Flint there was an epidemic of sit-downs, bringing with them a furor of discussion about their significance, their origin, and their economic and social morality.

. . . .

It is only where there appear to be threats to introduce strikebreakers and discharge the sitters that sit-down strikes have turned into plant seizures. That is what happened in the Fisher Body and Chevrolet Motor assembly plants in Flint, General Motors' "queen city." Military strategy occupied the minds of these strikers during their waking hours, which included most of the hours of the day and night. Nozzles and hoses were placed at a dozen windows and entrances to the plant. Many windows were barricaded with armor plate pierced both for nozzles and for "lockouts." Kegs of two- and three-pound automobile hinges were moved to the windows ready to be hurled at invaders. A picket shanty was constructed round the street valve which controlled the water supply of Plant Number One, and inside the shanty were stored gallons of gasoline, material for a wall of fire that would have made the valve unapproachable in the event of an attempt by General Motors forcibly to recapture its plant.

Inside the plants, for all the warlike paraphernalia, the peacefulness and good spirit of the strikers was such as would have touched the heart of a settlement worker. Both Fisher plants, like many others which have housed sit-down strikers in long-drawn-out strikes, had their own bands which made hill-billy music. While the vigilantes were recruiting their forces downtown, the strikers' women danced square dances on the lawn outside Plant One to the music of the Fisher Body Stay-In Band. The leisure hours of a long sit-down strike show fine creativeness. There was more substantial and original humor in a single session of the Fisher strikers' Kangaroo courts than in a season of Broadway musical comedies. Each sit-down strike inspires lyricists who sing the beauties of solidarity and the union, and the mean spitefulness of the bosses. The unbiased visitor comes away impressed with the resourcefulness, discipline, and courage with which men and women take hold of a million-dollar plant and, claiming the right of their families' need, defy ousting by force. The Flint sit-downers were talking business when they told the harassed Governor Frank Murphy that they would not give up the plants without a battle. They had decided, in their democratic daily general assemblies, that they would resist sheriffs' deputies or the police to the end, and that if the military turned machine guns on them they would not surrender until they had, by some sacrifice, conveyed to the nation the earnestness of their cause.

Union lawyers are hard put to it, under the existing state of law, to make a legal defense of the sit-downs. They hammer away on the contention that corporations which deny collective bargaining rights do not come into court with clean hands when they request injunctions. Affirmatively, some labor lawyers insist that the sit-down is no more an illegal interference with the right to own or use property than orthodox strikes and picketing, which were themselves illegal less than a century ago. The sit-down, like the strike and picketing, is being used, they argue, to equalize the bargaining powers of capital and labor. Many employers, as the La Follette committee has shown, use spies, strikebreakers, mercenary armed guards, tear and vomiting gases, not to mention arbitrary discharges and blacklisting. The sit-down is the only adequate weapon with which to resist these methods, it is held.

·   ·   ·   ·   ·   ·   ·   ·   ·   ·   ·   ·   ·   ·

5] Initial Battles and Final Victory at Ford

a] THE BATTLE OF THE OVERPASS

FIVE months ago began the onslaught of insurgent Labor upon Motors and Steel. Corporation by corporation John L. Lewis' organizing drive captured positions in these two great open-shop industries. By last week it had gained about two-thirds of Motors, better than half of Steel. Last week the United Automobile Workers were storming at the gates of Motors' inner citadel, Ford Motor Co. The Steel Workers Organizing Committee, having captured biggest U.S. Steel and most of the small fry, was pounding at the defense of three big steel independents: Republic, Youngstown, Inland. On both fronts there was blood and brutality. On one there was death.

On the Overpass

MEN with queasy stomachs had no place one afternoon last week on the overpass—across the street to streetcar tracks—at the No. 4 gate of Henry Ford's great River Rouge plant. The union had opened its Ford campaign by hiring two vacant bank buildings near the plant, as headquarters. Next step was to print handbills calling for "Unionism not Fordism," demanding a basic $8 six-hour day for workers, better not only than Ford's present $6 eight-hour day, but better than the terms obtained from any other motor company. Third step was to distribute the handbills to the 9,000 River Rouge workmen.

By announcing the event to the press an ample attendance of newshawks and cameramen as well as a batch of clergymen and investigators of Senator La Follette's civil liberties committee was insured. At the appointed time Organizer Richard Truman Frankensteen, head of the U.A.W. Ford drive, accompanied by his lieutenant, Walter Reuther and Organizers Robert Kanter and J. J. Kennedy, appeared. Leader Frankensteen, a husky 30 and a onetime football player (University of Dayton) led his friends up a long flight of stairs to the overpass to supervise the handbills' issuance. He was smiling for photographers as a group of Ford men approached. Someone shouted, "You're on Ford property. Get the hell off here!" Frankensteen started to obey, was struck from behind, turned around to fight. Four or five

FROM "Strikes of the Week," *Time* (June 7, 1937), pp. 13–14. Courtesy *Time*; copyright Time Inc., 1937.

men closed in on him. He was knocked down and his coat pulled over his head. He got to his feet and grabbed one of his attackers by the ear. Others slugged him fore & aft. Cameramen snapped these early stages of the battle, then fled before their plates were seized.

Organizer Frankensteen's own account of the battle, as given in detail to the Communist *Daily Worker* substantially agreed with the accounts of newshawks and clergymen. Excerpts:

They knocked me down again, turned me over on my side and began to kick me in the stomach. When I would protect my side they would kick my head. One of the attackers would say, "That is enough, let him go." Then they would pick me up and stand me on my feet, but I was no sooner on my feet than they would knock me down again. This went on about five times. They let me lie there for a while. . . . Every once in a while someone would grind his heel into me. They pulled my legs apart and kicked me in the scrotum.

By this time they had me driven to the steps. . . . I was bounced on each step. As I went down four or five steps I came to the landing. There were four or five more men who proceeded to administer the blows from that place. This continued until they had me on the cinders by the street car tracks. . . .

It was the worst licking I've ever taken.

The few Dearborn police in the neighborhood did not interfere. When newshawks picked him up a few minutes later, Frankensteen was a bloody pulp. The men with him got off little easier. Other organizers who had appeared at other gates were driven off; and women organizers who tried to get off street cars were promptly bundled back aboard, some of them claiming to have been kicked.

Personnel director of Ford Motor Co., as well as head of its company police (known as "service men") is Henry H. Bennett. This master of tough men occupies a special place in the esteem of mild Henry Ford, perhaps because he has for years been responsible for protecting the Ford grandchildren from kidnapping, of which the senior Ford is mortally afraid. One of Mr. Bennett's privileges is that he, almost alone of Ford lieutenants, can speak to the press in his own name. Last week Mr. Bennett declared:

The affair was deliberately provoked by union officials. . . . They simply wanted to trump up a charge of Ford brutality. . . . I know definitely no Ford service man or plant police were involved in any way in the fight. . . . The union men were beaten by regular Ford employes who were on their way to work. The union men called them scabs and cursed and taunted them. A Negro who works in the foundry was goaded and cursed so viciously by one organizer that he turned and struck him. That was the first blow struck. . . .

Unfortunately for Mr. Bennett's account as far as it concerned the beating of Organizer Frankensteen, there were too many witnesses. Newshawks reported recognizing Ford "service men" as the attackers, reported that these men had asked which were Frankensteen and Reuther. Also the Ford men were not quick enough to seize the plates of photographers. One group of cameramen were chased in a car at 60 m.p.h. and took refuge in the Melvindale police station where they were followed by three men who identified themselves as Ford service men. The pictures showed that Frankensteen & friends' were given no amateur beating but a standard job of mauling including well known gorilla tricks. One of the pictures disclosed a pair of handcuffs in the pocket of an attacker . . . and from the photographs it seemed likely that the Ford men would be identified. It looked very much as if that brutal beating might hurt Henry Ford as much as it hurt Richard Frankensteen. Last week in Massachusetts the Ford Motor Co. filed its balance sheet as required by State law, providing the annual glimpse which the public gets of Ford finances. It did not show, of course, what dividends had been paid but it showed an increase of $19,689,000 in profit & loss account, of $6,737,000 in reserves indicating that the company has salted away $26,-427,000 during 1936, over seven times as much as in 1935. With a total surplus of $600,000,000 Ford Motor Co. is well prepared for a costly strike now or later.

b] THE 1941 STRIKE BEGINS

Detroit, April 7

AT FIFTEEN minutes after midnight, Norman Smith, a hulking, unkempt, gentle-faced organizer who looks like Heywood Broun, stood on top of a C.I.O. sound-truck outside the main gate of the River Rouge plant. The hundreds of workers who had been milling around in the street, shouting and murmuring in the night, became pretty quiet. Then Smith roared: "The strike is on. Picket lines will be formed immediately."

The announcement sounded neat and unrhetorical, but the date—April 2—will be recorded in labor history. There was a lot of the incidental music of history in the setting. Over Smith's head, as he recited the strike call, was the overpass where C.I.O. organizers were so pitilessly slugged by Ford service men in the futile campaign of 1937. Smith himself took a terrific beating from Ford goons in Memphis, where another Ford plant was defying the C.I.O. But now, in the capital of the Ford empire, men had struck for the first time in the thirty-eight-year life of the Rouge plant.

It all happened with such incredible suddenness, and events moved so fast afterward, that the epic touch was almost overlooked. The words and sounds and signs were familiar strike routine. Yet this walkout, C.I.O. chiefs admitted, was close to a trade-union miracle. The basic and indisputable fact was that it was provoked by the company; that the C.I.O. strategists had not planned to strike for several weeks and had hoped that a walkout might be entirely avoided. Several months ago Michael F. Widman, Jr., leader of the C.I.O. drive at Ford, told me: "We won't let Harry Bennett pick the date for a strike if we have to have one." But Harry Bennett did.

The jaunty, shrewd chief of Ford's terror squad could easily have prevented the dismissal of eleven key C.I.O. workers from exploding into a strike. All that the C.I.O. asked was to discuss the firings. Bennett plainly believed that this was the time to fight it out, perhaps because the national temper was so inauspicious for labor, perhaps because he thought the C.I.O.

FROM James A. Wechsler, "River Rouge Revolt," *The Nation* (April 12, 1941), p. 426.

had gained so much ground at River Rouge that it had to be smashed now or not at all. He did not know that he was already too late. Neither did the C.I.O. leaders.

Throughout Tuesday evening the C.I.O. cabinet sat behind closed doors weighing a decision they had hoped to make under less feverish circumstances. As they met, stoppages—genuinely spontaneous—spread through the plant. When Ford officials refused to meet with the cabinet, retreat became impossible; it might have fatally demoralized the whole union. So at 12:15 the word sped into the cold Michigan night that Henry Ford's workers were going on strike.

After that the chips were down in this costly, desperate, long-frustrated campaign to organize the last home of anti-unionism in the auto industry, to make Henry Ford do what he had vowed he never would: recognize an outside union. What happened subsequently exceeded even the wishful thinking usually found in labor upsurges. It was a kind of mass rebellion against a tyranny that people had thought was immortal. Apparently the great bulk of the 85,000 workers employed at Rouge had decided, too, that this might be the last time they could fight it out with hope of success.

Once upon a time Henry Ford had insisted he would never close his plant in the face of a strike crisis; "We would stand to the last man." But twenty-four hours after the walkout Ford officialdom closed the plant, announcing it would not reopen while the war was being waged over mediation tables. The announcement was a confession that the C.I.O. had organized Ford. Thousands of workers signed union cards in the ensuing hours. The A.F. of L., in a frail and foolish effort to steal the C.I.O. show, called a mass meeting and preached back-to-work slogans; but less than 1,000 workers attended the meeting in the hall in which the C.I.O. had rallied 15,000 the night before. . . .

By the time this report appears, the strike may have been settled by a sudden compromise, or pending the Labor Board election, Henry Ford may have unleashed last-ditch violence against his employees. Whatever he does, there is a widespread convicton here that he has lost, and only the procedure of defeat is unsettled. Because while Ford publicists are lamely saying that "imported agitators" are behind the strike, they admitted the lie when they closed the plant.

c] FORD'S CAPITULATION

H ENRY FORD, American industry's most rugged individualist, pioneered again last week when, in effect, he made the C.I.O. a full partner in the largest privately-owned company in the world. He did it, as close observers indicated he would . . . by having his personnel manager, Harry Bennett, sign a union-shop, check-off contract with the United Automobile Workers Union.

The union can be considered Ford's partner in the sense that it is given

FROM "Ford's Partner," *Business Week* (June 28, 1941), p. 40. Reprinted by special permission of *Business Week*.

absolute suzerainty over every one of the 130,000 employees below the rank
of foreman who works for the company. So iron-bound is the bargain between union and company that, from now on in, Ford and U.A.W. are in
business together.

Asked and Received

FORD'S action was of his own volition. When Bennett conferred with C.I.O.
officials, he found them asking (1) wage increases ranging from 5¢ to 30¢
an hour to make Ford wages the highest in the industry, (2) abolition of the
service department often charged with carrying on anti-union espionage,
(3) a shop steward system with one steward for every 550 workers, (4) time-
and-a-half for all work over eight hours in one day and double time for
Sunday and holiday work, (5) two hours of call-in pay for employees called
in to work and finding no work available, (6) a strict seniority system governing lay-offs and rehiring, and (7) reinstatement without prejudice of thousands of employees allegedly fired for union membership.

Ford granted all these things, satisfying the union completely, and received in return the union's pledge of no labor trouble, a promise to drop
all Labor Board and court cases against the company (in which the NLRB
concurred), and the right, offered to other automobile manufacturers under
union contract but never accepted before, to put a union label on Ford
cars.

A Chat With Murray

WHEN it came time to incorporate these items in a signed agreement which
gave U.A.W. bargaining rights for the River Rouge and Lincoln plants,
where it had won recent Labor Board elections . . . Bennett told negoti-
ators that he would like to chat with C.I.O. President Philip Murray in
Washington. Crestfallen, U.A.W. officials felt that their mutual congratula-
tions had been premature. Recalling a series of undisciplined slow-down
strikes which had occurred in the Rouge plant while negotiations were in
progress, they thought the company had reconsidered, that Bennett would
argue with Murray for better terms.

A "Present"

IF BENNETT had asked for concessions he would have got them, for U.A.W.
was prepared to modify its demands to avoid a strike. Instead, his object in
seeing Murray was, in the words of an executive of a competing company,
"to make him a present of the whole goddamn industry."

Not that Ford is the whole automobile industry; but Ford's action is considered as giving the C.I.O. a stranglehold on automotive production and no
union which has secured the check-off from a big employer has ever been
undermined. Under the Ford-U.A.W. contract, the company's paymaster will
be sending a check for $130,000 each month to the union's treasurer. With-
out a "by your leave" it's going to be deducted from each Ford employee's
pay. No one familiar with labor organizations will suggest that the money
will be used for any other purpose than to campaign for identical arrangements with all the rest of the industry.

Off the Target Range

THUS, as the company, in the words of Edsel Ford, "decided to go the whole way" with the union after 38 years of unmitigated opposition to unionism, its first positive benefit becomes apparent. Ford is off the C.I.O.'s target range, and its competitors are going to be incessantly sniped at until they make the same kind of a deal.

The second economic gain for the company is that it comes off the blacklist of its most important customer, which could, if it chose, give Ford a great deal more business. That customer is, of course, the government, which under the New Deal has done everything it could under the law to buy from Ford competitors. Intermittent bitter controversies over defense contracts for the company . . . have highlighted the New Deal's attitude. From now on, employing only dues-paying union men, the Ford Motor Company can expect preferential treatment, whenever possible, from Washington. And if the preference flags, the powerful C.I.O. lobby can be counted on to do its share of prodding, since every worker Ford employs means another $1 a month in C.I.O. coffers. And, besides government business, there is the prospect of selling more cars to unionists in their own consumer rôle.

"Union Protection"

A THIRD benefit which Ford apparently expects is of a negative variety—a freedom from the labor troubles which beset companies, like all the other auto manufacturers, not operating under an agreement which makes union membership compulsory. In positive terms, it is "union protection," a kind of plant policing by the union for the company.

Where union membership is not a condition of employment, a labor organization must ever be active if it is to anchor the loyalty of employees and keep them convinced that it is to their interest to pay their dues. To achieve this, it constantly seeks "grievances," and where they cannot be found it often manufactures them.

The Industry and the Economy

INTRODUCTION

AFTER World War II, the patterns of production, finance, management, marketing, and labor relations initiated by the automobile industry during the first four decades of this century became relatively regularized and routinized. Other forces took over as primary creators of change in the American business economy. The demands of national defense and the increasing application of science to industrial products and processes through systematic research and development became more significant than the automobile. But the story of the impact of the motor-vehicle industry on the American economy cannot omit some reference to its vital contribution to the aggregate growth of the economy as well as to the way it functioned.

Clearly the automobile industry was of critical significance to the amazingly swift growth of the American economy in the three decades following the depression of the 1890's. In the period between 1897 and 1929, national income rose fivefold from slightly under $20 billion to slightly more than $100 billion. The swiftest growth came between 1908 and 1924, the very years of the automobile industry's greatest expansion. In that period alone, the national income increased almost $60 billion. The automobile industry not only contributed to this expansion by providing new wages, salaries, and profits of its own but also by increasing those in many other industries, including iron and steel, copper, nickel, oil, rubber, plate glass, leather, and road and housing construction. During these three decades only the electrical industry had anything like a comparable impact on American growth, and its major effect appears to have come before 1910.

This volume began by printing statistical tables emphasizing the impact of the automobile on the economy. Particularly significant are Tables 3 and 4. In closing, this volume makes the same point in a more analytical way by presenting selections from Joseph A. Schumpeter's monumental study, Business Cycles (New York, 1939). This eminent Austrian scholar, who taught for many years at Harvard, concentrated his attention on the dynamics of economic change. His particular interest was in the entrepreneur and his innovations as agents of long-term change. And he was one of the first economists to point out the critical role the automobile played in American economic growth.

In his broad study of the course of business cycles in the Western world since the British Industrial Revolution, Schumpeter devised a scheme of *analysis using long- and short-term waves. The long waves he called Kondra-tieff, after the Russian economist who first identified the occurrence of three such long-term waves of business activity since the 1780's. According to Schumpeter, the first wave ran from 1787 to 1842, the second from 1843 to 1897, and the third began in 1898. The short-term waves, normally averaging ten years in length, he called Juglars, for Clement Juglar, who had initially made a study of these shorter cycles. In indicating the vital importance of the automobile industry to the development of the third long Kondratieff wave and the shorter Juglars within it, Schumpeter added his own perceptive comments on the history of the industry.*

In studying this selection, the reader should keep in mind the ways in which the growth of the American economy would have differed if the large-scale production of the automobile had not come when it did. In so doing he should consider the impact of the automobile on sectors of the economy other than those covered in these readings. What, for example, might have been its effect on road and housing construction, on retail marketing, on resort areas, on the recreation industry, and the like? What does Schumpeter indicate about the ingredients and nature of economic change? Do the readings presented in this volume on the changes in economic functions and processes support his views?

THE READING

1] An Eminent Economist Analyzes the Dynamic Influence of the Industry on the Economy

. . . .

THE AUTOMOBILE industry affords a good example of a purely entrepreneurial achievement turning to new uses not only existing resources but also existing technology, *viz.*, the Lenoir-Otto internal combustion engine, the principle of interchangeable parts, the possibilities offered by steel developments and modern machine tools. Among modern industries it also was, in its beginnings, almost in a class by itself with respect to financial methods. Its own productive process consisted in assembling intermediate goods which it was possible to buy on credit (on 60 to 90 days' open account, for instance), so that the resulting product, sold for cash, could directly pay for itself. Later on, the retailer, or institutions that financed him, came in to bridge the gap by remitting not only in advance of his sale to the consumer, but also of delivery to him. Thus, the manufacturer need not borrow at all from banks and may still induce expansion of deposits to an extent amounting to inflation. No better instance could be found to show how credit creation for the purpose of innovation can hide. This industry, though not a starter yet one of the most important carriers of this Kondratieff, revealed its full meaning for the economic process and for civilization— it has altered the style of life and the outlook on life probably more than any prophet ever did—in the downgrade span after the war, exactly as cotton textiles asserted themselves fully in the downgrade of their Kondratieff. In the prosperity it did not get so far.

The problems of assembling were solved in Germany and France. G. Daimler and K. Benz produced vehicles in the eighties; Elwood Haynes, C. and F. Duryea, R. E. Olds, by 1893; A. Winton, in 1894. Half a dozen small companies, with a quantitative importance practically equal to zero, were founded in the next six years by these men (Duryea Motor Wagon Company, 1896; Winton Motor Company, 1897). Registration in this country totaled 8,624 in 1899, and in 1900 the Olds Motor Works of Detroit started what to them seemed mass production, reaching the figure of 4,000 in 1903. Ford, somewhat hampered in the nineties by a struggle with the Selden patent—this and similar struggles soon led to an understanding about pooling non-essential patents and to a considerable measure of cooperation which

FROM *Business Cycles* (Vol. I, pp. 415–18; Vol. II, pp. 772–77), Joseph Schumpeter. Copyright, 1939. McGraw-Hill Book Company, Inc. Used by permission.

it would be interesting to analyze—reached incorporation stage in 1903 ($100,000 capital, $28,000 paid up). Mortality among pioneers was as high as in such a case we would naturally expect. With the (temporarily) successful ones, profits paid for expansion. Along with the gasoline car came the gasoline mower. The first bus routes and stage lines were established about 1905. Between 1902 and 1907, 322 companies started operations. In the latter year, 8,423 cars were sold for about 5½ million dollars, of which 1 million was profit. The year 1908 closes the first stage.

In that year innovation turned against itself. The great new thing appeared in the shape of the light and cheap four-cylinder Ford car for the masses, which drove from the field many of what by then were old firms in our sense. That the increased mortality—the modal firm founded in 1902 lasted until 1910, and the modal firm founded in 1908, also—was mainly among firms under four years of age, does not contradict this statement, because in a period of such rapid change a great many new foundations will start on a plan that has already become obsolete, although the failure of others was no doubt due to unsuccessful innovations of their own. General Motors, founded in 1908 (Durant), provided the first occasion for bankers to enter the field (1910), which until then had been entirely outside their sphere of influence and substantially remained so to the war. Ratio of net profit to net worth, though declining, remained on a level about twice as high as in the post-war period and equal to, according to Professor Epstein's [1] estimate, six or seven times the "normal rate of interest." Prices, also declining, moved on a level still further above that of the twenties, which loose statement applies even if no account be taken of the difference in quality, which defies comparison, and of the change in the price level. Product per man-hour (*Monthly Labor Review*, 1930, p. 502), whatever it may mean in such a case, rose (logarithmically) more sharply between 1909 and 1914 than ever before or after. Designs became more stable, parts more standardized, after 1912—the year that closes the heroic age of the industry. In 1914, 338 firms (the 1914 census of manufactures gives, however, 415, not counting producers of electric vehicles) produced a total of 573,114 cars (Bureau of Foreign and Domestic Commerce), to which Ford contributed almost one-half. The importance of the industry and of its demand for the products of other industries was, therefore, perfectly adequate to "ignite" the second Juglar, although, even in 1914, value added was only 210.6 millions. Subsidiaries developed quickly. In 1914, 971 firms existed producing bodies and parts, and motors infused new life into the rubber industry.

Also in this country, there had been a considerable amount of enterprise in the field of rubber clothing fabrics in the thirties of the nineteenth century, but it ended in failure and disappeared in the crisis of 1837 to 1839. Vulcanization accounts for a new start that was a minor feature of the first Juglar of the second Kondratieff (from 1842, on). The next event, following upon a long period of quiet and rather passive expansion, was the merger that combined 10 concerns into the United States Rubber Company (incorporated in 1892), which conquered more and more ground in the Kondratieff prosperity under discussion (later on it also acquired plantations of its

---

[1] [Ralph C. Epstein, author of *The Automobile Industry* (Chicago, 1928).]

own). This industry felt the impulse of the new demand from the motorcar innovation soon after 1908, when production of tires (fabrics; the innovation of high-pressure cords, which in 1913 were only 2 per cent of total tire output, did not become important till 1918), tubes and other accessories began to count in production programs.

The oil industry also became almost a subsidiary to the gasoline engine. In 1899, only 12.8 per cent of crude oil on stills went to the production of gasoline, kerosene still absorbing 57.7 per cent; but in our period the former and the use of oil for fueling purposes in general approached their postwar importance. From the standpoint of the industry, this was but a favorable external fact, without which decay would have been unavoidable, and the considerable development during the period—value added in petroleum refining increased from about 21 to about 71 millions between 1899 and 1914, and output of crude petroleum from about 60 million to nearly 250 million barrels between 1897 and 1913—was primarily a case of "being drawn along" or of passive adaptation. The rise which occurred in prices bears witness to that. Pipe lines, tank ships, and tank cars were no longer novelties. There was progress in the methods of prospecting, in drilling to greater depths—the rotary drill came after the war—and in rational treatment of oil fields by gas and water pressure. Refining was still done in "skimming" and in complete straight-run plants, and gasoline yield from crude was still only 18.6 per cent in 1914—the cracking process was to increase it and hydrogenation to raise it to 100 per cent in postwar times. Profits were high all the time and partly financed new investment, particularly within the Standard Oil concern. Its dissolution by judicial decree in 1911 did not, within our period, affect the division of labor between the constituent companies, although it did so later.

.   .   .   .

The automobile industry led in every upswing and out of every downswing throughout the period, in fact beyond it, and continued in the Kondratieff recession to qualify as well for the role of standard example for the processes embodied in our model as it had done in the upswing. Employment in motor-vehicle factories, not including production of parts, tires, and bodies, increased from about 253,000 in 1922 to 427,500 in 1929, the corresponding wage bill from about 396 to about 775.5 million dollars. Passenger-car registration as of Dec. 31 increased without any break from the beginning of the series (1895:4) to 1929 (23,121,589), though of course at a decreasing percentage rate, depressions affecting the latter only. Even in the world crisis and in the year of minimum registration (1933) the total automobile retail and service business, including accessories, filling stations, garages, and also retail sales by wholesalers, figures out at $4,831,800,000. Over 1.1 million persons were engaged in distribution and servicing, among them 756,000 employees (part-time included), receiving wages and salaries amounting to 801 millions. Quantitative expansion and qualitative improvement, falling costs, prices, and rates of profit are obviously the expected as well as the actual characteristics of this industry's history during our decade. However, since there is no satisfactory way of measuring qualitative improvement, and since there was an almost uninterrupted shift from larger, heavier, and dearer to smaller, lighter, and cheaper cars—in 1903, for instance, 4.2 per cent of automobiles produced cost $675 and less, in 1924 nearly 60 per cent—even quantitative expansion becomes elusive, while indices of quoted prices, which should moreover be corrected for variations in the allowances made for old cars "traded in" and for other forms of rebates, cannot indicate more than a tendency which, of course, they understate. From 1916 on, profits of individual firms not only fell but also became more nearly equal.

The industry did not simply expand in function of the increase in real income but helped to bring it about. The former nexus, however, steadily gained in importance at the expense of the latter, as had been the case with cotton after the Napoleonic wars and with railroads from the eighties on. Innovations, increasing in number while individually decreasing in importance, are typically of the downgrade type. From 1912 on, designs became more stable. Considerable progress in the standardization of parts and in the rationalization of assembling reduced costs as did progress in subsidiary industries—tires, nitrocellulose lacquers and fast-drying solvents, and so on. Equally important or more so were the changes in organization and financing that were in part induced by the struggle for survival within the industry, in which incessant innovating and expanding into the low-price market was a matter of life and death. Competing-down went on at a rapid rate. The rise in price level after 1916 helped to keep failures and exits at a low and decreasing figure, and even the setback of 1918, when both production and wholesale value fell absolutely for the first time, cost few lives. But after 1921, when production and wholesale value again fell absolutely, exits—not necessarily failures—increased sharply *in the midst of spectacular expansion* of the industry as a whole, reaching 21 per cent in 1924. In 1923 and 1924 no less than 29 firms went out of business, 17 of them war and postwar foundations. Of the 101 plants—makers, not concerns—whose annual production of passenger cars was 5,000 or less in 1920 only 11 survived in 1930; of the 23 whose annual production was from 5,000 to 25,000, also 11; while we still find all of the 10 which produced over 25,000 in 1920. By 1918, 70 per cent of all automobiles produced in this country and Canada came from the three largest producers, by 1921 80 per cent, and by 1935 nearly 90 per cent.

Considering that the car of the masses became a reality, while the industry, which had always been monopolistically competitive, developed a typically oligopolistic situation, we cannot help being painfully aware once more of the somewhat less than realistic character of the general conclusions arrived at by the leading theorists of monopolistic competition. In fact, it should be obvious that the behavior of the motorcar industry during our decade [1919–29] could be described much more convincingly in terms of perfect competition working under the conditions of a new industry in the course of being absorbed by or inserted into the economic system. In the course of this development, ever since about 1916, methods of financing changed significantly. "Outside capital" began to play a greater role. We need, however, only mention the direct contact established by General Motors with the open market and its policy—followed by the other concerns—of financing

the consumer. Nevertheless, owned capital accumulated from profits and retailers' and furnishers' credit remained the industry's most important sources
of means, and this accounts for much which strikes the observer as particularly "sound" about it. Net tangible assets of motor-vehicle manufacturing
plants reached their maximum of about 2.1 billion dollars in 1926 and then
steadily fell, though up to the crisis but slowly. However unreliable any in-
ference from this may be, it seems clear that, barring the Ford plant, the
great wave of investment belongs to the third and not to the fourth Juglar.

In order to prove with quantitative precision how much of the processes
of the period and of the behavior of aggregates can be explained by the
motorcar developments alone, it would be necessary to go fully into what
they meant for the steel, copper, and equipment industries and so on. We
will, however, confine ourselves to one remark on the petroleum and another
on the rubber industry. Innovations that have already been mentioned
(. . . flooding, cracking, hydrogenation, extension of new uses such as fueling of locomotives and ships, by-products) and the discovery and development of new oil fields account for the fall in gasoline prices (excluding tax)
from $0.2411 per gallon in 1919 to $0.1557 in 1929 and—gasoline consumption did not fall until 1932—$0.1178 in 1931, which shows that the petro-
leum industry was not passively drawn along by the growth of demand. Yet
it comes sufficiently near to this pattern to qualify as an instance. This is particularly evident at the beginning of the period. In 1920 prices of oil and
gasoline rose considerably (peak of the period), so much so as to throw
them out of line with those of competing fuels and as to restrict the use of
fuel oil by railroads—the Great Northern, for instance, converted 70 locomotives into coal burners. This followed upon the doubling of automobile
production in 1920 as compared with 1918, with which the gasoline production was then unable to keep pace. An oil boom started accordingly, which
almost coincided with deep depression in other lines. Issues of oil securities
were at a peak early in 1920 and again toward the end of the year and at the
beginning of 1921. It is worth while to mention that the only cities in the
country which experienced greater building activity in November 1920 than
in November 1919 were Los Angeles, Baltimore, and New Orleans, and that
the Californian cities all showed large gains in their clearing figures while
these declined in the rest of the country. . . .

The rubber industry was, of course, also "drawn along." But its own
innovations were much more in evidence. As we have seen elsewhere, beginnings date far back (Goodyear vulcanization to 1839, for instance) or at any
rate to the Kondratieff prosperity (reclaiming, e.g., 1899, acceleration of the
vulcanizing process 1906; but commercial success of synthetic rubber came
after our period), the use of various pigments in order to increase the durability of rubber compounds (1916) being the only "inventive" innovation
of the twenties. It was again the "spreading" by means of discovering new
and developing old industrial uses for rubber (flooring, rubber cushions,
rubber linings, mountings, bumpers, and so on) which was a feature of the
period under discussion. In the field of the most important article the
great new thing—though also invented long ago (R. W. Thompson, patented
1845)—was, of course, the pneumatic tire (1916), which followed upon the

success of the cord and may be said to have imparted immediately a significant impulse to long-distance trucking, although at as late a date as July 1, 1920, the *India Rubber World* (p. 633) professed itself unable to believe that the solid tire, which had greatly improved in reaction to the intrusion of the new competitor, would be crowded out. At the same time the commercial opportunity for low-pressure tires for passenger cars manifested itself in the habit of many motorists to underinflate their tires for the sake of comfort. By 1923, 21 companies, among them practically all the leaders of the trade, were making such tires, experimentally or commercially, and several automobile manufacturers had adopted them as part of the regular equipment of their cars, while others listed them as optional. A "revolution" in tire making, the more important because it involved considerable new investment, announced itself. There was still resistance to overcome. But improvement and standardization—as to rim requirements—carried the innovation suddenly to definitive success about 1925, after one of the tire companies had taken the bold step—in the midst of doubts about practicability and the probable reaction of the public—to bring out balloon tires for all standard rims and thus to make a bid for immediate replacement of practically all tires in use. The aspect of the market changed within a few months, and the "host" followed the innovator promptly. There is no need of going into the illustrative virtues of the case or the quantitative importance of it for the fourth Juglar.

·   ·   ·   ·   ·   ·   ·   ·   ·   ·   ·   ·

CONCLUSION

THE PROFOUND impact the automobile industry made on the American economy resulted from the acts and decisions of many men. One distinctive feature of the auto industry was that those whose actions brought new ways of handling economic functions and contributed so much to economic growth carried on their activities through the giant industrial enterprise. The two great enterprises, Ford and General Motors, which loom so large in the history of the industry, were listed among the very largest of American corporations before either was a decade old. Their only successful competitor was a comparable giant created by Walter Chrysler after he purchased the Dodge interests and developed his own line of cars, including the low-priced Plymouth. As Schumpeter suggested, giant enterprise means oligopoly—that is, the domination of an industry by a few firms. Throughout most of its history, the automobile industry has provided a fascinating example of oligopoly, or monopolistic competition.

As the twentieth century progressed, giant enterprises became increasingly common in industrial America, as did the attendant oligopoly. In the first third of the century, too, the mass consumer market became more and more important to American industrialists. Major industries, like those manufacturing electrical machinery and chemicals, turned from making goods for other businessmen to manufacturing products for the final consumer. Thus the patterns of production, finance, marketing, management, and labor perfected by the automobile companies quickly spread through the industrial economy. By mid-century these methods and techniques were almost taken for granted by American industrialists, businessmen, and the general public. In these same years, the demands of the cold war and the explosion of scientific and technical knowledge were bringing new patterns of economic action and providing new sources for economic growth.

SUGGESTED READINGS

(Books and articles from which selections have been reprinted in this volume are not listed below.)

BEASLEY, NORMAN, *Knudsen: A Biography*. New York, 1947.

BORTH, CHRISTY, *Masters of Mass Production*. Indianapolis, 1945.

BOYD, T. A., *Professional Amateur: The Biography of Charles Franklin Kettering*. New York, 1957.

BURLINGAME, ROGER, *Henry Ford: A Great Life in Brief*. New York, 1955.

CLEVELAND, R. M., and S. T. WILLIAMSON, *The Road Is Yours*. New York, 1951.

CHANDLER, ALFRED D., JR., *Strategy and Structure: Chapters in the History of the Industrial Enterprise*. Cambridge, Mass., 1962, Chapter 3.

DALE, ERNEST, "Contributions to Administration by Alfred P. Sloan, Jr., and GM," *Administrative Science Quarterly*, Vol. 1 (June 1956), pp. 30–60.

DRUCKER, PETER, *The Concept of the Corporation*. New York, 1946.

EPSTEIN, RALPH C., *The Automobile Industry*. Chicago, 1928.

KENNEDY, E. D., *The Automobile Industry*. New York, 1941.

MACMANUS, THEODORE F., and NORMAN BEASLEY, *Men, Money, and Motors*. New York, 1929.

NEVINS, ALLAN, and FRANK E. HILL, *Ford: The Times, the Man, the Company*. New York, 1954.

———, *Ford: Expansion and Challenge, 1915–1933*. New York, 1957.

———, *Ford: Decline and Rebirth, 1933–1962*. New York, 1963.

POUND, ARTHUR, *The Turning Wheel*. New York, 1934.

RAE, JOHN B., *American Automobile Manufacturers: The First Forty Years*. Philadelphia, 1959.

———, "The Fabulous Billy Durant," *Business History Review*, Vol. 32 (Autumn 1958), pp. 251–71.

SLOAN, ALFRED P., JR., *My Years With General Motors*, John McDonald and Catharine Stevens, eds. New York, 1964.

———, in collaboration with BOYDEN SPARKS, *Adventures of a White Collar Man*. New York, 1941.

SORENSEN, CHARLES E., in collaboration with SAMUEL T. WILLIAMSON, *My Forty Years With Ford*. New York, 1956.

VANDERBLUE, HOMER B., "Pricing Policies in the Automobile Industry," *Harvard Business Review*, Vol. 17 (Summer 1939), pp. 385–401.